A Global Environmental Right

The development of an international substantive environmental right on a global level has long been a contested issue. To a limited extent environmental rights have developed in a fragmented way through different legal regimes. This book examines the potential for the development of a global environmental right that would create legal duties for all types of decision-makers and provide the bedrock for a reformed system of international environmental governance.

Taking a problem-solving approach, the book seeks to demonstrate how straightforward and logical changes to the existing global legal architecture would address some of the fundamental root causes of environmental degradation. It puts forward a draft global environmental right that would integrate duties for both state and non-state actors within reformed systems of environmental governance and a rational framework for business and industry to adhere to in order that those systems could be made operational. It also examines the failures of the existing international climate change regime and explains how the draft global environmental right could remedy existing deficits.

This innovative and interdisciplinary book will be of great interest to students and researchers of international environmental law, climate change, environmental politics and global environmental governance as well as those studying the WTO, international trade law, human rights law, constitutional law and corporate law.

Stephen J. Turner is a Senior Lecturer at Kingston University, UK where he leads the LLM course in Environmental Law and Sustainability. He also teaches Company Law.

Routledge Explorations in Environmental Studies

Nuclear Waste Management and Legitimacy
Nihilism and Responsibility
Mats Andrén

Nuclear Power, Economic Development Discourse and the Environment
The Case of India
Manu V. Mathai

Federalism of Wetlands
Ryan W. Taylor

Governing Sustainable Urban Renewal
Partnerships in Action
Rory Shand

Employee Engagement with Sustainable Business
How to Change the World Whilst Keeping Your Day Job
Nadine Exter

The Political Economy of Global Warming
The Terminal Crisis
Del Weston

Communicating Environmental Patriotism
A Rhetorical History of the American Environmental Movement
Anne Marie Todd

Environmental Justice in Developing Countries
Perspectives from Africa and Asia-Pacific
Rhuks Temitope Ako

The Political Economy of Global Warming
The Terminal Crisis
Del Weston

Climate Change and Cultural Heritage
A Race Against Time
Peter F. Smith

A Global Environmental Right
Stephen J. Turner

A Global Environmental Right

Stephen J. Turner

Routledge
Taylor & Francis Group
LONDON AND NEW YORK

earthscan
from Routledge

First published 2014
by Routledge
2 Park Square, Milton Park, Abingdon, Oxon OX14 4RN

Simultaneously published in the USA and Canada
by Routledge
711 Third Avenue, New York, NY 10017

Routledge is an imprint of the Taylor & Francis Group, an informa business

British Library Cataloguing in Publication Data
A catalogue record for this book is available from the British Library

Library of Congress Cataloging-in-Publication Data
Turner, Stephen J. (Stephen James)
A global environmental right / Stephen J. Turner.
pages cm
1. Environmental law, International. I. Title.
K3585.T85 2013
333.7--dc23
2013007127

ISBN13: 978-0-415-81159-0 (hbk)
ISBN13: 978-0-203-07015-4 (ebk)

Typeset in Times New Roman
by Fish Books Ltd.

Contents

List of acronyms and abbreviations

ACHPR	African Charter of Human and Peoples' Rights
ACHR	American Convention on Human Rights
CBDR	common but differentiated responsibility
CDM	Clean Development Mechanism
CER	certified emission reduction
CERES	Coalition for Environmentally Responsible Economies
COP	Conference of the Parties
CSR	corporate social responsibility
DECO	Direct Environmental Compensatory Offset
DSB	Dispute Settlement Body
ECHR	European Convention on Human Rights
EEC	European Economic Community
EIA	environmental impact assessment
EIT	economies in transition
EKC	Environmental Kuznets Curve
EPI	Environmental Performance Index
ERU	emission reduction unit
ESV	enlightened shareholder value
ETS	Emissions Trading Scheme
EU	European Union
FAC	Food Assistance Convention
FAO	Food and Agriculture Organization
GATS	General Agreement on Trade in Services
GATT	General Agreement on Tariffs and Trade
GCF	Green Climate Fund
GDP	gross domestic product
GEF	Global Environmental Facility
GEO	Global Environmental Organization
GER	Global Environmental Right
GHG	greenhouse gas
HRC	Human Rights Committee
IBRD	International Bank of Reconstruction and Development
ICCPR	International Covenant on Civil and Political Rights

ICESCR	International Covenant on Economic, Social and Cultural Rights
ICJ	International Court of Justice
IFC	International Finance Corporation
IMF	International Monetary Fund
IOS	International Organization for Standardization
IPCC	Intergovernmental Panel on Climate Change
ISO	International Standards Organization
ITO	International Trade Organization
JI	Joint Implementation
LULUCF	Land-Use, Land-Use Change and Forestry
MDB	multilateral development bank
MDG	Millennium Development Goal
MEA	Millennium Ecosystem Assessment
MNE	multinational enterprise
NAFTA	North American Free Trade Oganization
NGO	non-government organization
OAS	Organization of American States
OECD	Organisation for Economic Co-operation and Development
ppm	parts per million
SARL	Société à Responsabilité Limitée
SEA	strategic environmental assessment
SPS	Agreement on the Application of Sanitary and Phytosanitary Measures
SRSG	Special Representative of the Secretary General
TBT	Agreement on Technical Barriers to Trade
TLA	timber license agreement
TRIPS	The Agreement on Trade-Related Aspects of Intellectual Property Rights
UCC	Union Carbide Corporation
UDHR	Universal Declaration of Human Rights
UN	United Nations
UNCED	United Nations Conference on Environment and Development
UNCHE	United Nations Conference on Human Environment
UNECE	United Nations Economic Commission for Europe
UNEP	United Nations Environment Programme
UNFCCC	United Nations Framework Convention on Climate Change
WEO	World Environment Organization
WMO	World Meteorological Organization
WSSD	World Summit on Sustainable Development
WTO	World Trade Organization

Acknowledgements

There are many people that I want to thank for their support and help in relation to the writing of this book.

Primarily I wish to express my immense gratitude to Dr Olga Martin-Ortega for the advice and discussions throughout the research and writing process. I am especially thankful for the helpful advice relating to the structure of the book and for reading through specific sections and providing invaluable comments.

I would like to thank Professor Matthew Humphreys at Kingston University for providing me with the time to be able to work on this project. Additionally I want to thank all of my colleagues at Kingston University for their endless good humour and for making it a great place to work. However I specifically would like to thank Dr Wang Wei Lin, Dr Hiroko Onishi and Dr Vincenzo Bavoso for reading through sections of earlier drafts and providing helpful comments.

I would like to thank Mr Michael Woods and Professor Surya Subedi for helpful discussions related to this work, which have assisted in its overall development.

I specifically want to thank Sra. Patricia Iturregui for providing helpful comments in relation to the climate change chapter and for the associated discussions.

Additionally, I would especially like to thank Professor Malgosia Fitzmaurice for advice and for help with my earlier work in this field which helped in bringing this book to fruition.

I would like also to thank Associate Professor Anna Grear for help with related projects. Additionally I am grateful to the Global Network of Human Rights and Environment (GNHRE), which provides a vital focal point for those interested in and working in this field.

In the process of writing this book I have become indebted to all those whose work and research I have used, learned from and relied upon. They are listed in the bibliography.

I would like to thank Ms Gulay Varan for practical help and Mr Narayana Harave for invaluable technical assistance.

I want to thank Khanam Virjee, Ashley Irons, Helen Bell, Charlotte Russell, Jennifer Birtill, Charlotte Nixon, Samantha Freeman and all the staff at Routledge for their kind support and guidance during the publishing process. I also want to thank Karl Harrington from Fish Books for all his painstaking work and tremendous patience. Additionally I would like to thank Liz Riley for proof-reading and helpful advice.

It goes without saying that any errors in this book are entirely my own.

Finally on a personal level, I want to thank all those who have helped me in countless different ways over the years to be in the position to be able to write this book. I thank all of my family and friends but especially my parents Olive and Alan Turner. I also thank Alison, Jon, Philip and Sarah and all of my aunties and uncles and wider family for everything, great and small.

Stephen Turner
London, May 2013.

For
Alison, Jon, Philip and Sarah

Preface

In the summer of 2000, I came across an interesting and brilliant book in Waterstones called *Human Rights Approaches to Environmental Protection*.[1] At that time I was not involved in environmental law but found the book fascinating all the same. It described the extent to which human rights were being used for environmental protection. I was surprised to see what little impact they were having in that field. As an outsider to the subject it seemed strange that human rights should not figure more prominently in the pursuit of environmental sustainability, bearing in mind how fundamental the environment is to the existence of the human race and the future well-being of the planet. For me personally it represented the point at which I embarked on the study and research of environmental law.

In my own work, I had seen how human rights could evolve from concepts and notions into practical, workable systems that function effectively on a day-by-day basis. For example, I had seen how the human right to a fair hearing had gradually been operationalized in practice. The development of the right had taken place through the evolution of a range of duties for all of those actors that dealt with or had some kind of interface with suspects and defendants. Therefore everyone who had anything to do with a suspect or defendant, whether as an arresting officer, a custody sergeant, a judge, a solicitor, a witness, a doctor, a scientist or a barrister was under a strict set of legal duties in the way that they treated him or her and any related information, to ensure that they ultimately had a fair hearing.

As I embarked on the study of international environmental law, I came to see that a corresponding comprehensive range of duties did not apply in the same way. Not all of the actors that could influence or harm the environment were under strict legal duties to protect it. It was therefore little wonder that the legal regime that had developed was failing to achieve sustainability.

It was from these basic observations that the journey, which ultimately led to this book, originally began.

1 Introduction

The purpose of this book is to put the case for a global environmental right. The premise is that at both the national and international levels, certain key aspects of the current global legal architecture are pre-disposed towards an outcome of environmental degradation that includes increasing greenhouse gas (GHG) emissions. It observes that such degradation can have a negative impact upon basic human rights. Therefore it puts forward an approach that would seek to remedy this deficit in the law by creating fundamental legal duties for all types of decision-makers (both state and non-state actors) to protect the environment. It argues that this could be achieved through a framework treaty, which is presented in Chapter 4, the draft Global Environmental Right (GER).

Therefore, while the approach within this book looks to the creation of duties for decision-makers, the main emphasis is ultimately environmental governance. It argues that sustainable environmental governance can be achieved through the integration of rights-based environmental duties into the global legal architecture upon which states, business, industry, communities and individuals all operate. (The term 'global legal architecture' in the context of this book, is used to describe the framework of laws that are common to most countries, which determine how business, trade and governmental decision-making relating to the environment is conducted.) In this sense it anticipates a role for an environmental right to directly influence not just the law that relates to state constitutions but also other crucial areas of decision-making relating to the environment such as corporate law and World Trade Organization (WTO) law.

There have been numerous developments within the field of human rights and the environment over the last 40 years. For example, many national constitutions now contain environmental provisions, as do numerous state constitutions within federal states such as the United States. On an international level, there has been the adoption of laws (known as procedural environmental rights) that entitle individuals to the right to make legal challenges to decision-making relating to the environment, to be furnished with information relating to the environment and also to be able to participate in decisions relating to the environment. However at the same time, on an international level, there is currently no globally accepted substantive environmental right. In other words there is no globally accepted international agreement or treaty between states acknowledging that all people have the right to have the environment protected to a specified standard. Naturally there are always obstacles in the way of any international agreement but more fundamentally, there is the question of whether or not such a treaty is desirable, and if it is, what form it could take.

The increasing number of environmental provisions within national constitutions however, is hardly surprising owing to the connections that exist between human rights and the environment. The very fact that we rely on the environment and ecosystems for our survival, is an indication of the nexus between the environment and rights such as the right to life and the right to health. In recent years, concern relating to the challenge of climate change has intensified and that too has multiple links with existing human rights.

Notwithstanding the fact that there have been significant developments within the field of human rights and the environment, there has been an overriding factor that renders the significant developments in the field of environmental rights still wanting. This is that despite developments within this field, ecosystems and the environment are still facing significant and ongoing degradation. The significance of the scale of environmental degradation currently taking place not only forces the global community to seek methods of discovering less damaging methods of sustenance and production, but indicates an underlying failure of the existing global legal architecture, which has allowed such a state of affairs to occur and to continue.

On the global scale, developments by the international legal community in the field of environmental law or sustainable development are often characterized by a declaration of a set of goals that states then seek to achieve. For example this can be said of the Rio Declaration,[1] the Millennium Development Goals (MDGs),[2] the outcome of World Summit on Sustainable Development (WSSD)[3] and the outcome of the Rio + 20 conference.[4] This approach creates common ground and paves the way for individual treaties within specific sectors and international agreements within specific fields. However, it is an approach that thus far fails to identify and address the root causes[5] and drivers of environmental degradation, which this book argues are built into the global legal architecture of national economies, business and trade, and hence it fails to ensure that economic development is carried out within overriding ecological constraints.[6]

This book argues that environmental degradation is a natural consequence of a global legal architecture, which has certain features. Therefore it identifies a number of legal mechanisms that are built into the very fabric of the way that we work and do business. It explains that these legal mechanisms were historically included within our global legal architecture for very good reasons but goes on to show how they have gone on to stimulate many of the problems that we are currently facing. It is crucial to understand these legal mechanisms as they embody key root causes of decision-making within economies that lead to environmental degradation. Inherent in this analysis is a piece of good news: if it is possible that key root causes of environmental degradation are built into the functioning of a system of global legal architecture that was designed long before modern environmental concerns came to the fore, it is also possible to redesign that system.

Therefore the main purpose of this book is to consider the redesign of the existing global legal architecture in favour of a legal framework that would be predisposed to bring about environmental, economic and business sustainability. Such a system could potentially ease the burdens on governments, especially in the field of climate change. Potentially in relation to climate change, a global legal architecture that was predisposed to environmental sustainability could enable governments to focus more readily on adaptation by reducing their burdens in the field of mitigation. However, for such a system to be introduced, the global legal architecture would need to be clear, unequivocal and easily applicable for governments and business; therefore the design of such a framework of environmental governance is crucial.

To these ends, this book is comprised of four main chapters. The first of these is Chapter 2, which summarizes the reasons why there are needs for change. It looks in depth at the current state of the environment on a global level, emphasizing the scale of the problems and the links that the environment has with existing human rights. It also assesses the extent to which existing environmental rights have been effective in addressing the global environmental degradation that is taking place. The next stage is found in Chapter 3. This seeks to expose the reasons why the existing system of international environmental law is (often) failing to lead to sustainable outcomes. To do this it examines the global legal architecture and the way that it affects the environment. It therefore analyses corporate law on an international level and why it is that corporate directors are often under a legal obligation to make decisions that are detrimental to the environment. Additionally, it examines the law of the WTO and discusses the legal framework for international trade and shows how the system of rules that it contains often leads to environmental degradation. It then analyses the obligations that states have, taking into account national sovereignty and national constitutions, to highlight why it is that states are not only free to adopt policies and laws that lead to further environmental degradation but are often compelled to do so by a varying range of factors. From the overview of these legal frameworks, it is possible to gain a clearer perspective of the reasons why the mechanisms that have developed under international environmental law are so often limited in their effectiveness.

Armed with a clearer understanding of the deficits in the existing global legal architecture, Chapter 4 puts forward the design of a draft framework treaty that could pave the way for the development of clear legal obligations for all of those decision-makers that can affect the environment. It bases this framework on the premise that there should be a fundamental human right for all peoples to live in a good, clean and healthy environment.

It proposes the changes that are arguably required to provide the type of global legal architecture that would inevitably lead to sustainable outcomes. Therefore it puts forward the initial steps that would need to be made for corporate law to be amended, how the constitution of the WTO and regional trade organizations would need to be reformed and obviously how state law would need to be reformed too. Additionally it provides the basis for the amendment of the obligations of financial and banking institutions to ensure that the obligations of all types of commercial decision-makers could be streamlined.

However, Chapter 4 goes further than this. In addition to proposing a framework of new legal obligations for decision-makers, it also proposes a business and institutional framework that is designed to ensure that the obligations are clear and workable in practice. This aspect is important to ensure that businesses worldwide could operate on a level playing field. It therefore anticipates the oversight that would be required on a global level to achieve those objectives and suggests how it could be instituted. While the draft GER puts forward a range of reforms in this regard, the commentary explains that many of those reforms are either extensions of existing developments or the iteration of proposals that have been made in the past. Finally, the chapter emphasizes the need for a process of transition for those changes to take place in order that businesses and national economies could have appropriate timescales for adjustment.

The fifth chapter focuses on analysing the new global legal architecture that is proposed under the draft GER, in terms of its direct application to climate change. It has been argued by some that climate change is the most serious and pressing problem facing the international community. It clearly represents an issue that has not been met with an adequate solution internationally. Therefore, special consideration is given to illustrating the manner in which the draft GER could provide an effective method of achieving the levels of GHGs desired on an international level, within the timeframe necessary, through a fair and equitable process that would benefit states in all stages of development and make business environmentally sustainable.

In 2005, the United Nations published the Millennium Ecosystem Assessment (MEA) that made it clear that, '[p]rotecting and improving our future well-being requires wiser and less destructive use of natural assets. This in turn involves major changes in the way we make and implement decisions'.[7] Ultimately this book is a direct response to that challenge. It proposes a sustainably designed global legal architecture for all decisions that can negatively affect the environment.

Constitutional law, human rights law, corporate law, trade law and international law are usually viewed as separate and distinct disciplines both academically and in practice too. However, it can be argued that they are all component parts of the global legal architecture that affects the environment. When viewed in a piecemeal fashion, it is possible that the reasons for the underlying failures of the system remain unacknowledged and unaddressed. It is argued that when the overall system of global legal architecture is viewed as a whole, key flaws in that architecture can be properly identified and remedied.

By analogy, any architect who is designing a new building will always begin with a design of the whole structure before beginning to work on the finer details. While it is important to address those finer details at a later stage, it should only be done when the overall architecture has been designed in such a manner that it achieves the main design criteria. The same can also be said of the global legal architecture that affects the environment. It is necessary for us to view the entire framework as a whole to understand its faults in order that specific aspects of it can be redesigned to achieve overall global environmental sustainability. Once the central global legal architecture has been redesigned accordingly, it is then possible to turn attention to fine tuning the design of the individual disciplines of which it is comprised.

Therefore the approach adopted within this book, has been taken in order that a specific perspective can be achieved. It deliberately treats various legal disciplines as component parts of the global legal architecture, rather than simply as discrete disciplines in their own right. As such, while it would be tempting to be drawn into more detailed analysis of many of the areas of law that are covered, it would not be logical to do so as that would detract from the overall purpose of providing a picture of the way that the global legal architecture operates.

As will be seen, in certain respects the existing global legal architecture is highly dysfunctional in the sense that it is comprised of bodies of law that often pull in opposing directions. Arguably these dysfunctions contribute significantly to the root causes of environmental degradation. This book therefore seeks to provide the broader picture in order that these inherent dysfunctions can be identified and remedied accordingly.

In other words, the approach of this book is that of 'macro' legal analysis. It avoids being drawn into 'micro' legal analysis in order that it can achieve its overall objective. It is argued that it is only when such 'macro' legal analysis is carried out, that a deeper understanding can be gained of what this book describes as the 'global legal architecture'. Therefore this book is about that basic overall design. It is about looking to the reform of the global legal architecture that affects the environment by placing it on firm foundations, through logical design, so that it can be fully functional, fully sustainable and fully protect people's human rights.

2 The state of degradation of the planet's environment, the impact upon human rights and the current status of the development of environmental rights

2.1 Introduction

This chapter sets the scene for the following chapters in the book by providing the vantage point from which the overall picture of the global legal architecture relating to the environment can be seen. It provides a basic overview of the current state of the world's environment, a broad summary of the human rights which are affected through environmental degradation, and an overall assessment of the current state of development of specifically 'environmental' rights. Therefore it seeks to link two worlds, those of the science and the law. This process is a necessary one if we are to ascertain the extent to which human rights are affected by environmental degradation and also the extent to which existing human rights mechanisms are effective in responding to environmental degradation.

The first part of the chapter focuses on the environment itself by detailing the ways in which different aspects of environmental degradation affect human rights. It is impossible to completely compartmentalize key components of the environment, as they do not operate in isolation. For example it can be difficult to discuss forests without ultimately discussing the impacts of forest loss on desertification, biodiversity and climate change. Similarly it can be difficult to discuss land use conversion without discussing issues such as water supply. Therefore although these different types of environmental challenges are presented in different sub-sections, those sub-sections are inevitably not mutually exclusive.

Within each of the sub-sections that relate to the state of the world's environment, an indication is provided of the key 'established' human rights that are affected by the degradation described. (In other words it discusses how environmental degradation affects those human rights, such as the rights to life and health, that were not originally instituted specifically for the protection of the environment.) This leads to the second part of the chapter, which discusses those established human rights in more detail. It discusses how, within a contemporary context, their meanings have been broadened to encompass direct relationships with environmental degradation. Equally importantly, it provides an indication of the extent to which existing human rights mechanisms respond to that degradation, if at all.

The chapter subsequently proceeds to discuss the new 'environmental' rights that have developed both under national and international law. It provides an overview of the different types of rights that have been instituted, the extent to which they have developed and the extent to which they have actually been used effectively for the protection of the environment in the light of the environmental degradation that is described in the first part of the chapter.

The key purpose of this chapter is to elaborate on three key questions, which are as follows:

1 To what extent does the current state of environmental degradation impact upon people's human rights?
2 How have 'established' human rights developed to respond to those impacts?
3 To what extent have new 'environmental' rights been developed as a response for the protection of the environment?

2.2 The state of the planet's environment and its relationship with human rights

The international community is very fortunate in that a huge amount of work has been done in researching the science of the planet's environment. The United Nations under the leadership of Kofi Annan commissioned the MEA in 2000; the final series of reports was published in 2005.[1] The Intergovernmental Panel on Climate Change (IPCC) produces periodic reports on the latest research data relating to climate change science. Additionally, different parts of the United Nations (UN) such as the Food and Agriculture Organization (FAO) actively produce well-updated reports on aspects of the environment such as fisheries and forests. Also there are many individual initiatives by government institutions, universities and independent or semi-independent scientific groups, which add to the growing knowledge and understanding of the science that relates to the planet's environment.

The understanding that has grown from the science has ceased to be purely about assessing the harm that is being caused to individual species or individual geographical areas but extends to an understanding of complete ecosystems and natural systems. It is from this science that policy-makers, economists and lawyers must be informed if they are to design systems that adequately respond to the needs of existing generations, future generations and the requirements of the global environment itself.

The development of environmental science means that the concept of 'ecosystem services' is now at the heart of the dialogue that emanates from the research. As global recognition has taken place of the failure of markets to take into account the loss of natural capital as a result of industrial processes, a dominant theme is the loss of ecosystem services caused by environmental degradation within specific sectors.

With this in mind there are certain themes that have become prevalent. This overview seeks to review those themes as well as highlighting specific stresses to the environment and natural systems. Therefore, this chapter will begin by reviewing the concept of natural capital, as it is crucial to understanding the kind of legal framework that is required for the protection of the environment. It will then look at the state of the planet in terms of certain key components; these include the atmosphere and climate change, land use, water use, fisheries and coral reefs, biodiversity and the impact of population growth.

2.2.1 Natural capital

A core concept that now underpins the development of environmental policy, environmental law and environmental economics is that of natural capital. Natural capital in the context of this book can be described as the stock of ecosystems and natural systems across the planet that provide ecosystem services for present and future generations.[2] Therefore, examples of these might be the reefs, fish, forests, river systems and climatic systems that all provide valuable services upon which humans depend but which have the capacity to be eroded or degraded by human activity.

This concept has emerged from the acceptance that throughout the industrialized era, humankind has often exploited and degraded the natural capital of the planet without restoring or replacing it. During this era, many have been able to benefit financially and materially from doing so but the costs to the planet have not been included in the market costs of the goods or services produced. During this period, the systems of law and production had not seriously addressed this issue, owing to the seeming limitlessness of the planet's resources and the seeming unlikeliness of business and industry to seriously deplete or degrade them.

Increasingly there is an awareness of the inter-linkages between the ecosystems and natural systems that make up the stock of natural capital.[3] Examples of the provision of valuable ecosystem services are the purification of water and prevention of soil erosion through vegetation; the pollination and germination of plants by birds and insects; the protection of coastlines by coral reefs; the absorption of carbon dioxide by plants and trees; the regulation of air quality, water quality and local climatic conditions by forests; and the filtration of pollution and the flood prevention services of swamps and wetlands. These complement the more easily recognizable types of services provided by the planet that include the food provided by fisheries and the timber provided by forests (these are the types of services that relate directly to products that are sold as commercial goods).

The MEA found that over 60 per cent of the world's major ecosystem goods and services covered in the assessment were degraded or used unsustainably.[4] The MEA made an analysis that broke these services down into 24 categories.[5] It concluded that although four of those services were increasing their ability to benefit human populations, 15 were in decline.[6] The other five were found to be in a stable state but in trouble in some parts of the world.[7] This state of decline was further reflected in the United Nations Environment Programme (UNEP) report *Towards a Green Economy* in 2011.[8] Partha Dasgupta provides a clearer understanding of the vulnerable character of natural capital and ecosystem services:

> [e]cosystems are capital assets. Like reproducible capital assets...Ecosystems depreciate if they are misused or are overused. But they differ from

> reproducible capital assets in three ways: (1) depreciation of natural capital is frequently irreversible (or at best the systems take a long time to recover); (2) except in a very limited sense, it isn't possible to replace a depleted or degraded ecosystem by a new one; and (3) ecosystems can collapse abruptly, without much prior warning.[9]

Therefore, in assessing natural capital assets it is not always possible to merely consider replacement costs. Consideration of the value requires a deeper understanding of the asset and how, if at all, loss or degradation can be reversed or compensated. As will be seen the degradation of natural capital can have a direct impact on human rights.

2.2.2 Water use

Freshwater scarcity has already become a global issue. On a regional basis it causes immense stresses and forecasts predict an increasing gap between freshwater demand and renewable supply by 2030.[10] The amount of water taken from rivers and lakes to irrigate fields, to meet industrial needs and to provide household supplies has doubled since the 1960s.[11] The MEA reported that humans now use between 40 and 50 per cent of the freshwater running off land that is accessible by the majority of the population.[12]

There is also an ongoing problem of lack of improved sanitation for 1.1 billion people and 844 million people still lack access to clean drinking water.[13] As a result of the existing over-use of some water supplies, many rivers now transport much less of the sediments that bring food supplies to estuaries, which support ecosystems of shellfish, fish and birds, which can in turn affect the livelihoods of local communities.[14]

In addition, water quality in many areas has been progressively degraded owing to a variety of agricultural practices. Intensification of agriculture has been the main source of water pollution in many developed and developing countries.[15] Intensive forms of livestock production have also been the cause of large-scale water pollution. Additionally, excessive use of chemicals in farming has the effect of contaminating waterways, which can lead to dead-spots.[16]

In terms of the human rights affected, the lack of potable water or the pollution of available water can have a direct impact upon the right to life, the right to health and also of course right to water itself, which has developed in the last two decades.

2.2.3 Land use, land-use conversion and degradation

Between 1950 and 1980, more land was converted to cropland than in the 150 years between 1700 and 1850.[17] Now approximately one quarter of the Earth's land surface has been converted for cultivation.[18] While the conversion of land for the production of food can be beneficial, it can also have negative effects on biodiversity, water ecosystems, other ecosystems services and of course the climate.[19]

Land degradation generally is the long-term decline of land, driven mainly by poor land and water management, which can include over-cultivation, over-grazing, deforestation and inadequate irrigation.[20] The UN's 2011 report entitled, *World Economic and Social Survey: The Great Green Technological Transformation*, states that:

> [a] range of fundamental natural resources (such as land, water, air and biodiversity) provide the indispensable base for the production of essential goods and services upon which human survival depends. During the past half-century, shrinkage in the availability of natural resources occurred more rapidly than in any comparable time in history, driven in great part by human intervention in the environment in the form of agricultural activities. Although vital to the production and supply of food, feed and fuel, these have had negative environmental and socio-economic consequences, such as land degradation, water pollution, climate change, biodiversity loss, reduced long-term productive capacity, poverty, migration and ill health.[21]

Depending on the type of land degradation that has taken place, a variety of human rights can be affected either directly or indirectly. Naturally on a local level the degradation of land through land-use change, which affects water supplies or food supplies, can have a direct impact on the rights to life, health and water. On a wider scale the effects that land-use change can have upon climate change and biodiversity loss can impact upon the rights to life, health, water and food. Additionally, the loss of land or a change in its character can have an impact on the right to property.

2.2.4 Forests

The UN FAO has produced a comprehensive assessment of the world's forests in the *Global Forest Resources Assessment* 2010 (FRA 2010).[22] These data were included in the FAO's 2011 report, *The State of the World's Forests*.[23] The FRA 2010 tells us that the world's total forested area is just over 4 billion hectares. It states that there are five countries whose forested areas account for over half of the world's forested areas (i.e. the Russian Federation, Brazil, Canada, the United States of America and China).[24]

Overall, these reports confirm that global rates of deforestation are still alarmingly high.[25] They show that in recent years the rates of annual deforestation have decreased from approximately 16 million hectares per year during the 1990s to roughly 13 million hectares per year in the new millennium.[26] The reports confirm that the majority of afforestation has taken place in the temperate zones, while the tropical regions have continued to be subject to a high level of deforestation.[27]

The figures are summarised by UNEP in *Towards a Green Economy* 2011:

- 1990 World forest area: 4.17 billion hectares
- 2010 World forest area: 4.03 billion hectares
- 1990 World planted forest area: 178 million hectares

- 2010 World planted forest area: 264 million hectares
- 1990–2000 Annual net forest loss: 8.3 million hectares/year
- 2000–2010 Annual net forest loss: 5.2 million hectares/year
- 1990–2000 Annual deforestation: 16 million hectares/year
- 2000–2010 Annual deforestation: 13 million hectares/year
- 1990–2000 Annual increase in planted forest: 3.36 million hectares/year
- 2000–2010 Annual increase in planted forest: 5 million hectares/year[28]

In terms of the natural capital that forests represent, it has long been acknowledged that the 'market value' is usually only the value of the timber itself on the open market. The sale of the timber itself does not represent the loss of the natural capital in terms of the ecosystem services that may include: water control, local climate regulation, the absorption of carbon dioxide, provision of genetic resources, habitat for biodiversity, flood protection, protection of soil and protection against desertification.[29]

The loss of forests can have a direct impact on the right to property, especially for indigenous communities. The impact of the loss of forests can also lead to a loss of food for communities who are dependent upon forests for their sustenance. Therefore, in that direct sense the right to food can be impacted. In an indirect sense, as the loss of forests can exacerbate climate change, the loss of biodiversity, flood protection and water control, deforestation can also have an impact upon the rights to life and health.

2.2.5 Climate change

The IPCC was set up by two United Nations organizations UNEP and the World Meteorological Organization (WMO) in 1988. It produces periodic reports on the science related to climate change which include forecasts of the likely projected outcomes for climate, weather patterns, ice melt and the corresponding effects for civilization in terms of agriculture, migration and incidences of natural disasters. The IPCC does not carry out its own research but bases its assessments on the work of over 800 scientists from around the world. The concern amongst the scientific and indeed the international community, is that the increasing concentrations of GHGs in the atmosphere, may be having a forcing effect upon the natural variations which occur in the global climate. Therefore increases in the temperature may be due to anthropogenic emissions.

Of the GHGs caused by human activity, carbon dioxide causes the most concern. The global atmospheric concentration of carbon dioxide rose from pre-industrial levels of 280 parts per million (ppm) to 379 ppm in 2005.[30] International action related to GHG emissions has failed to redress the issue. The average annual carbon dioxide concentration growth rate was significantly greater between 1995 and 2005 than it had been in the period between 1960 and 1995.[31] In spite of international efforts, the amount of carbon dioxide being emitted into the atmosphere has increased steadily since 2000 by 3 per cent per annum.[32]

The temperature of the atmosphere has risen 0.7 degrees Celsius since the nineteenth century.[33] Of the 12 years between 1995 and 2006, 11 were among the 12 warmest years in the instrumental record of global surface temperatures (i.e. since 1850).[34] The IPCC now states that, 'most of the observed increase in global average temperatures since the mid-20th century is very likely due to the observed increase in anthropogenic GHG concentrations'.[35]

The use of fossil fuels has accounted for the largest proportion of GHG emissions. In 2005, it was fossil fuels that accounted for 85 per cent of global primary energy supplies.[36] (In addition to fossil fuels, nuclear power accounted for 6 per cent, hydroelectricity for 3 per cent, biomass for 4 per cent and modern renewables for less than 1 per cent).[37] During the 2000s numerous countries greatly increased their coal power capacity, which has been one of the key contributing factors to the increased emissions of GHGs. China is an example of an emerging economy that has greatly increased its number of coal-fired power stations. During the 2000s it added more coal power capacity annually than the total installed capacity in the United Kingdom.[38] This phenomenon has not been restricted to developing economies. Numerous developed countries have continued to increase their coal-fired power station capacities to meet an increasing demand for energy.[39]

The IPCC has recommended that the international community takes action that will meet a target concentration of carbon dioxide in the atmosphere of 450 ppm by 2050. It was envisaged that such a target would provide a 'reasonable' chance of stabilizing temperatures at 2 degrees Celsius above pre-industrial temperatures and thus create a reasonable chance of avoiding catastrophic consequences on humans and ecological systems.[40] This target was agreed upon by the UNFCCC in Mexico (Cancun) in 2010.[41] It is anticipated that for such a target to be achieved, it would be necessary for global GHG emissions to be reduced by 50 to 80 per cent below 1990 levels by 2050 and then become negative in the latter half of the century.[42]

Clearly there are difficulties in forecasting what effect the changes in the climate will have in the future. There have been various different models used to predict likely outcomes. Research and knowledge in this field is being augmented continuously. The IPCC forecasts a variety of possible outcomes and naturally the severity of the temperature increase of the planet will heavily influence the severity of those outcomes. Additionally, effects in different regions will vary and those variations will be contingent on numerous factors such as latitude, geology, existing climate, altitude and different types of vegetation. It is not the purpose of this section to detail all of the potential impacts in all areas. There is a wide range of authorities that provide detailed analyses. However, it is necessary to highlight the range and types of problems that could be faced.

Coastlines could be affected by increasing sea-level rises. Predictions vary but include a rise of up to 79 cm by 2100. Some small island states could be rendered virtually uninhabitable. Populations who rely on river deltas such as those in Bangladesh and those on the Nile delta could be severely affected. Many other coastal regions around the world could also be adversely affected.

In recent years there has been an increased incidence of storms and extreme weather events such as hurricanes in some regions. It has been predicted that such events will continue to increase as a result of global warming. With such events come the concomitant potential for flooding and the risk of loss of life.[43]

As well as increased storm activity, the propensity for heat waves could increase and these would be more intense in certain regions. Associated with this phenomenon is the increased likelihood of droughts in certain regions. It has been emphasized that many of the countries that could be worst hit by the impacts of climate change would be developing countries that are least well equipped either to deal with natural disasters or to mitigate for their potential occurrence. With heat waves and droughts come loss of life and the onset of disease related to the lack of fresh drinking water.

Clearly the health of the human population of the planet could be severely affected (as has already been the case) through the impacts of climate change. Lack of fresh drinking water could be a major issue in many areas, owing in part to the existing water stresses that many regions already face. The rates of river run off, the slower replenishment of groundwater supplies, increased evaporation and the potential for some water supplies to become salinated (through rising sea levels) could have deleterious effects on freshwater supplies.

Climate change can additionally have the effect of spreading diseases. Vector-borne diseases (in other words those that are carried by another organism) could be particularly prone to spread in some regions. Such diseases are sensitive to rainfall, humidity, temperature, wind, soil moisture, surface water and changes in plant life and forests.[44] Therefore there could be a spread of certain diseases such as malaria.

Associated with the general impacts on health can be the impacts on agriculture globally and regionally. There are predictions that the crop production potential of some regions may improve as a result of climate change but that in other regions drought and changing weather conditions may result in a loss of output.[45] There is uncertainty on the overall effects and the localized effects. What is clear is that developing countries are much more vulnerable to impacts on their agricultural production than developed countries that have a greater capacity to adapt. The potential for certain regions to be without freshwater and food may lead to ill-health, loss of life and large-scale migration.[46]

In terms of biodiversity there could be numerous impacts. Certain species that are not able to migrate would be liable to become extinct if their habitats are lost. Such species include polar bears, mountain gorillas and the bengal tiger. Some regions could face widespread extinctions if habitats are transformed making it impossible for certain species to survive.[47]

One of the associated problems of the increased levels of carbon dioxide in the atmosphere is the increased quantity of the gas that is absorbed by the planet's oceans. This creates a greater quantity of carbonic acid, which can have a negative impact on certain species and has the potential to disrupt food chains. Such acidification can be particularly harmful to some types of ecosystems. For example, coral reefs are particularly threatened. Coral reefs provide not only a major resource in terms of fish but they also provide a major form of coastal protection.

In terms of the economic costs of climate change, predictions vary and are naturally contingent upon the scale of the changes, the type of changes that take place and the level of preparation that takes place prior to the full onset of those changes. Some economists have estimated the economic costs running into hundreds of billions of dollars a year.[48] With such a range of different impacts and with so many variables associated with them, there are difficulties in estimating any precise costs. For example in the area of flood damage mitigation, recent research in the UK has estimated that if expenditure on flood defences is maintained at existing levels, the annual damage levels for England and Wales could rise to between £1.6 billion and £29 billion by the 2080s. The fact that many of these changes would be likely to occur at a time far into the future also makes economic planning particularly difficult.[49]

Clearly the effects of climate change on water supplies, food supplies, desertification, flooding, loss of land owing to sea-level rise, and the prevalence of disease can have direct impacts upon the rights to life, health, water, food and property.

2.2.6 Fisheries

The MEA provides an overview of the world's different fish stocks.[50] It states that at least one quarter of marine fish stocks were over-harvested. It states that inland fisheries had also suffered as a result of overfishing, changes to habitats and the withdrawal of fresh water.[51] This process impacts particularly on those communities and regions that are heavily reliant on fish as a source of protein. Further scientific analysis published in 2009 of a range of fish stocks worldwide, showed that efforts in certain regions to manage fish stocks more effectively have resulted in a reduction in exploitation rates.[52] However, that research states that 63 per cent of the fish stocks that were assessed still needed rebuilding and that even lower exploitation rates are required to stop the further collapse of vulnerable species.[53]

The 2010 FAO report *The State of World Fisheries and Aquaculture*[54] provides details particularly in economic and production terms and it indicates the severity of the problems that are faced. It states that globally, fish provide over 1.5 billion people with 20 per cent of their average intake of animal protein and 3 billion people with over 15 per cent.[55] However, the proportion of over-exploited, depleting or recovering stocks increased from 10 per cent in 1974 to 32 per cent in 2008. It states that the proportion of fully exploited stocks remained relatively stable between 1970 and 2008 at 50 per cent.

Certain fishing techniques have caused severe damage not only to fish stocks but also to the marine environment.[56] Prior to the 1980s sea beds, coral reefs and many sensitive ocean-bed ecosystems had been avoided by industrial trawlers as their nets could snag and tear. Since that time however, new types of trawling gear, which include heavy rollers, have been developed. These systems avoid this problem but cause systematic long-term damage on the ocean floor.

The use of cyanide in coral reef areas to stun fish to make them easier to catch is a method that has been employed in some regions since the 1960s. The problem with this method is that the cyanide subsequently kills coral and other aquatic life.

Coral reefs take thousands of years to grow, making this damage irreversible. Ghost fishing is a term that is given to gear that is lost or discarded at sea, but that continues to catch or snare fish, and thus causes further damage. Another problem has been bycatch, which is a term used for the fish or aquatic creatures caught unintentionally during fishing for specific species. Bycatch is often discarded and thus becomes a further waste of natural resources.[57]

The loss or collapse of fish stocks can have a direct impact on the right to food, the right to health for some communities and maybe even the right to life for certain communities too.

2.2.7 *Coral reefs and mangroves*

The MEA states that since about 1980, '35% of mangroves have been lost, while 20% of the world's coral reefs have been destroyed and a further 20% badly degraded or destroyed'.[58] In 2006 the UNEP World Conservation Monitoring Centre published a report that related to the degradation that has been caused to coral reefs and mangroves and the effect that this has on coastal protection from natural weather events.[59] It confirms the MEA's statistics but also states that some countries have lost up to 80 per cent of their original mangrove cover. This degradation has been caused through the conversion of coastal areas to aquaculture, through timber extraction, the use of wood for fuel and charcoal production and through diseases and storms.[60] It states that about 30 per cent of reefs have been seriously damaged and that around 60 per cent could be lost by 2030. This comes about through overfishing, destructive fishing methods, coral mining, anchor damage, pollution, sedimentation and damage through tourism.[61]

Reefs and mangroves are particularly important in buffering waves from storms and hurricanes. It is estimated that 70 to 90 per cent of the wind energy generated in storms and hurricanes is absorbed through coral reefs and mangroves.[62] Therefore the protection that they afford human communities can be significant at normal times and crucial during the occurrence of extreme weather events.

Owing to the potential impact of the increased risk of flooding, storm damage and the impact that this can have on rural communities, the loss of coral and mangroves in certain regions can have a direct impact on the rights to life, health, food and property.

2.2.8 *Biodiversity*

The MEA states that 12 per cent of birds, 25 per cent of mammals and at least 32 per cent of amphibians are threatened with extinction over this century.[63] It is estimated that the rate of global extinctions may have increased by up to 1,000 times the 'natural' rate that is associated with the history of the planet.[64] This loss is largely attributed to the conversion of areas of land to agricultural use.[65] The United Nation's World Economic and Social Survey Report 2011 entitled *The Great Green Technological Transformation* emphasizes the importance of biodiversity to humans, especially in terms of food security:

> [b]iodiversity underpins agriculture and food security through the provision of the genetic material needed for crop and livestock breeding, and raw materials for industry, and other ecosystem services. The past century has seen the greatest loss of biodiversity through habitat destruction, primarily through the conversion of forests for agriculture.[66]

Therefore there are numerous reasons from an anthropocentric perspective why biodiversity should be protected. For example, strains of disease, which attack crops, are continually evolving; it is therefore necessary to maintain wild strains of crops that can be developed and introduced for agricultural purposes as a safeguard against this process. Additionally, many important chemical compounds such as medicines are found in or are derived from wild organisms.[67] Also, many species help to control pollution through the removal of toxins from air, soil and water.[68]

It can be seen that from the pollination of plants by bees to the cleansing of river waters by aquatic plants, biodiversity provides a rich, life-giving range of services to the human population. The depletion of these services is naturally another cause for concern. The loss of biodiversity can have an indirect impact on the rights to food, life and health.

2.2.9 Poverty

Levels of poverty in the world not only posit a pressing imperative, but the integral relationship of poverty with the environment (as indicated above) requires that its current status be assessed.

The United Nation's *World Economic Social Survey* 2011 states that using the poverty line of $1.25 per day, '1.4 billion people, representing about 26 per cent of the developing world's population, lived in poverty in 2005. The incidence of poverty was 50.4 per cent in sub-Saharan Africa and 40.3 per cent in South Asia'.[69] Additionally, the food price rises in 2007–2008 and the economic crisis meant that globally the number of undernourished people was over 1 billion in 2009.[70] Although since then the position in Asia has improved, in 2010 there were still 925 million people who were undernourished.[71] Additionally, malnutrition contributes to the deaths of approximately 6 million children each year.[72]

One of the factors affecting the cost of food, which resulted in the ongoing crisis, is the increasing cost of oil used in food production. Additionally, the conversion of some corn production to the production of bio-fuels has had the effect of raising food prices.[73] As indicated above, the negative effects of climate change can have an aggravating impact on people suffering from insufficient food in numerous regions.

Another key factor is the availability of water. Over 2 billion people live in dry regions of the world and as a result suffer from malnutrition, infant mortality and diseases related to water contamination to a much higher degree than other regions.[74] With 844 million people lacking access to clean drinking water,[75] there can be a conflict between the use of water for industrial purposes and the basic living rights of affected individuals and communities. Associated with this is the fact that some areas such as sub-Saharan Africa have seen a decline in the amount of food produced per each living person.[76]

The relationship between poverty and the environment has been emphasized through the Environmental Performance Index (EPI) produced by Yale and Columbia Universities.[77] The links between poverty and the environment indicate a relationship whereby a failure to protect the environment can increase poverty and an increase in poverty can in turn lead to degradation of the environment. The existence of poverty is an indication of the failure to achieve certain human rights standards such as those anticipated to satisfy the rights to life, health and food.

2.2.10 Population

At around AD 1, there were probably about 100 million people in the world.[78] By 1960 that number had grown to 3 billion. In the last 40 years, the global population has increased to 6.8 billion.[79] It has been estimated that if the current population growth continues at the same rate, there could be 9.4 billion people by 2050.[80] Clearly the increasing population of the planet places even greater stresses on already fractured ecosystem services.

It can also be noted that increases in population can have an indirect impact on human rights owing to the stresses that can be caused in protecting and providing for the rights to life, health, water, food and housing and shelter.

2.3 The response of human rights to environmental degradation

It is clear and has been widely acknowledged that environmental degradation can have extensive impacts upon various human rights.[81] The narrative provided above illustrates the potential for degradation to the environment to particularly impact the well-established rights to life and health.[82] It has also provided clear evidence that other rights such as the rights to water, property, food, shelter/housing and private and family life can also be adversely affected. However, when discussing human rights in this context, there are two caveats that must be mentioned. First, while some human rights such as the right to life, for example, are very well established in a number of different human rights treaties, other human rights are less well established. Not all countries have acceded to the 1966 International Covenant on Economic, Social and Cultural Rights (ICESCR)[83] for example. This means that whereas in theory human rights are designed to be universal, in practical application this is not always the case. The second caveat relates to the meaning of specific rights. Naturally there can be disagreement as to the contents of specific rights and the precise obligations that states owe to the relevant rights holders. Therefore this section seeks to present an overall picture only, a framework that provides a broad understanding of the degree to which existing rights are potentially activated through environmental degradation. It is this broad picture that is required to provide the analysis in the concluding part of the chapter.

2.3.1 The right to life

While it is clear that the framers of the right to life, in the years following World War II, did not originally intend that such a civil and political right should be construed for the protection of the environment, it is certainly the case that certain forms of environmental degradation, referred to above, can ultimately lead to the loss of life. The meaning of the right to life has been expanded over the years. For example, the UN's Human Rights Committee (HRC) to the International Covenant on Civil and Political Rights (ICCPR)[84] developed its interpretation in General Comment 6, which states that:

> 5. . . . the Committee has noted that the right to life has been too narrowly interpreted. The expression 'inherent right to life' cannot properly be understood in a restrictive manner, and the protection of this right requires that States adopt positive measures. In this connection, the Committee considers that it would be desirable for States parties to take all possible measures to reduce infant mortality and to increase life expectancy, especially in adopting measures to eliminate malnutrition and epidemics.[85]

Although 'General Comments' under the UN system are interpretive tools that are non-binding on parties to a treaty, they have a normative value as they are often readily accepted as reflecting the correct interpretation of the original provisions of a treaty. The right to life is one of the fundamental and basic human rights that is included within numerous international and regional human rights treaties.[86] Within these regimes, it has in a small number of cases been deemed to have been violated as a result of severe environmental degradation.[87] Those cases that there are have been well documented and relate to issues such as the construction of a highway through an area of the Amazon that introduced diseases and caused the deaths of members of an indigenous community,[88] the failure of a government to deal with dangerous gases being emitted from a refuse site, which subsequently exploded causing the deaths of 39 people[89] and the failure of a government to take adequate legislative and administrative steps (to deter the threat to the right to life) in an area prone to mudslides that was subsequently hit by a slide in which eight people died.[90]

In addition to human rights, the corresponding constitutional 'right to life' has also been deemed, by courts in certain jurisdictions, to have been violated in cases of extreme environmental degradation. For example, these have included the discharge of effluent by tanneries into agricultural water and local drinking water which became severely polluted,[91] the pollution of drinking water in remote areas by mining operations[92] and the contamination of a river from a waste disposal plant.[93]

In practice it can be seen that in numerous cases, which often represent quite extreme instances of environmental pollution or harm that has affected local communities or individuals, the right to life has been activated effectively. However, from the interpretation of the right to life that is provided in General Comment 6 above, and from the summary of the current state of the environment, it would appear that there are numerous other impacts on the right to life that do not activate direct responses from human rights mechanisms.

If the right to life is to be interpreted as requiring a state to take positive steps to 'eliminate malnutrition and epidemics' for example, it can be seen that many aspects of environmental management are encompassed. These could include for example policies relating to the production of GHGs that contribute to climate change and its adverse effects,[94] domestic and international policies and rules relating to trade that exacerbate climate change and its adverse effects,[95] policies relating to the use of agrochemicals which contaminate waterways reducing the capacity for people to fish and meet nutritional needs,[96] agricultural policies and practices that lead to land degradation and malnutrition,[97] forestry practices and policies that reduce the capacity of local communities to feed themselves effectively and which therefore amplify the potential for ill-health and disease,[98] fishing policies that can lead to fish stock collapses, or fishing practices that harm aquatic life and lead to the potential of malnutrition,[99] policies that lead to the loss of biodiversity that can have a negative impact upon an effective system for the retention of important genetic resources, and pollution control policies that can impact upon the life and health of communities.[100]

2.3.2 The right to health

Similarly, at the time that the 'right to health' was enunciated as part of the ICESCR in 1966,[101] it was not envisaged that environmental degradation could have the severe impact on health that has been described above. The right is now well established within different human rights regimes.[102] The UN has clarified the meaning of the right through the Committee on Economic, Social and Cultural Rights in General Comment 14, which states *inter alia* that:

> 4. …the right to health embraces a wide range of socio-economic factors that promote conditions in which people can lead a healthy life, and extends to the underlying determinants of health, such as food and nutrition, housing, access to safe and potable water and adequate sanitation, safe and healthy working conditions, and a healthy environment.[103]

This has resulted in the greater inclusion of environmental factors within the reporting requirements under the ICESCR.[104] Additionally within the regional human rights regimes, there have been numerous complaints in which it has been determined that the right to health has been adversely affected due to the effects of environmental degradation.[105] It should be noted that the European Convention on Human Rights (ECHR) does not contain a right to health as such but its Article 8, relating to respect for 'private and family life', has been used successfully in cases of severe environmental pollution at the local level.[106]

It can therefore be seen, in a similar manner to that noted for the right to life, that the right to health has been developed to encompass new aspects of national governance. However, when these developments are seen in the light of the scale of the environmental problems that affect the right to health, which were detailed in section 2.2 of this chapter, it is clear that they are still quite limited.

Under the meaning provided by General Comment 14, it is apparent that governments are potentially obliged to take much more stringent measures related to environmental protection. The full range of areas of concern would, as detailed in section 2.2, include all those aspects that affect the right to health such as industrial GHG emissions,[107] national and international trade policies and rules, agricultural laws and policies, fishing laws and policies, forestry and the rules relating to the management of biodiversity including aspects such as coral reefs and mangroves.

It can also be noted that while the International Court of Justice (ICJ) has not provided a specific judgement relating to the status of the 'right to life' and the 'right to health', in a separate opinion in 1997, Judge Weeramantry stated (famously) that:

> [t]he protection of the environment is likewise a vital part of contemporary human rights doctrine, for it is a *sine qua non* for numerous human rights such as the right to health and the right to life itself. It is scarcely necessary to elaborate on this, as damage to the environment can impair and undermine all the human rights spoken of in the Universal Declaration and other rights instruments. While, therefore, all peoples have the right to initiate development projects and enjoy their benefits, there is likewise a duty to ensure that those projects do not significantly damage the environment.[108]

2.3.3 The right to water

The right to water has drawn much of its legitimacy from a number of rights which include the right to an adequate standard of living, the right to the highest attainable standard of health and the right to life.[109] General Comment 15 to the ICESCR made clear that all peoples have a right to sufficient, safe, acceptable, physically accessible and affordable water for personal and domestic uses.[110] Additionally in 2010, the United Nations General Assembly made a resolution that recognized that access to clean water and sanitation is a human right.[111] In 2011 a resolution by the Human Rights Council of the United Nations called on states to ensure that there is enough financing for the sustainable delivery of water and sanitation services.[112]

The right to water is in the process of developing, so it will take a lengthy period of time for its contents to properly evolve and for the precise expectations that are required of states to develop. It leads to some particular challenges in terms of the environment because the issue of available potable water has twin dimensions. These are that it relates first to the need for water to be unpolluted and drinkable, therefore there is a responsibility on states to ensure that the water that people drink is of a certain quality. However the other dimension of the right to water in many jurisdictions is that of distribution and access. Many regions of sub-Saharan Africa for example are subject to water stresses and this issue leads inevitably to how populations will acquire adequate supplies of potable water. This distributional aspect of the right leads to issues of the management of the available water supplies on the one hand and on the other, to the wider issues of the overall causes of depleting water supplies in certain regions.[113]

As has already been noted, human rights have been used in the context of water pollution in certain jurisdictions, where access to potable water has been regarded as fundamental to the right to life and or health.[114] However, in terms of overall law and policy, the right to water does not directly result in legal mechanisms that are designed to reverse some of the causes of water stresses that certain regions face. For example it does not create a direct mechanism relating to climate change laws and policies, in spite of the fact that the effects of climate change are beginning to contribute to specific water stresses in certain regions of the world.

2.3.4 The right to food

The right to food[115] and the right to be free from hunger[116] are now well established.[117] The ICESCR states that everyone has the right to 'an adequate standard of living for himself and his family, including adequate food'.[118] Additionally it states that everyone has 'the fundamental right to be free from hunger'.[119] General Comment 12 states that the right to food shall:

> 6. …therefore not be interpreted in a narrow or restrictive sense which equates it with a minimum package of calories, proteins and other specific nutrients. The *right to adequate food* will have to be realized progressively. However, States have a core obligation to take the necessary action to mitigate and alleviate hunger…[120]

Manifestations of the right include international efforts to alleviate hunger such as the UN Food Assistance Convention (FAC) 2012.[121]

The links between the right to food and environmental degradation, especially the impacts of climate change, are self-evident.[122] However, the measures relating to the right to food that have developed on an international level tend to relate more directly to the provision of aid in times of crisis rather than creating new legal mechanisms that, for example, reduce GHG emissions on the basis of the lack of food that may result from some of the negative consequences of climate change. At this time, in this respect, the influence of the right to food is limited to providing a persuasive argument that policies should avoid negatively impacting the provision of food in the future.

2.3.5 The right to housing or shelter

The right to housing or shelter also needs to be considered. This right is also derived from the right to an adequate standard of living under the ICESCR.[123] General Comment 4 states that it:

> 7. …should not be interpreted in a narrow or restrictive sense which equates it with, for example, the shelter provided by merely having a roof over one's head or views shelter exclusively as a commodity. Rather it should be seen as the right to live somewhere in security, peace and dignity…[124]

One of the greatest possible impacts of climate change for the future is the potential displacement of large numbers of people in certain geographical areas. This may be due to lack of adequate water supplies in certain regions, the lack of food in some regions, the flooding of certain areas and also potentially due to conflicts that may occur as a result of those environmental stresses. Such displacement and the creation of significant migrant communities could severely impact the right to housing or shelter.

Predictably there are at this point in time no direct mechanisms from this human right that create legal obligations related to the mitigation of climate change, such as the reduction of emissions of GHGs.

2.3.6 The right to property

The right to property is evidenced in numerous international human rights treaties[125] and it is also present in most national constitutions. There are a number of different ways in which the right is linked with environmental protection, environmental regulation or the management of natural resources.

First, there is the potential failure of governments to take adequate environmental measures, such as those to mitigate climate change, which could have the effect of displacing communities from their land. There is only sparse evidence at this time of legal claims of this type related to the right to property.[126]

Second and conversely, there is the potential for the right to property to be invoked in cases where the government has taken environmental measures that in themselves have an impact on the property rights of landowners.[127] However, generally in such cases, the human rights tribunals allow states a wide margin of appreciation in their decision-making relating to land use and the measures they employ for the protection of the environment.[128]

Third, for indigenous communities living in remote regions, which do not have well-established property rights, there have been cases in which states have been instructed by international human rights tribunals to demarcate boundaries to ensure that the traditional lands that the communities inhabit are better protected from the environmental impacts of industrial projects.[129]

In addition to the different ways that the right to property can be impacted or used for the protection of the environment, property rights are sometimes granted in natural resources themselves and this in itself can have widespread impacts. For example, there is the possibility of property rights being created in water, which can negatively impact the access that local people have to it. This can be particularly problematical where monopolistic concessions are granted to corporations relating to water supplies, leaving local communities subject to excessive charges for access to what is a basic human requirement.[130]

2.4 The development of environmental rights internationally

Environmental rights have developed at a considerable pace over the last 40 years. The concept of the further development of environmental rights is one that has attracted a wide range of supporters and detractors along with a wide range of arguments about the types of rights that should possibly be developed. These arguments are illustrative of how recently these concepts have emerged. Unlike many of the founding precepts of public international law, which emerged in the seventeenth century, the emergence of environmental rights has taken place in the post-World War II era.

In 1949 Aldo Leopold stated that:

> [t]he extension of ethics to this third element in human environment is, if I read the evidence correctly, an evolutionary possibility and an ecological necessity…[t]he land ethic simply enlarges the boundaries of the community to include soils, waters, plants, and animals, or collectively: the land.[131]

Later the scientist and pioneering environmentalist Rachel Carson, stated in the 1960s that individuals should be guaranteed freedom from lethal poisons by the Bill of Rights.[132] In 1972 Christopher Stone wrote a groundbreaking essay in which he put forward the case for natural objects to have legal rights.[133] In 1974 the French Nobel prize-winning lawyer René Cassin declared that over the previous 20 years, the notion of an environmental right had emerged.[134] In 1976 W. P. Gormley wrote a book entitled, *Human Rights and the Environment: The Need for International Cooperation*, in which he asserted the existence of a new human right to a 'minimum decent environment'.[135]

Since then there has been a steady growth of developments within the law itself. This evolution requires attention owing to the different types of rights that have developed and also due to the differing levels of effectiveness that they have in practice. This part of the chapter seeks to provide a summary of these developments with a view to considering the overall impact that they have had in relation to the scale of environmental degradation that is affecting the environment. It therefore considers rights that have developed within international human rights law and also those within international environmental law. It mentions the significance of environmental rights that have developed under state constitutions although these are considered in more detail in Chapter 3. It also notes the work that has taken place within the UN.

Within the field of environmental rights generally, there is a distinction between what are known as 'procedural' rights and 'substantive' rights. Substantive environmental rights entitle the holder to an environment of a specific standard, whereas procedural environmental rights entitle the holder to engage in processes that are normally classified as the right of access to information, the right to participate in decision-making and the right of access to justice. Access to information may for example amount to the right to access information that local or national authorities hold relating to pollutants in a particular locality. The right to participate in decision-making might, for example, be the right to be consulted in local hearings relating to proposed new developments. The right of access to justice may for example amount to the right to challenge a planning process for a development project in the local or national courts.[136]

2.4.1 Procedural environmental rights

Although many of the philosophical arguments relating to environmental rights have centred around substantive environmental rights, many of the practical developments in this field have involved the inclusion of procedural environmental rights in decision-making processes. These rights owe their origins to concepts of fair governance that precede environmental concerns and that were embodied in the Universal Declaration of Human Rights (UDHR) 1948.[137] The concept of participatory rights relating to the environment emerged during the 1970s and 1980s and came to prominence in 1992 when they were embodied in Principle 10 of the Rio Declaration.[138] The general strengthening of participatory rights within human rights law in recent decades has had the effect of strengthening the development of environmental procedural rights and their integration into international environmental law.[139] Therefore states have been ready to accept the inclusion of procedural rights within a wide range of multilateral environmental agreements such as those related to the protection of biodiversity, climate change, specific watercourse regimes and agreements relating to environmental cooperation in specific regions.[140]

These developments show that the lines between human rights law and environmental law can become blurred. Procedural environmental rights represent a practical and functional hybrid between human rights law and environmental law. This is shown clearly in the United Nations Economic Commission for Europe (UNECE) Aarhus Convention,[141] one of the most important international developments in this field. It is of specific interest for a number of reasons. First, because as an international treaty, its purpose and focus are solely related to procedural environmental rights. Second, it has been widely accepted within Europe (indeed by the European Union – EU) and a number of other states that are members of the UNECE.[142] Third, it includes innovative features such as a compliance mechanism that allows complaints from members of the public to its 'Compliance Committee'.[143] This has been particularly effective in providing a practical facility to enable individuals and non-government organizations (NGOs) to place pressure on their home states to provide procedural rights that conform to the treaty regime's developing standards.[144]

The ICJ can be important as although its judgements do not amount to the creation of law and strictly speaking do not create binding precedent, its judgements often provide a respected analysis of the state of the law. A judgement in 2010 was significant as it recognized that it was a requirement under 'general international law' that an environmental impact assessment (EIA) be carried out prior to developments taking place that could potentially harm the environment of a neighbouring state.[145] Such a procedure inevitably activates the duty for the state concerned to provide information and a process of consultation with those affected. Therefore this case reinforced the status of procedural environmental rights at the international level.

Additionally, specific procedural environmental rights have been included in the state constitutions of 30 national constitutions.[146] More general procedural rights that could have application to environmental issues are included in many other national constitutions.[147] Often the effectiveness of these national regimes will depend on the system of laws and regulations that implement such rights and of course the administrative and judicial infrastructure in the country concerned.[148] However they have increasingly been relied upon in numerous jurisdictions to good effect.[149] In practice procedural environmental rights are often seen most prominently in the consultation requirements of EIAs[150] and strategic environmental assessments (SEA).[151] The efficacy of those regulations will also have a key impact on the effectiveness of the procedural rights in the given jurisdiction.

Finally, procedural environmental rights are now extensively included within the operational policies of international financial institutions such as the multilateral development banks (MDBs). These institutions will require that development loans be tied to EIAs and SEAs that are accompanied by the provision of adequate procedural rights.[152]

2.4.2 Substantive environmental rights

In terms of substantive environmental rights there has been less development within international law. To many, the United Nations Conference on Human Environment (UNCHE) in Stockholm (1972) marked the dawn of modern international environmental law. Also it laid down a foundation stone for those seeking to develop concrete links between environmental degradation and human rights. Principle 1 stated that, '[m]an has the fundamental right to freedom, equality and adequate conditions of life in an environment of a quality that permits a life of dignity and well-being, and he bears a solemn responsibility to protect and improve the environment for present and future generations'.[153] As a declaration, it did not establish a new environmental right under international law, but it was of considerable influence especially in terms of the way that established human rights such as the 'right to life' and 'the right to health' went on to be interpreted and developed.

However at the United Nations Conference on Environment and Development (UNCED) in Rio de Janeiro in 1992 it was the concept of 'sustainable development' that emerged as the policy choice of the international community and this meant that references to human rights for environmental protection faded in comparison.[154] Therefore the Rio Declaration used language that largely avoided references to human rights.[155] It stated that, '[h]uman beings are at the centre of concerns for sustainable development. They are entitled to a healthy and productive life in harmony with nature'.[156] Neither the WSSD Conference[157] in 2002 or the United Nations Conference on Sustainable Development (Rio + 20)[158] in 2012 produced declarations similar to those of UNCHE and UNCED. At the Rio + 20 conference, a declaration made by the UN General Assembly reaffirmed all of the principles from the original Rio Declaration.[159]

There have been some significant developments in the field of regional human rights treaties. Within the regime of the American Convention on Human Rights (ACHR), the Additional Protocol in the Area of Economic, Social and Cultural Rights (The Protocol of San Salvador) 1989 provides in Article 11 that states should 'protect, preserve and improve the environment' and that citizens have the right to 'live in a healthy environment'.[160] Additionally, Article 24 of the African Charter of Human and Peoples' Rights (AFCHPR) 1981 states that citizens have a right to a, 'general satisfactory environment favourable to their development'.[161]

The aforementioned provisions are clearly drafted in wide terms, which leave much open to interpretation. Within the human rights system of the Organization of American States (OAS)[162] there has been limited use and development of the environmental provisions of the Protocol of San Salvador. There has been much more active use of other rights such as the rights to life and property rather than Article 11.[163]

Similar comments can also be made of the AFCHPR.[164] The treaty does have its own commission and court that consider complaints. However, this system is hampered by a lack of real authority and political influence.[165] Article 24 of the treaty was invoked in a case filed against Nigeria that related to the environmental harm caused to a community by the activities of a multinational oil company.[166] It could therefore be argued that the treaty provision and the Commission, at very least, have the potential to raise awareness and increase political pressure in relation to certain cases.

The Arab Charter on Human Rights came into force in 2008. It does include a right to a healthy environment within Article 38 but the charter does not have an effective enforcement mechanism and therefore time will tell precisely what impact it will have in the region.[167]

It should also be noted that judgments of the ICJ have not advanced the case for specific recognition of a substantive environmental right under international law.[168]

In spite of the limited development of substantive environmental rights on an international level, there has been a significant growth of constitutional substantive environmental rights at the national level. Of the 193 nations recognized by the United Nations, 147 countries include specific references to environmental rights or responsibilities for the protection of the environment.[169] This is a dramatic scale of adoption when it is considered that this process began in the 1970s.[170] However, it must also be remembered that since World War II, 113 new states have been recognized by the international community and in the drafting of their constitutions it would seem reasonable to include provisions relating to the environment owing to its importance as a national issue.[171] Additionally, national constitutions are generally speaking not static in terms of their content; in fact they are remarkably ephemeral in this respect. On average they are changed every 19 years and in any given year have a 38 per cent chance of being amended.[172] Between 1990 and 2000, over half of the world's national constitutions were amended and of those, 70 per cent adopted completely new constitutions.[173]

Therefore when constitutional amendments are made, it can be seen as natural to include environmental provisions. One of the few countries that has traditionally not amended its constitution is the United States of America. However, many of the individual states within the US, have amended theirs and do now contain environmental provisions.[174] The EU does not have a constitution as such but many of its member states have environmental provisions within their own constitutions. The EU did create a non-binding Charter of Fundamental Rights in 2000 that does make certain references to the protection of the environment.[175] It also acceded to the European Convention on Human Rights in 2009, although it is currently unclear what the precise implications of this step will mean in terms of environmental rights.[176]

In South America groundbreaking developments have taken place with the introduction in 2008 in the Constitution of Ecuador of 'the right of nature to exist'[177] and the introduction of a law in Bolivia that also grants rights to nature.[178] It is difficult to predict the precise impact of these developments, although it is fair to say that they are generating a lot of interest on the international level, including in 2012 a paragraph in the Rio + 20 outcome document, *The Future We Want.*[179]

As has already been observed, constitutional rights to life have been used quite frequently in claims relating to extreme pollution that could have a detrimental effect on the health of individuals.[180] Increasingly however specific environmental rights are also used in claims in many different countries. Not all of the environmental rights contained in constitutions are justiciable (entitling citizens to use them to take a legal claim again the government in court). However, many of them are used in litigation, the results of which have included: stopping an environmental authority from authorizing the discharge of polluted groundwater into local rivers (State of Montana, USA),[181] the ordering of a clean up of a polluted river that led to World Bank funding for a sustainable development project (Argentina),[182] declaring that an ordinance by a local authority to convert an area of wetlands from recreational use to commercial use was unconstitutional (Peru),[183] ensuring that a governmental authority take measures to protect endangered sea turtles within a national park (Costa Rica),[184] making an order that certain timber license agreements (TLAs) should be cancelled (Philippines),[185] rejecting a challenge to a government ban on highly polluting vehicles (Nepal)[186] and annulling a development plan for new businesses in the vicinity of a lakeland area (Slovenia).[187]

There is also the potential for regional human rights courts to use constitutional environmental rights as a basis upon which to find that a state has failed in its duties towards its citizens *vis à vis* the environment (Europe).[188] It is widely recognized that the judiciary in certain regions, such as many of the jurisdictions in South America, have been ready to use constitutional environmental provisions as a means of providing environmental protection. Additionally, although there is no justiciable environmental right within the Indian constitution, its judiciary has famously expanded the meaning of the constitutional right to life and pioneered innovative measures to secure protection of the environment.[189] The few cases above are mentioned solely to provide a very broad overview of the types of cases that have been contested successfully on the basis of substantive environmental rights within national constitutions. Certain authors have carried out very useful and extensive studies of this area of jurisprudence.[190]

It can be observed that where constitutional environmental rights can have a direct impact is in cases of severe environmental pollution or degradation at a local level. There are numerous examples in a variety of jurisdictions, as noted above. However, it has been noted that invariably where attempts have been made to use constitutional rights (whether that be the right to life, the right to health or an environmental provision) to challenge national development projects, they have mostly failed. Examples include the Narmada Dam project in India,[191] the Camisea natural gas extraction project in Peru[192] and more recently the Belo Monte Dam project in Brazil that is due to flood 516 square kilometres of land (mainly standing forest) and displace 20,000 people.[193] There are some exceptional cases where national constitutional provisions have been used to successfully challenge national level development projects.[194] These include an action taken to reject the development of an offshore oil extraction project in Costa Rica.[195] Similarly, it can also be observed that so far, state constitutional provisions have only been used occasionally to strike down legislation that would result in increased degradation of the environment.[196]

Therefore it must be noted that on a global scale, substantive environmental rights have had only limited impacts. They have not resulted in the creation of mechanisms for addressing the root causes of much of the environmental degradation that was described above. For example they have not resulted in the creation of distinct mechanisms to control GHG emissions, the causes of loss of biodiversity, the causes of loss of forests, the causes of loss of fisheries and coral reefs; all of which can ultimately have significant impacts on people's human rights, as was detailed above.

2.4.3 Developments within the United Nations

The links between human rights and the environment have long been recognized by the UN.[197] Whereas the ICJ (itself an organ of the UN) has not taken a proactive stance in developing environmental rights, other organs of the UN have been particularly active. As has already been noted there have been certain key initiatives such as numerous General Comments that have developed the meaning of rights, such as the right to life and the right to health in order that they include environmental factors.[198] Additionally, the reporting requirements in relation to the ICESCR have expanded to include environmental concerns.[199]

A significant development occurred in 1989 when the UN appointed a Special Rapporteur to carry out a five-year study of the links between human rights and the environment.[200] The final report included a draft international environmental right (comprised of a number of rights).[201] Although the newly drafted right was not taken any further, it represented the first attempt at the international institutional level to draft a substantive human right for the protection of the environment.

General continuing interest within the UN in relation to the issue of human rights and the environment led to the General Assembly announcing a 'Mother Earth' day in 2009 following Bolivia's creation of a law for the right of nature to exist.[202] Further work has included a Human Rights Council resolution in 2011 for a new study to be undertaken on the relationship between human rights and climate change.[203] In addition, the Human Rights Council made a resolution in 2012 to appoint an expert for a period of three years to make recommendations relating to the human rights obligations that pertain to the enjoyment of a 'safe, clean and healthy and sustainable environment'.[204]

2.5 Conclusion

One of the characteristics of this field is that authors differ in their opinion as to whether or not a right to 'clean' or 'healthy' environment has actually evolved. (Different authors have produced different versions of a potential environmental right. These have included, 'a right to environment' and a right to a 'healthy', 'clean', 'adequate', 'decent', 'satisfactory', 'safe' or 'viable' environment.)[205]

Some authors argue that as a result of the culmination of developments that have taken place within the field of environmental rights, an actual right to a 'clean' or 'healthy' environment has emerged on an international level.[106] There is certainly a very strong case to say that procedural environmental rights have emerged as customary international law. The claim that a substantive environmental right, such as a right to a 'healthy' or 'clean' environment has emerged is more difficult to argue. Most lawyers are of the opinion that if it exists at all, it does so as an emerging right. Strict adherence to international law rules of interpretation would probably affirm that position.[207]

What is more important however is not the label that is given to the variety of new rights which have emerged over the last 40 years but the state of their effectiveness in the face of the scale of environmental harm that is occurring on national and international levels. There are three key points that are clear from the information that has been provided in this chapter.

First, environmental degradation is without doubt a human rights issue within the contemporary understanding of human rights. It can be seen that the modern interpretation of core rights such as the right to life and the right to health now encompass responsibilities that states have in relation to issues relating to the environment. This has been seen especially through the General Comments of the UN's HRC and the Committee on Economic, Social and Cultural Rights. For example under the right to life, there is the responsibility of states to take positive measures to eliminate malnutrition and epidemics.[208] This would indicate that there are human rights responsibilities upon states in relation to a number of the environmental problems that have been summarized such as climate change, loss of biodiversity, loss of water, land use change and degradation, loss of fisheries and loss of coral and mangroves.

Second, human rights mechanisms are only able to respond to a very small percentage of those impacts. It has been seen that existing human rights mechanisms and mechanisms within state constitutions for the protection of constitutional rights have had limited application in terms of the scale of environmental harm that is currently affecting and is forecast to affect peoples' human rights. It has been observed that usually where litigation does occur successfully in this field, it is in relation to local authority decision-making rather than national authority decisions or policy-making.

Third, it is clear that other traditional or existing mechanisms are also failing to respond adequately to those issues, otherwise we would not see the scale of degradation that we are currently witnessing. Therefore we are seeing not only the impact of environmental degradation on human rights and the failure of existing human rights and constitutional rights mechanisms to adequately respond to those problems but also an inadequacy of those systems of national and international environmental law that have been instituted to deal with those challenges. As such, on an international level, we are witnessing a climate change regime that is struggling not just to address the problem but even to define an acceptable approach; we are seeing an international regime for biodiversity that similarly is struggling to address the mounting challenges that are faced globally; we are experiencing the struggle of international regimes to adequately manage fish stocks; and we are observing corresponding challenges in most other aspects of international environmental governance.

Therefore this chapter highlights the fact that environmental degradation is very much a human rights issue and that existing human rights mechanisms do little to address the majority of the severe environmental problems that occur on a global level. Additionally, it highlights the fact that existing approaches through international environmental law are currently inadequate in dealing with the problems that are faced. This final issue raises the question of whether or not there is something fundamentally flawed in the approach that is currently being taken by the international community to environmental degradation and whether or not human rights (in one form or another) have a meaningful contribution to make to create mechanisms that can stem the tide of the environmental degradation which is occurring.

This point leads to the next chapter that considers the fundamental flaws with existing approaches to global environmental governance, the root causes of environmental degradation in terms of the global legal architecture that has developed and what that could mean for the future.

3 Global environmental governance, the global legal architecture and the root causes of environmental degradation

3.1 Introduction

The previous chapter highlighted the extent of environmental degradation on a global level and the relationship that this has with existing human rights. The international community is challenged at this current time, not through a lack of initiatives for the protection of the environment but through the failure to clearly define and adopt systems that can resolve the problems at hand. Despite an ever-increasing international will to establish programmes of action that will lead to the levels of environmental protection that are required, efforts often lead to minimal improvement and in the case of the climate change regime, a system that has overseen an overall deterioration rather than an improvement.

This chapter explores the reasons why the existing systems of international environmental governance so often fail to bring results and frequently leave us with an ever-worsening legacy. It therefore seeks to expose the root causes of environmental degradation in terms of the global legal architecture. This is a key analysis that is required if future environmental governance on a global scale is to avoid replication of systems that lead to the outcomes and impacts on human rights that were described in the previous chapter.

The chapter develops in three phases. The first phase analyses the existing approaches to international environmental governance. It demonstrates that from an academic and institutional point of view at least, there has been an emphasis (unsurprisingly perhaps) on the functions of existing international environmental law. However, it goes on to note that increasingly scholars are looking beyond traditional international environmental law, given the preponderance of non-state actors that now have an impact on global environmental governance. Therefore it not only registers the change of emphasis that has occurred within the field of environmental governance but acknowledges a global legal architecture that to a great extent exists quite separately from international environmental law but within which some of the root causes of environmental degradation can be found.

Therefore the second part of the chapter examines this global legal architecture and it focuses on three key areas to emphasize some of the drivers or root causes of environmental degradation. Those three areas are the laws that relate to corporations (companies), the law relating to the WTO and the constitutional law relating to states themselves.

In terms of corporations, this chapter seeks to show the precise legal obligations that corporate directors have in their decision-making relating to the environment. In terms of the WTO, it seeks to show the legal framework of obligations relating to the environment that membership of the WTO creates for states. While the effectiveness of environmental provisions within constitutions was considered within Chapter 2, this chapter examines national constitutional provisions within the wider obligations that states have and exposes the *reasons* why they are of limited effect in terms of constraining the decision-making of governments in relation to the environment. Within each of these areas, a historical perspective is provided to illustrate how the global legal architecture has developed. The historical perspective is important as it demonstrates that the global legal architecture did not evolve in an *ad hoc* manner, but was developed through careful and deliberate design. It explains how the very design of the law itself is fundamentally predisposed to environmental degradation and forms part of a dysfunctional global legal architecture which cannot achieve environmental sustainability.

The final part of the chapter therefore concludes that with the existing dysfunctions within the global legal architecture, international environmental law is unlikely to succeed. It concludes that adjustments to the design of the framework of laws which make up the global legal architecture are required.

3.2 Existing approaches to global environmental governance

There has been a wide range of different approaches to the issue of global environmental governance. It certainly is not possible here to provide anything other than a broad summary of some of the dominant themes that have emerged within this field. However, in doing so, it is possible to identify certain features that recur frequently, and certain observations that resonate and pave the way for the type of approach that this book adopts.

The undercurrent of all of the work relating to global environmental governance is an acknowledgement that overall, international environmental law in its current form does not achieve the levels of environmental protection that are required in the long term. However it is necessary to be realistic in our expectations. The modern system of international environmental law is only just over 40 years old, is faced with problems that have taken much longer than that to develop and has in fact accumulated some considerable successes along the way.[1] While a fair assessment must include references to certain initiatives such as the Stockholm Declaration,[2] the Rio Declaration,[3] the associated development of principles of international environmental law and individual successes such as the Montreal Protocol,[4] the overriding state of the planet's environment as detailed in Chapter 2 is a testament to a system of international environmental law and international environmental governance that is struggling to meet the existing challenges.

3.2.1 The Westphalian system

For the challenges that are faced, the overarching question of the adequacy of the

Westphalian system is called into question.[5] This system emerged in the seventeenth century and established the state-centric model for international law and international relations. While such a system has been effective in certain respects, such as the resolution of individual disputes, there is a question as to its capacity to provide the requisite framework to deal with many issues such as transboundary pollution, climate change, the degradation of the global commons and to provide requisite control of multinational enterprises (MNEs). It was observed by commentators of international law, long prior to the current issues facing the environment, that the system of international law excluded non-state actors and the question of their inclusion had been a point of debate.[6] Contemporary commentators note that in certain respects global environmental governance is developing in a fragmented manner that no longer conforms to the traditional top-down approach; it is one in which non-state actors such as businesses, NGOs and even individuals can have significant influence.[7] This obviously raises questions of the appropriateness of the existing international legal system to adapt and respond effectively to this new 'multi-layered' and 'multi-faceted' reality.[8]

While the emergence in strength of new actors on the international scene and the development of new responsibilities for states and their leaders has evolved and affected the notion of 'sovereignty' since World War II, the framework for the creation of international law has remained fundamentally unchanged. Peel for example emphasizes that in spite of the influence of other actors, 'states remain far and away the most important actors shaping international environmental law'.[9] Generally the framework still functions on the basis of states acting as the sole subjects of international law. This system has advantages in terms of the representation of governments but potential drawbacks such as the reluctance of states to bind their countries to onerous commitments that may affect their economic competitiveness.

3.2.2 'Soft law' and 'hard law'

In terms of international environmental law, the Westphalian system has been criticized for the 'soft law' that has evolved as an integral component of it. Critics may argue that the evolution of 'soft law' commitments by states are a convenient cloak for both inaction by governments and a lack of political will to develop binding commitments. Others may point to the relatively short timescale that governments have had to address major environmental problems, the need for a process of gradual adjustment and institution building, and the helpfulness of 'soft law' commitments in terms of creating the groundwork for the development of new 'norms', international cooperation and practical responses to difficult problems.[10]

While 'soft law' can be viewed as being problematical, the development of 'hard law' has been no less controversial. In terms of sheer quantity, there has been no shortage of international environmental agreements. UNEP records show that between 1920 and the end of 1970, a total of only 50 international treaties in the field of the environment were agreed but in the next 30 years, between 1971 and the end of 2000, a further 193 such treaties were added to that number.[11] Additionally, in certain sectors there has been a high intensity of treaty creating activity. For example, some countries have ratified up to 30 multilateral environmental agreements relating to the atmosphere.[12] Although this process has slowed down over the last decade, it has produced a concept that has become known as 'treaty congestion'.[13] The number of treaties can have unwelcome side-effects such as an overlap between the subject matter of different treaty regimes, states (especially developing countries) finding it difficult if not impossible to resource the wide range of treaty commitments[14] and also the management of a wide range of treaties can create challenges for the associated international institutions or treaty bodies.

3.2.3 Compliance

Treaties often exhibit common issues in terms of their organization and management. One of the key challenges is that of compliance. The problem of ensuring that states comply with their treaty obligations is one that raises the issue of effective monitoring and enforcement. This is an area that has received significant attention from academics and practitioners.[15] International environmental law has generally relied on mechanisms such as reporting by state parties to demonstrate their levels of compliance. Reports however may not always be forthcoming or may provide an incomplete picture. Where they indicate a failure to comply, the responses that the treaty organizations generally employ are non-confrontational approaches that seek resolution through support and facilitation. This system can be fraught with difficulty as it can lead to states signing up to treaties but failing to attempt to comply with their obligations.[16] While innovative new techniques have been developed within certain treaty regimes to attempt to ensure compliance, states are traditionally reluctant to bind themselves to regimes that would lead to inspections by international bodies or punitive measures in the event of non-compliance.[17] For this reason the practical *modus operandai* of multilateral environmental agreements is one that leads to much critical debate and a range of different opinions as to what types of methods could or should be adopted to facilitate effective and comprehensive protection of the environment.[18]

3.2.4 A World Environment Organization?

The issue of 'treaty congestion', the associated proliferation of treaty secretariats and the ongoing debate about compliance has led some to look to the creation of new international institutions as a potential solution. Arguments for the creation of a World Environment Organization (WEO) have surfaced and re-surfaced since the mid-1990s.[19] In recent times the Rio + 20 conference was a forum for further calls from some quarters for the creation of a WEO.[20] There is no single model for a WEO. Different authors have different visions of the precise role that such an organization could fulfill, its structure, source of authority and make up.

However, there has been a growing acknowledgement that an organization such as the WTO is much more powerful politically and economically than either UNEP or the secretariats and treaty bodies of the multilateral environmental agreements. Therefore there is an argument that a WEO could have the potential to counterbalance the influence of major international commercial organizations such as the WTO by presiding as an authority relating to environmental standards. It can also be said that an organization such as the WTO may be ill-equipped to provide the level of expertise that is required to deal with trade disputes that involve issues relating to environmental standards. Additionally in terms of the levels of 'treaty congestion' that have been referred to, there are arguments that a WEO could provide an overall administrative authority to coordinate the work currently undertaken by different secretariats of various multilateral environmental agreements. While such a suggestion may appear attractive, the practicalities would undoubtedly create numerous difficulties and as much as there have been proponents of such a concept, significant opposition has also emerged.[21]

3.2.5 An expanded approach to international environmental law

Calls for a WEO are inevitably interlinked with the general make up of global environmental governance in terms of the existing international institutions that make decisions or have a role in the legal or administrative processes that can affect the environment. These include not just the WTO but the MDBs (of which the World Bank is the most prominent) and the various other international organizations. Peel points to this by stating:

> [t]hat we now look to the WTO and other economic institutions, as much as to international environmental organizations, for rules governing environmental matters attests to the extent of integration of environmental issues into aspects of economic and development institutions and law. This is a welcome development in that it signals the potential for international environmental law to have a transformative effect on broader institutional society.[22]

Additionally, the roles of MNEs and other non-state actors have grown in their capacity to influence decision-making on an international level. Increasingly scholars are looking at this wider institutional and administrative picture rather than solely the body of international environmental law that is found in multilateral environmental agreements. For example Sands *et al.* state that:

> a growing role for non-state actors of various kinds in international environmental law is shifting the focus from (exclusively) top-down strategies of law-making and implementation, with states and international organizations as the principle actors, to a bottom-up dynamic where international legal development may be driven to a greater extent by the actions of individuals, business and NGOs.[23]

Bodansky goes even further by stating that:

> [t]he boundaries of what constitutes an 'environmental' issue have already become blurred. Problems such as global warming and loss of biological diversity result from a wide variety of factors, including population growth, energy use, consumption patterns, and trade. If international environmental law is to address not merely the surface manifestations but the root causes of environmental degradation, then our understanding of what constitutes an environmental issue must grow to encompass economic, social, and trade policy. Indeed, if, as some claim, everything is interconnected, then everything becomes an environmental problem. For now, however, this kind of integration is still more of an aspiration than a reality.[24]

The suggestion that the 'root causes of environmental degradation' may be built into 'economic, social and trade policy' leads the reviewer of global environmental governance to a new viewing point. If that is the case, then one task for environmental lawyers is to analyse those root causes from a legal perspective to determine whether or not such causes are in fact built into the core systems of the global legal architecture. It is therefore at this point that this chapter turns its attention to elaborating further on this perspective.

3.3 The development of a global legal architecture

This section considers significant aspects and elements of the global legal architecture that may constitute or contribute to the root causes of environmental degradation worldwide. Therefore it considers the legal frameworks that determine how decisions are made within three of the most important types of actors on the international stage; these are corporations (companies), the WTO and states. As will be seen, the law relating to these actors has developed in such a way that it is applicable to the majority of countries in the world. For this reason it is possible to describe these frameworks of law as forming important parts of the 'global legal architecture'.

In assessing fundamental constitutional aspects of this global legal architecture, it is possible to show that key aspects of it are predisposed towards decision-making, which can cause environmental degradation. However, it is important to understand why these legal rules developed in the way that they did in order that appropriate re-design can be considered. Therefore in examining corporations, the WTO and states it is necessary to trace the historical development of their legal frameworks or constitutions. It is from this foundation that it is possible to contemplate a programme of reform that would lead to effective global environmental governance.

3.3.1 Corporations

Prior to embarking on this section, it should be noted that the term 'corporation' is used for convenience to encompass corporations, companies and other styles of incorporated businesses with limited liability in jurisdictions around the globe. As will become clear this narrative focuses on particular elements of the law that enable this generalization to be made.

Within much contemporary literature relating to the environment, the decisions of those in business and industry have often been severely criticized owing to the negative impact that their operations have caused to the environment and the impacts that they have had on human rights. This can be both helpful in exposing corporate decision-making but also unhelpful when it is accompanied by a failure to acknowledge the legal prerequisites that determine how corporate directors are obliged to make those decisions. Additionally, such an approach is often founded upon a presumption that corporations and the business community have a legal responsibility to protect the environment over and above the levels of protection that are required under the applicable national law.

It is understandable that the actions of corporations and their directors cause consternation or anger when news is received of the negative effects of their activities. These might be the construction of a highway through a tropical forest causing death to indigenous communities and loss of biodiversity, an industrial plant leeching poisons into groundwater threatening the lives and health of local communities, the development of mineral extraction activities destroying pristine aspects of nature or overfishing in areas containing depleted fish stocks and fragile ecosystems. However, directing attention purely at the results, and not at the underlying legal frameworks that cause such decision-making to take place, connotes a disconnect of understanding with a constitutional system of law that was designed by our forefathers two centuries ago. It is a system of law that has its origins in the very things that we all need, goods and trade and commerce. Therefore, for us to understand the legal system that affects the way that corporate directors make decisions, it is important to understand how and why it developed in the way that it did.

3.3.1.1 Historical development of companies

In going back to the origins of the modern corporation, we find the root causes of the legal constraints that company directors are bound by in the way that they treat the environment and how that legal architecture developed. The concept of individuals or groups of individuals carrying out their working activities in the forms of businesses or what could be regarded as the earliest forms of corporations can be traced back to some of the ancient civilizations. For example, in 1800 BC, the King of Assyria granted a group of merchants the right to form a trading organization.[25] In those early times, groups of merchants or tradesmen would often work together to reduce overheads and maybe to share the use of vessels, expertise, labour, raw materials or specialist equipment. Of course such arrangements did not entail the legal ramifications of incorporation as we know it today but they represent the early origins and the natural tendency for merchants and tradesmen to work together cooperatively for mutual benefit.

In mediaeval times monarchs had granted charters of incorporation to certain types of institutions such as ecclesiastical orders and public bodies.[26] The advantage of this was that it gave them a separate corporate personality and therefore they could enjoy certain rights and privileges such as owning land in the name of the incorporated organization and not in the name of the individuals who held offices within them.[27]

Additionally, there are records dating back to mediaeval times of powers being given by the monarch to traders in order that they could manage their businesses within the framework of organizations.[28] In Sweden for example a royal charter of incorporation was given to the Storra Kopparbergs in around 1288[29] (a company that incredibly still exists). In England, royal charters started to be used to incorporate trading organizations. However it was not until the late sixteenth century that incorporated trading organizations began to operate joint ventures between members.[30] This allowed individuals to invest in a particular venture, maybe in the cargo of a particular shipping voyage for example, and take a specified share of the profit.[31] In the rest of Europe similar developments took place, thus illustrating the importance of legal mechanisms that would allow individuals to invest in trading ventures, often as sleeping partners, with a view to realizing a profit on their successful completion.[32]

Although during this period, the types of incorporations that existed were still a distant relative to modern corporations, history shows the advantages of incorporation as a form for carrying out business and it also shows the inherent trend for individuals and groups of individuals to work together in business either to gain investment for trading ventures or to invest in ventures with a view to achieving profit. Therefore, it was during this period that these incorporated organizations or early corporations enabled the public to invest in what were the earliest 'joint stock' corporations. During the seventeenth century the opportunities for investment in businesses became recognized to the extent that in England stock-broking became a recognized profession formalized by statute.[33]

What is important to recognize in terms of the relationship between business and the environment is the nature of these business enterprises. Even during these formative years, certain features were being built into their design that would eventually have huge impacts on the environment in the modern era. As has been stated, they were the formative examples of organizations that were incorporated with a separate legal personality. Therefore they could trade as entities in their own right rather than in the names of their members or investors. It also meant that if members of those companies died, the incorporated organization and the work of the ventures that they were involved in could continue. In 1765, Sir William Blackstone commented on this type of organization:

> [a]s all personal rights die with the person; and as the necessary forms of investing a series of individuals, one after another, with the same individual rights, would be very inconvenient if not impracticable; it has been found necessary, when it is for the advantage of the public to have any particular rights kept on foot and continued, to constitute artificial persons, who may maintain a perpetual succession, and enjoy a kind of legal immortality. These artificial personas are called bodies politic, bodies corporate (*corpora corporate*), or corporations.[34]

In England the use of incorporated organizations for business ventures became subject to a major setback in 1720. Owing to the frenetic trading in shares, along with large-scale fraud and corruption and also the major losses that were suffered as a result, Parliament passed the Bubble Act that made it much more difficult for businesses to become incorporated.[35] This situation was to last for the next 124 years. In other parts of the world however incorporation was beginning to be recognized as providing a valuable framework within which businesses could operate and within which investors could speculate.

3.3.1.2 The origins of modern companies and corporations

Following the American War of Independence, the newly independent states recognized the advantages of providing incorporation for businesses. Therefore certain states led the way by making it easier for people to set up corporations. They did this by passing legislation that enabled business ventures to be incorporated without requiring special legislative grants or charters.[36] Such legislative measures were adopted by North Carolina in 1795, Massachusetts in 1799, New York in 1811 and Connecticut in 1837.[37] These types of corporations paved the way for the modern corporation that we know today.

However, there were still important questions as to the precise manner in which they would function. These questions related to the issues of liability for debts, the protection of creditors and the need for businesses to be able to provide a secure framework within which investors could speculate. It was these questions that were answered during the first half of the nineteenth century (on both sides of the Atlantic) and that would go on to play and still play an enduring part in the way that corporations around the world treat the environment today.

It was already clear, and had been for a long time prior to this period, that there were distinct advantages for business organizations to be set up with separate legal personality, which is what incorporation provided. There were definitely advantages for investors as it meant that if a person purchased shares in a business, there was not a danger that the business would cease to exist if the proprietor himself were to pass away. However these advantages raised the thorny question of liability. If the incorporated business were to run into difficulties, how would those it owed money to (their creditors) be protected if the incorporated business was treated as a separate entity to its owners? Should the owners be liable for the debts of the corporation or should they enjoy limited liability? On the one hand, it made sense that those who invested in a corporation and who would enjoy the profits of the business venture should be liable for its debts. In this way creditors would be more likely to be protected and investors would justifiably be liable for the risks associated with their speculation. However, on the other hand, such an approach would not be attractive to investors and would be more likely to stifle enterprise and business growth.

In the states of America in those formative years, different approaches to this issue of liability were adopted.[38] However, when New Hampshire offered a system of limited liability for shareholders in 1816 the practice spread across New England as other states did not wish to provide less attractive business environments for investors. As a result of this, the practice of businesses being incorporated with limited liability spread across the whole of the US.

In Britain many businesses were using partnerships as a form with which to organize their businesses but these had the drawback that they were not separate legal entities, therefore a creditor potentially had to take legal action against each of the partners individually to recover debts. There was still much enthusiasm from individuals looking to invest in successful businesses but the lack of a coherent system made it more difficult for that investment to take place.[39] This situation was overcome by a general system of incorporation for businesses in 1844 with the Joint Stock Companies Act.[40] This, like the system that had developed in the US, enabled people to incorporate their businesses through a relatively straightforward process. In 1855 after much debate in Parliament, further legislation entitled shareholders to enjoy limited liability in the same way that those in the US were able to.[41]

3.3.1.3 The constitution of a corporation

Therefore at this time, on both sides of the Atlantic, the fundamentals of the modern corporation had been born. This however does not tell the whole story in terms of the nature of the legal architecture and how it could and would affect the environment right the way around the planet. To understand this, it is necessary to understand the full constitutional make up of corporations.

Within corporate law generally, the documentation that provides details of the directors and shareholders and also the associated documents providing rules on how an individual corporation will operate in terms of meetings and the voting rights of shareholders are generally regarded as the 'constitutional' documents of a corporation.[42] These documents are required when a corporation is registered and they are generally publicly available to allow transparency, especially for potential creditors. However, in relation to decision-making related to the environment, those documents do not contain the constitutional rules that determine the legal constraints on the decision-makers within corporations. Those rules are found within national corporate law in the form of what are known as 'directors' duties'.

As has been seen, historically investors have placed their money into business ventures with a view to making profit. This business practice and the need for investment for larger businesses was very much part of the *raison d'être* of making incorporation readily available for businesses. This development inevitably meant that there could be two groups of individuals involved with corporations. These were first, those that were running and controlling the corporation (now known as corporate directors) and second, those that were investing in them (now known as members or shareholders).

Therefore as these new incorporated businesses developed in the nineteenth century, they did so on this model. Naturally it was necessary, if investors were to have security in putting their money into corporations, that there were strict rules in place to ensure that those who were running them did not squander the money or use it for improper purposes. It is these rules that are now part of corporate law worldwide (subject to minor variations)[43] and that play a fundamental role in the manner in which corporate directors make decisions. Therefore these 'directors' duties' effectively form *de facto* constitutions for all corporations, constraining how their business decisions should be made. As these rules are effectively now common across the majority of all nations, they form a crucial part of the global legal architecture that impacts upon human rights and the environment.

3.3.1.4 Directors' duties

In Britain and America, the directors were regarded as being in a *fiduciary* relationship with the corporation. The term *fiduciary* is a reference to trust and confidence.[44] Therefore although directors are not trustees, they are entrusted as the persons responsible for the management of a corporation and therefore the fiduciary relationship denotes the responsibility that is attached to that role. In other words they owe a duty of responsibility to the corporation itself. What this traditionally meant in England and Wales was that directors, once appointed, should demonstrate 'the utmost good faith towards the company in their dealings with it or on its behalf'.[45] Essentially it meant that a director had to act in what he believed to be the 'best interests of the company'.[46]

These same principles have applied to the development of corporations in the US and other common law jurisdictions.[47] As Catá Backer states:

> [t]he common law approach to the regulation of the conduct of managers is distinctive among systems of corporate governance. This approach is shared by common-law countries, including the United States, Great Britain, Ireland, Australia and New Zealand, and many of the former British colonies in Asia and Africa. The approach is based on the imposition of 'fiduciary' duties on managers, principally directors of a corporation derived from and similar (but not identical) to the duties imposed on trustees generally under the common law.[48]

What this system means in practice is that directors and managers of corporations are under a legal responsibility to make decisions that are in the 'best interests of the company' and not necessarily decisions that are in the best interests of the environment.[49] If this mechanism did not exist within the law, it would be very difficult to persuade anyone to invest in a corporation, as there would be no guarantee that the invested funds would be used for the purposes of making a profit. The bottom line is that investors will invest in a corporation with a view to making a profit either through an increase in the value of the share price or through the distribution of dividends from the annual profits.

Therefore, there may be corporate directors who are faced with decisions that may have a harmful effect on the environment and who would personally rather take the most environmentally friendly option but who are constrained by the law and as a result have to take the option that is the most financially beneficial for the corporation. Of course it can be argued that when a corporation makes decisions that are more expensive but beneficial to the environment, the corporation can benefit as it can take the credit for an environmentally friendly decision and this may enhance its success. Although this approach may be true in some cases, the majority of managers and directors are concerned with reducing overheads to maximize profit because they are acutely aware that investors have invested their money to achieve a profit and not for other reasons. They are also acutely aware that to continue to be successful in a competitive commercial environment and to attract further investment, it is crucial to demonstrate a strong drive to achieve profit.

It can be argued that there are now categories of corporations that adhere to certain environmental reporting standards and thus attract investors who are concerned to ensure that their funds go into businesses that comply with such standards.[50] However, even in a corporation that has certain environmental standards, there is still a bottom line as it is a business venture that is designed for the creation of profit and therefore such standards can only go so far. If such a corporation has a decision to make between purchasing products that have been harmful to the environment and remaining solvent, or purchasing products that have not been harmful to the environment and going out of business, the law dictates that the directors must make the decision that will benefit the corporation and that would be detrimental to the environment, so long as that purchase itself is within the law.

What is telling however is that the system of using corporations as the predominant mode of doing business has been adopted not just by those common law jurisdictions mentioned above but by the majority of other countries right the way around the world. Even though the precise mechanisms that are used in those other countries may differ to that used in common law jurisdictions, the basic legal principles are present and operate in the same way. Therefore, the familiar pattern of the incorporation of a business as a separate legal entity will exist and that corporation will be made up of the owners (shareholders) and also the managers or directors. The significance of this is that right the way around the world, corporations operate with an intrinsic legal separation between ownership and control. This separation therefore requires duties of directors and managers that mirror those described above for common law countries.

Therefore in each jurisdiction there are very firm legal obligations to ensure that directors and managers do not use a corporation's funds for purposes outside of those that will bring benefit to the corporation itself. This means that corporate directors and managers should not allow conflicts of interest to arise in their service to the corporation. Alongside these responsibilities are always legal sanctions that can be exercised by the corporation itself and powers that the owners (shareholders) of a corporation can exercise in the event that a director is in breach of those duties. Typically a director's contract can be terminated by the owners if they wish.[51]

Therefore, in Germany a limited liability corporation is known as a GmbHG.[52] In order to protect the interests of the shareholders there are a range of duties and responsibilities that directors are subject to. The principal duty of a manager is to manage the corporation's affairs with the degree of skill of a conscientious businessman.[53] Generally managers can be dismissed at any time, although this may be limited to situations where there is good cause such as gross breaches of the managers' duties or through being unable to carry out those duties.[54] Under German law managers also potentially face criminal liability for the breach of certain specific duties. For example managers that disclose business or trade secrets that they have knowledge of as a result of their position, are liable to criminal proceedings.[55]

The French were early pioneers in this field and developed a law known as the Code de Commerce in 1807, which in turn influenced the law that was ultimately adopted in Germany and other parts of Europe.[56] The French equivalent of a corporation with limited liability is known as a Société à Responsabilité Limitée (SARL).[57] As stated, these too follow the internationally adopted formula of ownership by shareholders and management by one or more managers (known as *gérants*). The precise duties that are owed by the managers to the corporation will be set out in the corporation's statutes (the equivalent to articles under UK law).[58] Ultimately the managers are under the control of the shareholders who have the power to remove them through votes of members representing more than half of the corporation's capital.[59] The managers are individually and jointly liable for damages to the corporation in the event that they are in breach of their duties.[60] It is open to the corporation to take action or the shareholders themselves are entitled to take action under such circumstances.[61]

The examples of the corporate law of France and Germany show that the system spread historically throughout different regions of the world (whether they were civil or common law jurisdictions). This process indicates the success of the corporate structure in terms of providing investment for enterprise, for protecting the interests of shareholders and for providing single legal entities that other parties could do business with in relation to the products and services offered by the group of business people involved with the specific enterprise concerned.

The adoption of a different country's legal systems or rules by another country is sometimes called 'transplantation'.[62] Japan is a prime example of the transplantation process taking place. At the end of the nineteenth century it adopted a system of corporate law that mirrored that of Germany at the time. This system was then amended following World War II, with reforms that stemmed from specific legal rules derived from the US.[63] Now for instance under the new Japanese Corporate Law, there are the same systems of protection of the interests of investors that have been developed in other legal systems. Therefore for example the law 'recognizes the consequent need for the shareholders' right to dismiss a director who is not acting in the interest of shareholders'.[64]

Peruvian law provides an example from a South American jurisdiction of the way that directors' duties have developed in conformity with this internationally accepted model. The board of directors in a Peruvian corporation 'is empowered with legal and management representation, necessary for the administration of the corporation *within its purpose*'.[65] The Peruvian General Law of Corporations provides the scope of the responsibilities of corporate directors and also details of the strict responsibilities that they have to put the interests of the shareholders first.[66] Additionally the Peruvian law allows shareholders to remove a director who fails to comply with his or her duties.[67]

In China a similar model has been adopted. China's revised corporate law came into effect on 1 January 2006.[68] It too reflects the now standard format for corporations and the responsibilities that corporate directors have towards the corporations themselves and ultimately their owners. Its provisions state that directors bear the responsibility of 'fidelity and diligence' to the corporation,[60] that they must not carry out acts that are 'inconsistent with the obligation of fidelity to the corporation'[70] and that a director can be subject to pay compensation for acts that are in violation of his duty of 'fidelity to the corporation'.[71] Additionally, shareholders have the power to lodge a lawsuit against directors or senior managers where they damage 'the shareholders' interests by violating any law, administrative regulation or the articles of association'.[72]

Finally it should be noted that in the UK, a concept known as the 'enlightened shareholder value' (ESV) approach to directors' duties was adopted when new corporate legislation was introduced in 2006.[73] It amounted to the culmination of much debate that went into the reframing of directors' duties in terms of a theory known as the 'stakeholder theory of responsibilities'. This theory is that boards of directors should take into account a range of different stakeholders (including employees, local communities, and the environment). Owing to the weak nature of the provision in the legislation,[74] there is little evidence that it has brought about a significant change in the way that directors make decisions and it has arguably had little influence internationally.[75]

Having said that, this provision is of crucial importance as it demonstrates that the traditional model of directors' duties that was designed and developed two centuries ago can be redesigned. It shows that it is possible for directors to operate under a more contemporary constitutional model and be subject to different decision-making objectives. Ultimately it provides a basis upon which it can be argued that the system that we have inherited, which may have been appropriate until recent times, is no longer appropriate and can be amended accordingly. It shows that the traditional model that developed in the USA and Europe, at a time long before MNEs and contemporary environmental issues, does not need to remain unchanged; it shows that it is possible for directors to have different rules under which they operate and a different set of overall goals.

3.3.1.5 The effect that the decision-making of corporations can have on the environment

In practical terms there are a myriad of decisions that are made on a daily basis by corporate directors that have an impact on the environment. On the one end of the scale, a multinational may have to decide whether or not to proceed with an oil extraction project that has the potential to cause major harm to the environment or pursue the development of a more environmentally friendly project such as the development of a wind farm. However, a corporate director who does not properly pursue a profit-making venture could potentially be liable for a breach of his duties towards the corporation itself and the shareholders.

Other examples are corporations that work in the field of the development of nuclear energy. Naturally there are major risks to the environment from such projects both in the short and long term when the half-lives of spent radioactive fuel are taken into account. However, a corporate director or the board of directors working for such a corporation is under a legal obligation to maximize the potential profit for the business and ultimately those investing in it. They do not as directors have duties directly towards the environment and ultimately therefore, can only take the environment into account to the extent that the decisions they make will affect further investment and the profits of the corporation. Of course the directors will have the responsibility to comply with the safety and environmental laws that are in place at the time in relation to that particular industry.

On a more mundane but equally important level, all corporations have procurement decisions to make. These can range from the type of paper that is purchased for a photocopier, to the products used for the construction of a factory, to the materials used in a manufacturing process or to the types of chairs that are purchased for the corporation's offices. In all of these decisions, the legal requirement that directors must comply with is that which has been described above.

This will mean that regardless of the personal preferences of a particular director, his or her decision-making responsibilities have to be aligned with their fiduciary duty to the corporation and its success (even if those decisions do not correspond with the protection of the environment). As there is always a pressure on corporate directors to maximize profit, this may often mean that environmental concerns will be lost in procurement processes, as such decisions are often driven by a concern to minimize overheads rather than a requirement to make decisions with the least environmental or human rights impact.[76]

Finally, but of crucial importance, is the role that corporations can play in politics. With the purpose of benefitting the corporation itself directors sometimes use corporate funds to lobby governments in relation to policy and legislation. It has been argued that such interventions have had dramatic effects. It has been argued that the failure of national US climate policy can be attributed in part to energy policies that were the result of 'the great political power of the fossil fuels industry'.[77] The political power of corporations can also of course influence the development of international environmental law. Tienhaara *et al.* state that:

> [g]lobal corporations have significant resources at their disposal and access to new technologies; their acceptance of or support for a regime can therefore be crucial to its success. Conversely, if global corporations oppose a particular regime it can be politically and financially costly for a government to implement it.[78]

3.3.1.6 *Aspects of the global legal architecture arising from the separate legal personality of companies*

The concept of separate legal personality also requires some consideration. It is not harmful to the environment in itself, however there are certain key developments that are intrinsically associated with the separate legal personality of corporations that have resulted in un-redressed harm to the environment.[79]

The main issue, at this stage in the development of corporations worldwide, is that there is currently no international system of registration of groups of corporations at the point that they become MNEs.[80] Therefore, where a corporation in one jurisdiction may set up a subsidiary corporation in another jurisdiction, the subsidiary will (in law), be a separate legal entity to the parent corporation.

This can lead to specific consequences when the subsidiary is operating in a country with poor environmental standards or a poor institutional framework for regulating its environmental or technical standards.[81] In such cases where harm has occurred to the environment or to individuals as a result of the subsidiary's activities, it can be very difficult to bring the parent corporation to account as it is a separate legal entity and *prima facie* would not be liable for the environmental harm caused by its subsidiary. Dine emphasizes that, '[t]here are numerous cases, for example, of parent companies exporting dirty and dangerous business to poor countries where regulations are minimal or unenforced'.[82] Historically, this has caused immeasurable problems for claimants (especially those from developing countries) who have been seeking redress from a parent corporation (from another jurisdiction) whose subsidiaries have failed to compensate for the harms caused. (Sometimes the claimants are unable to make an effective claim against the subsidiary in the developing country either because the subsidiary lacks the necessary funds or because the legal system in the developing country fails to provide effective redress.) Generally there have been many obstacles for claimants from developing country jurisdictions to make claims against parent corporations in developed countries.[83]

There have been numerous famous cases where the separate legal personality of parent corporations within corporate groups has resulted in them seeking to avoid liability for the harmful acts of their subsidiaries. One of the most famous examples is that of the Bhopal disaster.[84] The American multinational, Union Carbide Corporation (UCC), had created a subsidiary company in India that operated a pesticides plant in Bhopal, Madhya Pradesh. Between 2 and 3 September 1984, a gas leak occurred at the plant that resulted in the death of 3,787 people living nearby.[85] It is estimated that many more have died subsequently as a result of gas-related diseases.[86] There was evidence that safety standards at the plant were extremely low and that this could have been a significant contributory factor in causing the disaster.[87] The courts in the US were opposed to the proposition of allowing the claimants in this case to take legal action against the parent corporation in the US. One of the key reasons for this was that the parent corporation by law is deemed to be a separate legal entity to the subsidiary in India.[88]

At first glance, the conduct of the corporations in these types of cases can appear to be at best hard-nosed and at worst inhumane. However, it is crucial to remember that the decision-makers within corporations operate within strict legal rules relating to the decisions that they make. As stated above, the legal duty that directors have across all major jurisdictions is to act in the best interests of the corporation within the law of the jurisdiction concerned. Therefore in addressing the reform of corporate law, one of the problems that must be resolved is this potential of avoidance of liability by parent corporations within MNEs. This is the consequence of the failure to adopt an international system of accountability for those corporations that are effectively operating in more than one jurisdiction albeit ostensibly through legally distinct entities.

3.3.1.7 Corporate social responsibility, soft law and other initiatives

Within the process of assessing the legal obligations of corporations with respect to the environment or human rights, it can be seen on a practical level that there are three key aspects of hard law that must be analysed in order that a proper assessment can be made.

First, it is necessary to analyse the national laws of the country in which the corporation is operating. It is also, as has been illustrated above, necessary to understand the extent to which the particular country concerned applies and enforces those laws.

Second, it is important to understand the corporate law that is applicable to the directors within the corporation. As has been seen, a consistent global legal architecture has evolved in which corporate directors are obliged to make decisions that are in the best interests of the corporation.

Third, it is important to understand the legal relationships that exist between parent and subsidiary corporations where they operate in different jurisdictions. This is due to the difficulty that can arise under the existing global legal architecture in making parent corporations liable for the torts of their subsidiaries in other jurisdictions.

However, there is also a fourth area, not of hard law but of developments within this field that requires understanding owing to its influence on corporate decision-making; this comes in the form of soft law, codes of conduct, guidelines and corporate social responsibility (CSR) initiatives. This is comprised of the many initiatives by different actors within the international community that have attempted to create higher standards for corporations in terms of their impacts on human rights and the environment. These initiatives are of particular relevance for those corporations that operate in countries where there are either low standards of environmental and human rights law, or where the laws that do exist are inadequately enforced.

Recognition within the international community generally of the negative impacts that corporations can have on local communities, the environment and human rights has led to a wide range of different responses from civil society and from international organizations and this in turn in many cases, has resulted in responses from industry itself.

There are those that claim that corporations have a moral responsibility towards the environment, communities and human rights.[89] Although there may well be ethical grounds for such an argument, the initiatives that have developed in this field do not override the legal responsibility that directors have towards their corporations. The very presence of many of these initiatives, however, represents an acknowledgement that corporations can and do often have severe negative impacts of the types described above. Therefore these initiatives can be seen as representing a symptom of a significant deficit in the existing global legal architecture.

Therefore although they do not in themselves amount to hard law, they are significant in two ways. First, they create a pressure on some (but not all) corporations to adopt higher standards than they would otherwise be obliged to follow; and second, soft law, codes of conduct and CSR standards can in some cases be adopted by national legislatures and become hard law.

Although these initiatives are not always mutually exclusive, they are summarized under the following four sub-headings: initiatives from business and industry, initiatives from civil society, initiatives from international organizations and initiatives from the UN.

3.3.1.7.1 INITIATIVES FROM BUSINESS AND INDUSTRY

Owing to the increasing scrutiny that many corporations have become subject to in recent decades, there have been initiatives from within the business and investment community to create codes of conduct or standards that should be adhered to. For example, following the Exxon Valdez tanker disaster in 1989 in which 11 million gallons of oil spoiled an area of pristine habitat on the coast of Alaska, a group of investors and corporations formed the Coalition for Environmentally Responsible Economies (CERES), that drafted a set of principles for associated corporations to follow, in the way that they carried out their businesses.[90]

Some corporations now engage in environmental reporting, which is sometimes linked to accreditation for groups of corporations that attract investors seeking businesses that comply with certain environmental standards. However, where corporations have voluntarily reported information relating to their environmental or human rights performance, the results can provide an unclear picture for the external observer owing to the lack of comprehensive and consistent requirements worldwide and the lack of consequences for the failure to report.[91] There has even been research that suggests that those corporations with the worst performance put more work into such reporting as they have more to hide.[92]

Many corporations now routinely invest in developing their own CSR initiatives. This can take the form of hiring specific staff tasked with assessing and advising the directors on ways in which the corporation can improve its CSR performance and many larger corporations include sections on their websites detailing their CSR policies. Many corporations go to great lengths to put across to their customers and to the public at large the positive steps that they take to maintain good CSR. This has sometimes led to accusations from civil society of 'greenwashing' the true nature of their corporate activities.[93]

It has to be stressed that codes of conduct or CSR policies do not in any way change the legal duties that directors of corporations have, although they may provide a reason or an excuse for a director *vis-à-vis* the board room or the shareholders to divert some potential profit into activities or procurements that fall into the categories of the principles concerned.

3.3.1.7.2 INITIATIVES FROM CIVIL SOCIETY

Civil society, including many NGOs, has been active in numerous ways in attempting to raise the human rights and environmental standards that certain corporations operate by. Additionally, many have been active in attempting to use litigation, with varying degrees of success, to hold corporations accountable for damage caused to the environment.[94] Some NGOs have been active in analysing the legal obligations that corporate directors are subject to and have attempted to influence new legislation to bring about greater corporate responsibility for the environment and human rights.[95]

3.3.1.7.3 INITIATIVES FROM INTERNATIONAL ORGANIZATIONS (OTHER THAN THE UN)

There are examples of international organizations (other than the UN) that have been active in attempting to create guidelines or codes of conduct for corporations. Among these is the Organisation for Economic Co-operation and Development (OECD), which originally developed a set of guidelines for MNEs in 1976. The OECD has updated these guidelines periodically and most recently in 2011.[96] However, it must be stressed that the OECD guidelines represent voluntary guidelines for states and do not create new legal obligations.[97] While they are purely non-binding, they do represent an acknowledgement among developed country states of the immense power that MNEs can have *vis-à-vis* developing countries. However, it can also be argued that they demonstrate the weaknesses of using non-binding obligations generally.

3.3.1.7.4 INITIATIVES FROM THE UN

There have been numerous initiatives from the UN both in terms of attempting to create guidelines for MNEs operating in developing countries and also concerning the broader framework of responsibilities that corporations have in relation to human rights and the environment. Among the most high profile is the UN Global Compact, which was launched in 2000.[98] It provides a set of principles to which corporations can subscribe. In doing so they are invited to post the steps that they are taking to comply on the Global Compact's website.

In 2004 a Sub-Commission of the UN Commission on Human Rights produced a draft set of 'Norms on the Responsibilities of Transnational Corporations and other Business Enterprises with regards to Human Rights'.[99] These were not adopted by the UN but helped to raise the profile of many of the issues related to corporations in this area and prompted a further major development. As such, in 2005 the Secretary General of the UN appointed Professor John Ruggie of Harvard

University as a 'Special Representative of the Secretary General on the issue of human rights and transnational corporations and other business enterprises' (SRSG).

The SRSG's work resulted in a number of reports, the final one being in 2011.[100] The reports ultimately did not recommend any changes to the legal architecture that corporations operate under, or the duties that directors have within corporate law around the world. However they received widespread support from the likes of the OECD, the EU, the International Finance Corporation (IFC) and the International Organization for Standardization (ISO).[101]

The reports put forward three principles that encourage states to protect human rights, businesses to respect human rights standards and for the facilitation for victims of human rights standards to have remedies available to them.[102] The reports of the SRSG have generated an approach in which there would be an expectation for corporations to carry out 'due diligence' assessments relating to the impacts of their business activities on human rights.[103] There is the potential that this type of 'due diligence' practice could ultimately be transformed by legislatures into hard legal obligations.

However, there have been those who have regarded the reports as inadequate because they do not lead directly to regulation by hard law.[104] Ruggie himself stated in 2004 that, '[a] related criticism is that voluntary initiatives undermine the prospect for more robust regulations or other public sector roles'. However, he then added:

> [b]ut this claim is premature at best. There is little chance of transnational firms becoming subject to legally binding regulations at the global level any time soon; the political will or even capacity simply is not there, and much of the corporate world would unite to fight it. In contrast, *voluntary initiatives over time may build an interest among leading firms for a more level playing field* vis-à-vis laggards, thereby realigning the political balance in the corporate sector.[105]

It can be argued that until obligations towards human rights and the environment are clearly designated and enforced within the laws of the jurisdictions in which corporations operate, the underlying existing legal obligations of corporate directors to make decisions that benefit the corporation will invariably take precedence.

3.3.2 Trade

It is clear that degradation of the environment has links with commerce and trade on national and international levels. The legal architecture relating to the types of goods that can be traded (or the level of environmental harm that is permissible in the process and production methods of traded goods) has a huge impact upon the environment and associated human rights. It is therefore necessary to examine the extent to which international trading rules facilitate environmental degradation, or constrain it.

In broad terms, the early development of approaches on the international level to encourage free trade between countries coincided with the industrial revolution in Britain in the nineteenth century. However the modern era of global trade rules began after World War II and this period corresponded with the commencement of industrialization in many developing countries. The trade aspects of the global legal architecture began with the advent of the General Agreement on Tariffs and Trade (GATT) in 1947 and subsequently the WTO in 1994. In addition to these core developments there are also regional trade agreements that play an important part in the relationship between trade and the environment. However for the purposes of this book, the focus will be on the system that has developed through the GATT and the WTO as this is not only the most important system globally but has a very powerful influence on the development of the regional systems too.

To understand the trade aspects of the global legal architecture, it is important to understand its origins. From this it is possible to gain an insight into the nature of the system, why it has developed in the way that it has and why there may be important legal features that are inherent in the design of the system that can cause harm to the environment and contribute to climate change. However, prior to examining the historical bases of the system itself, the following section reviews the different ways that trade itself can impact upon the environment.

3.3.2.1 The effects of trade on the environment

The question of the precise relationship between trade and the environment has been a vexed one, which has not led to simple or straightforward conclusions. There are complex links between trade and the environment as there are a number of different factors that have to be taken into account.[106] These include (but are not limited to):

1. The types of goods that are traded and the effect that they can have on the importer's environment (for example the importation of environmentally friendly goods such as wind turbines or by contrast the importation of environmentally unfriendly goods, such as machinery which produces pollutants).
2. The methods that were used in the production of the goods that are traded and the effect that those methods can have on the *local* environment of the exporting country (for example local pollution levels).
3. The methods that were used in the production of the goods that are traded and the effect that those methods can have on the *global* environment (for example contributions to GHGs).
4. Trade will often involve the transportation of goods. This also can have a harmful effect on the environment.
5. The beneficial effects of the export of goods on a nation's economic development and the potential for the creation of better environmental regulation and standards as a result (for example the provision of better sanitation and water quality for local communities).[107]

6 Increased demand for natural resources through trade can put pressure on the environment and lead to environmental degradation or the loss of specific natural resources.

7 The production of goods in countries with low environmental standards at low cost can lead to greater success of those industries in comparison to the production of the same goods in countries with higher environmental standards and lead to a net increase in the manufacture of those goods in the countries with lower environmental standards and hence a net increase in environmental degradation. (This concept is known as the creation of 'pollution havens'.)[108]

8 The success of 'pollution havens' can have the effect of states maintaining low environmental standards or turning a blind eye to the enforcement of environmental standards to attract industry to their country and hence create greater net environmental degradation. (This concept is known as 'regulatory chill'.)[109]

Different research in this area over the last 20 years has brought different results.[110] It has been noted that the type of methodology used can have a distinct effect on the results.[111] There has been sufficient research in recent decades for general conclusions to be drawn. The consensus that has become accepted is that trade itself can have positive, negative or neutral effects upon the environment.[112] Naturally the results of research within this field have an impact on the development of policy relating to trade and the environment. This is particularly sensitive as trade and investment can have a huge impact on both the economic development of individual states and also the individual success of specific businesses and industries.

A core theory that has been the subject of much research is the Environmental Kuznets Curve (EKC).[113] This model suggests that during the early stages of development, a country will pollute intensively and this will decrease as the country becomes wealthier and is able to take more effective pollution abatement measures. In recent years the research related to the effects of trade on the environment has produced more empirical research related to EKC theory.[114] It now appears that to a varying degree, the EKC model applies to many pollutants that have an impact on the communities local to the industry concerned, however, it does not apply to the production of carbon dioxide.[115] This has been credited to the fact that carbon dioxide and other GHGs do not just affect a community that is local to the industry causing the emissions but all nations and unilateral abatement action on the part of one country would be unlikely to have any meaningful impact.[116]

Although there is plenty of scope for a lot more research into the precise effects of certain types of trade on the environment, it is clear that trade in general can have a wide range of impacts. Therefore a major problem is that an increase in trade that causes a net increase in environmental degradation amounts to a dysfunction within the system. Additionally, it is also clear that an increase in the trade of manufactured goods that brings about a net increase in the emission of GHGs in their production represents another clear dysfunction in terms of combating rising emissions.

3.3.2.2 Historical development of trade

To understand the reason for the design of the trade rules that have been adopted and the reasons for the approaches of the international trade institutions, it is useful to have an understanding of the historical development of trade and the attitudes towards it.

As was noted previously, both national and international trade can be traced back to the very earliest civilizations.[117] In Greek and Roman times, there was of course no international system of trade. However, there was international trade, which attracted the attention of early writers. In around AD 100, Plutarch recognized that sea trading had brought 'mutual assistance and exchange' that had resulted in 'cooperation and friendship'.[118] He commented, among other things, on the benefits being brought to Greece by grain from other lands and by vines from India. However, in spite of this type of early intellectual recognition of the benefits of trade, there were also widespread negative opinions among many nations. For example in early Christian times, writers were concerned about the problems that the occupation of trade could have on individuals and communities. There were concerns that trading as an occupation led to covetousness, lying, cheating and fraud.[119] For example St Augustine wrote, '[l]et Christians amend themselves, let them not trade'.[120]

Also in China by the twelfth century, major advances had been made in industry and technology. The Chinese were already using water-powered machinery in their production of textiles and also coke blast furnaces for the smelting of iron. It would be centuries before such technology was used in the west.[121] However, the technological advances that the Chinese had achieved took place within a governmental system that did not make it easy for innovators and trades-people to thrive. There was an absence of institutionalized property rights and there were high levels of state control over commerce.[122] The Chinese state took over many thriving businesses and took to intervention in the prices of goods, which led to an environment in which it was difficult for good businesses to thrive. Attempts were even made to prohibit overseas trade and this led to smuggling, violence and punishment.[123]

These attitudes to trade reflect a very different world to that in which we now live. A combination of factors predominated in approaches by rulers. These included a desire of governments to control commerce, a fear of outsiders and a greater sense of self-sufficiency than exists in the modern globalized interdependent world. However, in Europe, by the Middle Ages, attitudes had begun to ease. By the sixteenth century not only had a more pragmatic approach to trade developed but also the neutrality of trade had largely been accepted, or in other words, it was not regarded as necessarily being harmful or beneficial.

In the seventheenth century Grotius wrote, '[u]nder the law of nations, the following principle was established: that all men should be privileged to trade freely with one another'.[124] The expansion of world trade and exploration meant that there were growing opportunities generally. No longer were merchants regarded poorly; they were now respected for the benefits that they brought to a nation. Therefore literature of the time reflected this recognition. For example Edward Misselden stated, '[f]or when trade flourishes, the King's revenue is augmented, lands and rents improved, navigation is increased, the poor employed'.[125]

Therefore, intellectual attention turned towards how trade should be managed and governed, rather than any perceived inherent morality or immorality This question led writers in the seventeenth century to consider different types of trade and the effects they could have on a nation's wealth. It was during this period that the development of 'mercantilist' theory evolved. At the heart of mercantilist doctrine was the belief that the state should intervene in a nation's trade to protect certain interests and benefit the wider good of the nation. This therefore predicated that some trade was in fact harmful and as such state intervention was required to contain it. It was widely held that all types of export were beneficial but that certain imports were harmful. It was frequently argued that a nation should avoid importing consumer or luxury goods because that took wealth out of the country. For example, William Wood argued that, 'it is our business to keep out as much as conveniently we can…all sorts of goods for consumption and luxury: and there is no other way of doing it, but high duties and impositions'.[126]

In the eighteenth century the mercantilist approach gradually became the subject of challenge through a new wave of discussion and writings that would eventually lead to the economic theory of 'free trade', which provides the cornerstone of the modern-day approach through the GATT and the WTO. In 1776 Adam Smith made the case for free trade and argued against protectionism in a work called *An Inquiry into the Nature and Causes of the Wealth of Nations*.[127] Smith elaborated on the following argument:

> [i]t is the maxim of every prudent master of a family, never to attempt to make at home what it will cost him more to make than to buy. The tailor does not attempt to make his own shoes, but buys them of the shoemaker. The shoemaker does not attempt to make his own clothes, but employs a tailor. The farmer attempts to make neither the one nor the other, but employs those different artificers. All of them find it for their interest to employ their whole industry in a way in which they have some advantage over their neighbours, and to purchase with a part of its produce, or what is the same thing, with the price of a part of it, whatever else they have occasion for.
>
> What is prudence in the conduct of every private family can scarce be folly in that of a great kingdom. If a foreign country can supply us with a commodity cheaper than we ourselves can make it, better buy it of them with some part of the produce of our own industry, employed in a way in which we have some advantage. The general industry of the country, being always in proportion to the capital which employs it, will not thereby be diminished, no more than that of the above mentioned artificers; but only left to find out the way in which it can be employed with the greatest advantage. It is certainly not

employed to the greatest advantage, when it is thus directed towards an object which it can buy cheaper than it can make.[128]

Though not all of Smith's arguments were accepted wholesale, a template had been laid for the advantages of free trade that established it as a 'central tenet of economics'.[129] In the early nineteenth century David Ricardo followed on from Smith's work by developing the theory of 'comparative advantage', which lent even greater weight to the arguments for free trade.[130]

It is at this point that it is worth commenting on the notions of free trade that were developing and the impact that trade could have upon the environment. In the eighteenth and early ninteenth centuries there was not the modern concern or understanding of the environment that we now have. For example there was no concern for the potential of climate change. Although the labour costs and total production costs were factored in to Adam Smith's and David Ricardo's theories, they did not factor in the costs to the local, national and global environment and the damage to natural capital and ecosystem services that result from different types of production methods.[131] This is an important absence that has affected the development of the international trading system, and in turn the effects that it has upon the environment and the levels of emissions of GHGs.

In Britain protectionist policies had been adopted in the late seventeenth century and had continued through the eighteenth century especially in the competition with Dutch merchandise.[132] However in the early nineteenth century the British had become extremely efficient and dominant in the manufacturing of many types of goods and they began championing free trade. However, the British were not always particularly successful in persuading other countries to adopt the free trade approach. For example, the rapid industrial growth of the US in the late nineteenth century was accompanied by the protection of developing industries with high import tariffs.[133] The philosophy of free trade had made significant headway but countries were still very cautious in implementing it.

The twentieth century saw further significant developments in the attitudes towards trade. These have had a crucial influence in the development of the trading system that we now have. In the 1930s, the Great Depression led to protectionism from major trading nations such as the US and Britain. The US Congress passed the now infamous Smoot Hawley Tariff Act in 1930, which raised import duties on over 20,000 different goods to unprecedented levels. Britain and its commonwealth states, which included Canada, Australia, New Zealand and South Africa, retaliated with reciprocal protectionism. As Zeiler puts it, 'a circle of retaliation characterized Anglo–American trade relations in the 1930s'.[134]

This pattern, and the corresponding financial crises, naturally affected other trading nations. The Great Depression had a particularly damaging effect on Germany, which had been economically devastated in the aftermath of World War I. The economic crisis led to widespread unemployment and many people turned to extremism, which ultimately assisted the rise to power of Adolf Hitler and his National Socialist German Workers Party.[135] On 1 September 1939, Germany invaded Poland in the first act of World War II. Many observers have subsequently attributed the protectionist trade measures that had been implemented in the 1930s as pivotal in exacerbating the economic depression, damaging international relations and ultimately creating the conditions for the rise of the Nazi party in Germany, which led to World War II.[136]

As early as 1941, there were questions related to the manner in which a post-war world would operate in terms of international trade. President Roosevelt was particularly anxious to take the lead in avoiding a repetition of the international and economic problems of the 1930s. In a meeting on the president's ship off the coast of Newfoundland in 1941, President Roosevelt and Winston Churchill agreed a charter that included the basis of an international system of liberalized trade.[137] Towards the close of World War II the real business of post-war reconstruction and reorganization began. At Bretton Woods in 1944 agreements were reached for the creation of two new post-war institutions, the International Bank of Reconstruction and Development (IBRD or the World Bank) and the International Monetary Fund (IMF).[138] Additionally in San Francisco in 1945 an agreement was reached for the United Nations Charter.[139]

In 1945, the US proposed a charter or a code that would limit governmental restrictions on international trade. Additionally it proposed the creation of an International Trade Organization (ITO) to oversee new trading arrangements.[140] The ITO did not come into being, following a lack of momentum from key states. However, 23 countries met over a period of six months in 1947 to negotiate import duties on a range of around 50,000 different items. Significant agreements were achieved that would have the effect of opening up international trade. To bind themselves to these new agreements, the parties agreed to a provisional arrangement; this was the GATT. It contained schedules of the agreed tariffs and also rules that countries had to abide by, which would safeguard the tariffs that they had negotiated. At the time, the GATT was regarded as a provisional measure as it was anticipated that the ITO would be created and take on the role of oversight of the negotiated agreements.

The GATT survived despite the absence of the development of the ITO and remarkably became the cornerstone of international trade up until the advent of the WTO in 1994. When the WTO came into being, the principle rules of the GATT remained and provided a template for further developments. The GATT was effectively a framework for the liberalization of trade between states but it also allowed for numerous exceptions to liberalization. This framework was attractive to states as it encompassed sufficient flexibility for them to exercise their sovereignty and protect key areas of concern.

There were certain core principles that provided the framework of the operation of the GATT. It required that member states would not impose quantitative restrictions on imports or exports.[141] It operated on the basis that import tariffs would be the standard method for a state in controlling the imports of goods. This had the appeal of being more transparent than using other methods. The GATT included a provision that each state should make its laws, regulations and measures relating to trade publicly available and transparent for other nations and traders to view.[142] Fundamentally, the GATT also required in Article I that any tariff that was agreed between two or more contracting parties had to be offered at the same rate to all other contracting parties. This was known as the 'most-favoured nation' standard. In addition in Article III, it required that each state did not discriminate between goods that were imported and those that were domestically produced in terms of regulations and requirements. This was known as 'national treatment'. Therefore the GATT offered an attractive package to states that sought the reduction of import tariffs and a greater flow of trade between nations.

As much as the GATT provided this framework it also provided a range of exceptions that allowed states sufficient flexibility to adjust to specific economic conditions, protect specific interests and maintain security.

Therefore although one of the primary aims of the GATT was that contracting parties did not impose quantitive restrictions, it did allow them to be introduced under certain circumstances. There was an 'escape clause' that allowed states to withdraw from agreed tariff levels at three year intervals under certain circumstances[144] and also a provision that allowed states to impose restrictions on certain imports if certain conditions applied that amounted to a serious threat to domestic producers.[145] The agreement also allowed for political exclusions,[146] measures for the protection of national security[147] and it did not require states to change their existing legislation.[148] On top of this there was a provision that allowed states to continue with existing preferences that they may have had with specific trading partners.[149] Additionally and of major importance, the GATT allowed for the development of customs unions,[150] therefore it had the flexibility to allow contracting states to develop the European Economic Community (EEC)[151] for example. It also allowed for regional trade agreements such as the North American Free Trade Agreement (NAFTA).[152]

Finally and of most interest to environmentalists and environmental lawyers, there were provisions that were contained in Article XX relating to 'general exceptions' that provided the potential opportunity for states to justify a ban on specific imports if the goods fell within certain classifications. (This article and the effects that it has had in relation to the protection of the environment will be discussed in greater detail in sub-section 3.3.2.4).

Therefore an agreement had arrived that established a *modus operandi* for nations to pursue a trade liberalization agenda but one that contained a large degree of flexibility; it was this flexibility that was the essence of its success. Although for some, the exceptions significantly weakened the potential of accomplishing a brave new world of free trade and the eradication of barriers to trade, it represented a significant achievement that was designed in a manner that did not deter states from joining and provided sufficient political and economic manoeuvrability, once they had become members. Zeiler states that the pursuit of trade liberalization ultimately meant that free trade ideals had to be left behind through the influence of protectionism.[153]

3.3.2.3 The development of the WTO

The success of the GATT led to new rounds of negotiations, in which contracting members would attend for the purposes of setting new tariffs on specific goods.

There have been eight rounds in total and a new round (The Doha Round) is currently underway. Whereas the ITO never materialized in the 1940s, the Uruguay Round was a major turning point which culminated in 1994, with the creation of the WTO[154] and numerous new agreements. The WTO took the formal role of coordinating the work of the different agreements that would operate under its umbrella and importantly, it housed the new Dispute Settlement Body (DSB).[155] Although under the GATT there had been a dispute settlement mechanism, it had shortcomings. The DSB effectively created a binding dispute settlement mechanism for trade related disputes that originated within aspects of trade covered by one or more of the WTO covered agreements.

At the Uruguay Round, the GATT itself remained largely the same as the agreement that had been adopted in 1947. However, there were new agreements that were designed to fill recognized gaps in the GATT system. These new agreements included the General Agreement on Trade in Services (GATS)[156] (which provided a framework for liberalization of the trade in services), The Agreement on Trade-Related Aspects of Intellectual Property Rights (TRIPS)[157] (which provided a framework for a set of minimum standards of protection of intellectual property rights across all member states), the Agreement on Technical Barriers to Trade (TBT)[158] and the Agreement on the Application of Sanitary and Phytosanitary Measures (SPS).[159]

3.3.2.4 The effect of measures within the existing trading regime on the environment

The issue for the purposes of this book however, is the overall impact that the multilateral trading regime has had upon the environment. Just as Adam Smith and David Ricardo did not factor in the effect on natural capital, ecosystem services or climate change into their analyses of free trade, nor did the framers of the GATT comprehensively provide for protection of the environment. Just as it could not have been expected of Adam Smith or David Ricardo at times when the environment was not a prominent issue, nor could it have been expected that the framers of the GATT in the years following World War II would have the protection of the environment at the forefront of their minds. In fact it is a credit to their foresight that they did in fact include two provisions in the GATT that relate to contracting parties' capacity to introduce domestic measures for the protection of the environment. As mentioned above these two provisions are found in Article XX as 'general exceptions' to the standard rules prohibiting discrimination. It is worth looking at Article XX in its entirety in order that the provisions concerned [sub-sections (b) and (g)] can be read in context (see endnote).[160]

There are three important points to note in considering sub-sections (b) and (g). First, they demonstrate that even in 1947 it was recognized that trade rules could have an impact on the environment (as well as many other aspects of life). Second, they demonstrate that if contracting members do implement measures to protect elements of the environment, relying on sub-sections (b) and (g), they need to comply with the overall purposes of the GATT and therefore those measures should not amount to 'arbitrary or unjustifiable discrimination between countries where the same conditions prevail, or a disguised restriction on international trade'.[161] Third, it is important to note that even though the GATT was slightly modified, in 1994 on the formation of the WTO, its content for the purposes of this discussion remained the same. (Additionally, it can be said that although the TBT and SPS agreements were also adopted in 1994 and added to the matrix of rules that member states had to comply with in relation to the measures that they take to protect the environment, the fundamental obligations that were created by the GATT 1947 in this respect were not changed).

What this meant in summary was that the GATT (in 1947 and in 1994) did not create obligations to ensure that states prevented degradation of the environment in the course of the international trade to which those trade rules applied. What it meant was that if states did decide to impose restrictions on the imports of certain goods on the grounds that those goods either had caused harm to the environment (in the production process) or that they could (or would) cause harm to the environment of their own state, then they would have to comply with the set of rules provided in Article XX of the GATT. (A comparable clause was also included in the GATS.)[162]

Therefore the system that was adopted did not provide a general system of rules that ensured that the environment was protected; what it did was left it to contracting parties (member states) to take unilateral action in this regard. This has resulted in numerous claims that some measures taken by importing states were in fact protectionist measures disguised as measures for the protection of the environment.[163]

A huge amount has been written about the various trade disputes that came to the GATT panels and later to the DSB of the WTO. The jurisprudence from these disputes provides interesting insights into the development of the DSB in relation to the integration of new environmental principles and the leeway given to states to take unilateral action in relation to the protection of the environment outside of their own territories.

The Agreement Establishing the WTO itself must also be considered. Whereas it did not create an obligation for member states to protect the environment or to ensure that the goods they export meet certain environmental standards, the concept of 'sustainable development' and 'protection of the environment' are both mentioned in the 'preamble' to the agreement. It states *inter alia* that:

> *[r]ecognizing* that their relations in the field of trade and economic endeavour should be conducted with a view to raising standards of living, ensuring full employment and a large and steadily growing volume of real income and effective demand, and expanding the production of and trade in goods and services, while allowing for the optimal use of the world's resources in accordance with the objective of sustainable development, seeking both to protect and preserve the environment and to enhance the means for doing so in a manner consistent with their respective needs and concerns at different levels of economic development.[164]

While the preamble itself does not amount to a legally binding obligation upon member states, it does indicate a recognition by the member states themselves of the links between trade and the environment and the potential negative effects that some trade can have on the environment. However, to date the approach of the WTO has been to limit its obligations towards the environment, leaving the burden of environmental protection with states and the specialist international organizations such as UNEP.[165]

It was noted earlier in this chapter that trade can be harmful to the environment in a number of different ways. Therefore, the approach of the GATT and the WTO system can be seen to contribute to a dysfunctional system of decision-making relating to the environment, which provides one of the root causes of the continuation of environmental degradation. This is not only because as a system it permits such a state of affairs to occur but it also creates obligations for states not to restrict imports of goods that have caused harm to the environment beyond the limits of the exceptions in Art XX of the GATT.

In fact in Daniel Esty's seminal study of the GATT published in 1994, he observes that:

> [f]undamentally, the GATT is asymmetrical; its rules only permit a decision that particular environmental standards 'excessively' intrude on trade prerogatives. The GATT provides no comparable process for declaring a nation's economic activities (and related trade) to be environmentally 'inadequate' – and therefore an unfair basis for trade. Thus, the GATT fails to satisfactorily accommodate environmental protection in defining the ground rules for trade.[166]

This is not to say that 'free trade' is harmful; intrinsically it is not. It is only certain types of trade that bring about harm to the environment. However, there is clearly much trade occurring in products that have caused degradation to the environment in their production and also much trade in products that cause degradation to the environment in their use and/or disposal. The fact that these processes take place within a 'trade liberalization' context does not mean that 'trade liberalization' in itself is harmful; it means that the constitution of the trading regime in question has not incorporated a system of rules that will eradicate those problems.[167]

Unfortunately, whereas there has been a large amount of academic literature examining the development of the law within the GATT Article XX exceptions, there has been less detailed attention to the global legal architecture that the WTO system is a part of.

Within this area, careful consideration has to be given to the linkages between development and trade. Many developing countries do not consider that the various rounds of trade agreements under the GATT and WTO system have led to a fair deal for them.[168] They wish for this situation to be redressed so that they are able to gain access to the markets of developed countries within key sectors (such as textiles and agriculture for example). There is also the fear of 'eco-imperialism', or in other words, that developed countries could create or impose environmental standards that would eradicate any comparative advantage that they may have in particular sectors.

The concerns and frustrations of developing countries in relation to the fairness of the outcomes of the previous trade rounds have been a major contributing factor to the failings of the most recent ongoing round of negotiations (the Doha Round). These frustrations coincide with the aspirations that more liberalized access to markets for their produce has the potential to act as a catalyst for development, lift people out of poverty and provide the wealth that enables those countries to provide adequate environmental protection for their citizens. Many developing countries would argue that they face other more pressing priorities than the protection of the environment and that the imposition of higher environmental standards for them is simply unfair.[169] Therefore any redesign of the system requires that these issues are factored in to the overall solution.

3.3.3 States

Naturally, states are the primary decision-makers relating to the environment and also they are subjects of international law. Therefore it is important to analyse their inherent responsibilities as legal entities to gain a more complete understanding of the range of actors that participate in environmental decision-making on domestic and international levels. To an extent the obligations of states towards the environment have already been discussed in sections 2.4.2 and 3.3.2 above.

Therefore this section takes a broad view in discussing the overall constitutional arrangements within states that play a fundamental part in determining their legal obligations towards the environment. This assists in understanding further deficits within the global legal architecture in terms of its relationship with the environment. States make a variety of different types of decisions relating to the environment, which include the creation of legislation, the development of policies relating to evironmental standards and the determination of the use of natural resources. It is governments that make policy relating to the types of energy resources that should be used, whether or not aviation sectors should be expanded or contracted and the levels of subsidization or tax relief that should be granted to different sectors. It is tempting to consider that such decisions are purely matters of policy for individual governments or heads of states. However, progressively over the centuries, restrictions have been placed on the use of power by monarchs, governments and heads of states for a variety of reasons. It has been argued that the most important role of constitutions:

> is to limit the behaviour of government. Constitutions generate a set of inviolable principles and more specific provisions to which future law and government activity more generally must conform. This function – which, as if to highlight its centrality to the concept is commonly given the namesake *constitutionalism* – is vital to the functioning of democracy. Without a commitment to higher law, the state operates for the short-term benefit of those in power.[170]

Many constitutions now contain environmental provisions. Therefore it is important to consider what powers states have to make decisions that are harmful to the environment. It is the consideration of these powers that provides an insight into an important aspect of the global legal architecture.

3.3.3.1 Historical development

To understand the developments (or lack of development) within national state constitutions towards the environment, it is important to consider the historical context. The historical background provides us with a picture of the way that national constitutions have developed and how they are still continuing to develop. Although it is not possible within this chapter to provide an in-depth account, a broad overview is mapped out, against which the developments of recent decades can be understood.

The concept of constitutions as a reference to the form of government of nations is recorded as far back as the writings of the early philosophers such as Plato and Aristotle.[171] During those early times, various translations of the word 'constitution' were used to refer to 'the higher law of political jurisdictions'.[172] Although Aristotle made accounts of the different types of constitutions and political regimes of his day, the features of modern constitutions that many states now adopt were yet to emerge.[173]

The development of the characteristic features of modern-day constitutions and governments has been a long, and arguably arduous, process but one that has been punctuated by key events that have had a significant influence on the evolution of ideas and practice. In AD 930, the *Althing*, the world's first parliament, began its first annual meetings. In 1215, King John of England signed the *Magna Carta*, which later became law and formed a significant foundation of the UK's constitution.[174] (It can be noted that the first instance in which the word 'constitution' was used in the *Oxford Dictionary* to describe the whole legal framework of a state was a reference made in 1610).[175] Later another significant development, following the English civil war, was the passage of the Bill of Rights in 1689 that laid down limitations on the powers of the sovereign and further established the rights of parliament by statute.[176] From the middle of the seventeenth century until the time of the American and French revolutions, a period known as the *Age of Enlightenment* occurred in Europe that involved the development of new thinking about the way that states should be constituted, the rule of law and the rights that individuals within states should have. In this period many sought to reject the feudalism that had existed within many forms of government.[177]

In quick succession, between 1789 and 1791, America, Poland and France instituted written national constitutions.[178] In 1776 thirteen of Britain's American colonies had declared their independence and formed an American union.[179] This was followed by the drafting of a written national constitution that came into effect in 1789. In Poland a written national constitution was instiued in 1791 following a period of political agitation. In France a revolution began in 1789. A document entitled the *The Declaration of the Rights of Man* was instituted that year and this became a foundational document for the French written constitution of 1791. This sequence of events illustrates the influence that political and constitutional developments on one continent can have upon others. These countries put in place a trend for nations to adopt national written constitutions. Today only a number of countries such as the UK, Israel, Saudi Arabia, New Zealand and Canada do not have constitutions that are formed in the style of a single written document.[180]

In terms of content and format, the constitution of the US has had an immense influence that is represented by the number of other countries that have followed that particular model for their own constitutions.[181]

During the nineteenth century, written constitutions became a necessary consituent of newly independent states as they sought to legitimize their sovereignty and establish government.[182] Additionally the 113 new states that have been recognized by the international community since World War II have largely followed the format of a written constitution as part of the establishment of their independent statehood.[183] Naturally the early written constitutions that were developed prior to the modern concern for the environment would not have included provisions relating to the protection of the environment.

3.3.3.2 Constitutional environmental rights

As has been seen in Chapter 2, in recent years there has been a growth in the number of constitutions that contain provisions for the protection of the environment. However, when discussing the scope that states have in terms of decision-making that can affect the environment, it is important to highlight the role of international law relating to sovereignty over natural resources. In other words, it is a basic principle of public international law that each state has the sovereign right to manage the natural resources within its own jurisdiction in accordance with its own policies, subject to certain constraints relating to the duty not to cause harm to other states. Sands *et al.* define this as follows, '[t]he principle of state sovereignty allows states within limits established by international law to conduct or authorize such activities as they choose within their territories, including activities that may have adverse effects on their own environment'.[184]

It should be emphasized that one of the main reasons for the development of this principle following World War II was to ensure that newly independent states could control the natural resources within their own territories.[185] Therefore it was particularly important in defining the legal relationships between developing country states and corporations that engaged in contracts to extract or exploit natural resources within their jurisdictions. While this principle has been important in establishing such authority, in an unbridled form it has the potential to lead to major negative impacts on the environment. Therefore it is important to view constitutional rights and duties within this context.

The different environmental provisions within constitutions vary in their characteristics. For example, they may confer substantive rights[186] or procedural rights.[187] Additionally, environmental provisions may be phrased in different ways in different constitutions and this can mean that it is often difficult to generalize about their meaning or content.[188] Notwithstanding these facts, it is possible to observe certain features that are crucial to the role that they play in terms of the global legal architecture.

Whereas it has already been noted that such rights may be activated in certain types of scenarios such as extreme degradation to the environment that can affect local populations,[189] this section seeks to explain why it is that there are so many aspects of the environment that can be harmed without triggering any response from constitutions or the environmental rights within them.

The first point is to recall that (as was stated in Chapter 2) the environmental rights that have developed are not always justiciable. Some are drafted in such a way that enables legal action against states for alleged breaches but others are policy statements that provide goals for the government to aim for but are not justiciable.[190] For example, the South African constitution contains the following provisions:

> 24. Everyone has the right –
> (a) to an environment that is not harmful to their health or well-being; and
> (b) to have the environment protected, for the benefit of present and future generations, through reasonable legislative and other measures that –
> (i) prevent pollution and ecological degradation;
> (ii) promote conservation; and
> (iii) secure ecologically sustainable development and use of natural resources while promoting justifiable economic and social development.[191]

This contains a justiciable right that is found in part (a) and also a policy statement that is found in part (b).[192]

The second point to note is that often environmental rights are phrased in general terms that lack the specificity to deal with certain types of environmental harm. For example the Norwegian constitution contains a right of everyone:

> 110(b). …to an environment that is conducive to health and to natural surroundings whose productivity and diversity are preserved. Natural resources should be made use of on the basis of comprehensive long-term considerations whereby this right will be safeguarded for future generations as well.[193]

This provision does not elaborate on what is meant by the term 'conducive to health' for example or 'natural surroundings whose productivity and diversity are preserved'.[194]

Another example is the constitution of Chile, which states that all persons are guaranteed:

> 19(8). …the right to live in an environment free from contamination. It is the duty of the State to watch over the protection of this right and the preservation of nature.

> The law may establish specific restrictions on the exercise of certain rights or freedoms in order to protect the environment.[195]

This provision does not provide more detail of the levels of contamination that would be required for a violation to have occurred, and therefore the government is left with a wide degree of discretion in terms of the legislation that is developed and the courts a similar degree of discretion in how the provision can be interpreted. There are numerous other examples that could be cited from a range of different types of jurisdictions.[196]

There are of course certain exceptions to this. Notably the Kingdom of Bhutan makes a specific requirement within its constitution that, '[t]he Government shall ensure that, in order to conserve the country's natural resources and to prevent degradation of the ecosystem, a minimum of sixty percent of Bhutan's total land shall be maintained under forest cover for all time'.[197]

Although the constitution of Kenya lacks the unique specificity of the constitution of Bhutan, it does show an attempt to provide a policy goal in a specific sector, which is an interesting development for one of the more recent environmental constitutional provisions. It provides that the state shall, 'work to achieve and maintain a tree cover of at least ten per cent of the land area of Kenya'.[198]

The third point to note is that the notion of furtherance of economic development is normally intrinsically part of the work of governments. In some cases the obligation of the government to pursue policies to develop the national economy are written explicitly into national constitutions. For example the constitutions of India,[199] Ghana,[200] China[201] and Ecuador[202] all have provisions within their constitutions that relate to economic development. Each of these countries also have provisions in their constitutions that relate to environmental protection or other rights that are used for the protection of the environment. Therefore, those environmental provisions will not be read in isolation but in the context of the overall goals that the constitution is seeking to achieve.

Constitutions have developed historically not for the purpose of environmental protection but for a number of reasons that include the organization of government, the conferral of rights on citizens and the creation of policy goals for the government in terms of social objectives. Therefore they contain a range of provisions and numerous of them, such as the provision of education, housing and health services for example are related to or are reliant upon a healthy economy for their furtherance. Therefore the economic development goals of a nation are usually an implicit if not always an explicit factor upon which constitutional provisions are understood.

Therefore national constitutions cater for an overarching policy goal of economic development that can often favour the increase of a nation's gross domestic product (GDP) over other concerns.[203] For this reason where a provision for the protection of the environment is included within a constitution, it will often be read in the context of the country's economic objectives. Therefore, if the environmental provision itself does not detail specific requisite standards, it can readily come into conflict with an implicit or explicit economic goal of the government and as such compromises can be legitimately reached.[204]

It is for these reasons that (as was discussed in Chapter 2) environmental provisions in constitutions are mainly used in litigation where there is very severe pollution at a local level. Therefore despite the inherent advantage of such provisions, through the educative and normative effects that they have, they are still often relatively weak when placed within the context of the driving forces of economic development and the rights that states have over the natural resources in their territories.

3.4 Conclusions

There are a number of conclusions that can be made from bringing together these different areas of law. The first set of conclusions relates to the study of the global legal architecture. The second set of conclusions comes from the relationship of the global legal architecture with contemporary concepts of global environmental governance. The third set of conclusions relates to the potential relationship that a global substantive environmental right could have with the global legal architecture and existing global environmental governance.

3.4.1 The global legal architecture

This chapter has shown the historical progression in the development of three aspects of the global legal architecture. It has also demonstrated that those three aspects of the global legal architecture, corporate law, WTO law and state law have elements or features that are predisposed to decision-making that can lead to environmental degradation. By that, what is meant is that, the very design of their systems has led to legal constructs or mechanisms that either lead to or allow environmental degradation to occur as a natural by-product of their functioning.

In each of these areas of law, the historical development has been outlined. There have been three key points that this historical development has exposed. First and most important, it has been possible to demonstrate that the legal frameworks that have been instituted, in corporate law, the WTO and within state law, that ultimately cause harm to the environment, did not come about through negligence, ill will or any kind of malicious intent. This leads to the second point that the historical development has shown, that the features within these systems that cause degradation to the environment were deliberately designed to achieve legitimate and worthy objectives. The third point that the historical perspective helps to highlight is the fact that all of those elements of the global legal architecture developed within certain times in history: in the case of corporate law (around 200 years ago), WTO law (since 1948) and constitutional law (in recent centuries). It is only in the post-World War II period that these systems have been operating together and clearly it is within this timeframe that environmental degradation has greatly increased.

A further conclusion is that in all of those three areas of law, the developments that have taken place are truly global in nature. However, in each of these different areas of law, this global nature manifests itself in different ways.

Within corporate law, it has been seen that although there is no central international organization that governs corporations,[205] there are aspects of the law that are crucial to the environment and that are consistent regardless of the jurisdiction. In WTO law, a truly international system of law has developed owing to the success of the organization itself and its widespread membership. Therefore the rules that it has developed, and that have an impact on the environment, inevitably are global in nature. Finally, in all parts of the world, nations operate through systems of government with national constitutions. Therefore the consistency of key features of the constitutional make up of governments that can have negative impacts upon the environment, combined and supported by the principle of sovereignty over natural resources, also creates a truly global framework.

Another conclusion is that although in each of these systems there are design features that lead to environmental degradation, these design features are distinctive to each of these individual areas of law.

In corporate law it is principally the system of directors' duties that legally oblige directors to put the interests of the corporation ahead of the interests of the environment, thus leaving harm to the environment as an 'externality' that others outside of the corporation would have to redress.

In WTO law, there is no system that requires that all goods and services that are traded internationally should be benign in their overall impacts upon the environment in terms of their production, use and disposal. Under the existing rules, any trade measures that states take for the protection of the environment have to be compliant with the strict rules contained within the trade disciplines.

Within state law, national constitutions do not contain provisions that require complete sustainability within their economies. Economic growth is generally a priority and this is sometimes tempered by environmental provisions within national constitutions, which are often only activated in the cases of severe environmental harm. These conditions prevail within a corpus of international law that has established state sovereignty over natural resources, even to the extent that degradation may be caused by a state to its own environment so long as harm is not caused to other states in the process.

A final comment is that it is usual to view this global legal architecture in terms of its component parts. Therefore there is much literature that is devoted to each of these sub-systems. For example there is much literature devoted to the WTO and the environment or separately to corporations and the environment or separately again to national constitutions and the environment. It is argued that this detailed approach to individual systems of law should be accompanied by the examination and analysis of the entire system as it is here that an overview of some of the 'root causes' of environmental degradation emerges.

3.4.2 The relationship between the global legal architecture and global environmental governance

It has been seen that there are a number of different approaches that have been taken to global environmental governance. Often approaches focus on how existing international environmental law can be made to function more effectively. The inhibitors to its effective operation, such as compliance, treaty congestion and the weaknesses of international organizations, are therefore subjected to close scrutiny. However, studies of those aspects of international environmental governance sometimes overlook the 'root causes' or 'drivers' of environmental degradation.

Therefore when the system of international environmental law is placed alongside the system of global legal architecture that has been described above, there are few links. International environmental law focuses on transboundary harm or a variety of different sectors such as biodiversity, climate change and fisheries. What international environmental law does not currently do effectively is address those elements within the global legal architecture that are predisposed to environmental degradation; in other words it does not address those underlying causes of environmental degradation.

Therefore international environmental law, as a system of law, is attempting to superimpose itself upon the global legal architecture without addressing its underlying features. As such, there are two bodies of law in place that operate in parallel: one is a system of international environmental law that is attempting to reduce and control environmental degradation; the other is the global legal architecture, that contains component parts that are legally predisposed towards economic goals at the expense of the environment. Therefore the complete picture is that of a dysfunctional system that contains parallel sets of legal agendas that are frequently pulling in opposite directions.

Therefore it can be observed that in spite of the proliferation of international environmental law treaties that cover a range of different sectors, the difficulties of resolving environmental governance remain. This is because currently our existing approaches do not deal with the 'root causes' of the problem but attempt to superimpose solutions upon the symptoms. Such an approach is destined to failure or at best only muted success.

3.4.3 To what extent can human rights respond to this global legal architecture?

It was emphasized in Chapter 2 that many aspects of environmental degradation have negative impacts upon human rights on an international scale. It also showed that climate change especially can have numerous negative impacts upon human rights and increasingly the international community is acknowledging this. Equally however, Chapter 2 noted that existing human rights mechanisms are often limited in the manner in which they respond to environmental degradation. Therefore a question that must be asked is, 'should human rights be part of the solution in addressing the existing state of the global legal architecture and the existing levels of environmental degradation?'

It can be argued that human rights are at their best and most potent when they create legal duties for decision-makers. While traditionally human rights have been designed to create legal duties for state actors, it has been argued that they should be designed in such a manner that they create direct legal duties for non-state actors too.[206] If that could be achieved, they would have the potential to create a valuable framework of legal obligations that could constrain decision-making processes within the global legal architecture described above. Therefore there is a case for the development of a new type of environmental right that creates duties not just for state decision-makers but also for non-state actors.

It has been seen that the precepts within corporate law and WTO law create regimes that effectively govern how the environment is treated or how decisions are made relating to it. While such legal frameworks do not amount to formal constitutions, it could be argued that they are *de facto* constitutions by virtue of the effects that they have on decision-making. This in itself creates an argument for the creation of obligations at the highest level for those non-state actors to ensure that their legal regimes are designed to protect the environment. It can therefore be argued that a rights-based approach that created legal duties for those non-state actors could play a constructive role.

As noted above, Elkins *et al.* provide an argument for the use of constitutions to constrain decision-making:

> [a]rguably, the most important role of constitutions is to limit the behaviour of government. Constitutions generate a set of inviolable principles and more specific provisions to which future law and government activity more generally must conform. This function – which, as if to highlight its centrality to the concept is commonly given the namesake *constitutionalism* – is vital to the functioning of democracy.[207]

It is argued that until the global legal architecture is redesigned so that its 'constitutional' elements are consistent with the goal of sustainability, international environmental law will continue to be hampered in its attempts to superimpose itself upon it. It is argued that once the problems with the global legal architecture and hence some of the most important 'root causes' of environmental degradation have been addressed, international environmental law can focus on its true task, which should be standard setting alongside a global legal architecture that is predisposed towards complete sustainability. The subsequent chapter provides a breakdown of how a global environmental right could be framed, to provide the necessary amendments to the law to achieve this.

4 A Global Environmental Right

Draft with commentary

4.1 Introduction

This chapter presents a draft GER, which is a draft treaty designed to create duties for both state and non-state actors relating to the environment and in doing so, lead to sustainability that in turn would protect those human rights that are affected through environmental degradation. The duties that the draft GER proposes are founded on the premise of addressing the 'root causes' of environmental degradation by creating effective, pragmatic national and international systems of business and trade that are predisposed to sustainable outcomes. Therefore the chapter follows on directly from the conclusions of Chapter 3 relating to the inadequacies that currently exist in the global legal architecture. The draft is accompanied by a commentary that provides an explanation for the provisions where necessary.

The proposals that the draft GER contains are to a large extent reliant on the observations and suggestions for reform by academics in the various sub-sectors concerned. Where the draft GER is perhaps unusual is in bringing together a framework of legal obligations for different types of actors within one document. It is argued that it is this type of legal reform that is required if a coherent system of international protection of the environment is to be achieved. Therefore it seeks to link a range of reforms, within what are ordinarily regarded as discrete legal disciplines, but under an overarching framework that streamlines the legal duties for both state and non-state actors to protect the environment.

There are certain key elements that have not been included in any depth as they require more detailed analysis and development, which is outside the scope of this book. This is particularly the case with Article 18 of the draft GER that deals with 'Transitional Arrangements'. In other words it does not include the timetabling for the introduction of the draft GER, or the special arrangements that would be required for its application to different types of actors (both state and non-state).

One important feature of the draft GER is that it includes proposals for the institutional arrangements that would be required for the integration of the types of obligations that the treaty would create. Accordingly, it can be seen that the provisions of the treaty can be categorized into two types. First, there are those provisions that relate to the duties and obligations that are required of specific actors to ensure that the overall quality of the environment is maintained. Second, there are those provisions that relate to the institutional and business frameworks that would be required to enable those responsibilities to be put into practical effect. The institutional aspects raise numerous crucial issues for the proper development of any form of international legal architecture. These issues include those related to sovereignty, equity between states, legitimacy and efficiency. All of these issues are critical factors that need to be addressed within the overall design and development of such a framework, and therefore it is argued that they should be incorporated in the overall design at the earliest possible time.

Another related feature of this chapter is that, in addition to providing a framework within which business decision-making and business systems can be structured to lead to sustainable outcomes, it indicates the way in which new businesses would inevitably evolve from the architecture provided. In fact a key component of the right that has been suggested, is the facilitation of private investment in new business entities and technologies that would be a necessity worldwide for the reformed legal architecture to function.

What this and the following chapter seek to show is that there is an incentive for states to adopt such a right and reasons why business could benefit from it. Incentivization is a crucial requirement in treaty making. As Hathaway notes, states need to have sound reasons to enter into international agreements and will therefore weigh up the costs and the benefits of doing so.[1] Therefore, although any measures that result in changing business and industrial practices are bound to provoke opposition from those seeking to protect specific interests, key advantages to states, business, industry and communities are detailed as part of the commentary.

4.2 Background

Chapter 2 emphasized the strong relationship that exists between human rights and the environment in terms of the way that environmental degradation can impact upon existing rights, such as the right to life and the right to health. However, Chapter 2 also demonstrated that legal mechanisms within human rights systems have unfortunately had only a very limited effect in stemming the tide of environmental degradation that leads to those impacts upon human rights.

Certain writers have highlighted issues relating to human rights and the environment over the last two decades.[2] In recent years the study of human rights and the environment has become increasingly sectoral, or focused on specific types of rights. Therefore there are writers who have focused on specific aspects of human rights and the environment such as procedural rights,[3] human rights and climate change,[4] and the right to water[5]. What is consistent within all of these areas of literature is the acknowledgement that environmental degradation has significant impacts upon existing human rights and that there is the question of how human rights as legal mechanisms can respond.

Chapter 3 went on to describe how the design of the global legal architecture in terms of state law, corporate law and trade law unfortunately contains features that mean that it is often fundamentally predisposed to outcomes of environmental degradation. This has highlighted the failure of existing systems of global environmental governance, usually through multilateral environmental agreements, to either adequately respond to that global legal architecture or provide corresponding protection for the environment in those sectors that are affected.

This area of study stands alongside the recognition of the failure of international law to impose direct legal responsibilities on non-state actors. This has led to what Sands has described as a 'quasi-feudal' system that excludes many of the actors that play pivotal roles in the functioning of an increasingly globalized world.[6] There have been specific arguments relating to the functions of non-state actors and the responsibilities that they could or should have in relation to both the environment and human rights. This is particularly true of MNEs. However such arguments have usually taken place outside of the discussions relating to the developments of environmental rights.[7] Therefore the disconnect between state and non-state actors that is inherent in the nature of international law can in turn lead to a lack of connection between the development of environmental rights and the development of responsibilities for non-state actors towards human rights and the environment.

A further disconnect has also been observed between human rights and specific disciplines that detail the impacts of environmental degradation. For example in the field of climate change, Humphreys notes that there is a lack of acknowledgement of the human rights issues at stake in the IPCC reports.[8] These dissonances, which are found both between academic disciplines and between different areas of law, can hinder the integration into reform of the wide range of different factors that are necessary for coherent and efficient systems of governance and the comprehensive protection of human rights and the environment. They therefore represent a strong case for taking a broader approach that takes a view of the entirety rather than solely focusing on the individual components and tenets of each specific sector or discipline.

This has raised the question of how the global legal architecture (especially relating to commerce and trade) can be redesigned in order that the 'root causes' of environmental degradation can be properly addressed. Therefore the draft right presented here seeks to bring into one space an approach that addresses the problematical issues detailed in the former chapters, along with those mentioned above. The design represents work that not only draws heavily on the work of many academics within this field but also on earlier foundational analysis.[9] The product of earlier foundational analysis was the formulation of a one-paragraph draft right in the following terms:

> [a]ny decision by a person, group of people, organisation or government that brings about or could bring about degradation of the environment, is contrary to the human right to a good environment and as such is fundamentally unlawful. It is a human right to be able to challenge such decisions throughout the process of decision-making and in courts of law and tribunals. Environmental degradation can be rendered lawful when brought about to satisfy other basic human rights and where other less environmentally degrading alternatives are not viable. In the event that such decisions are sanctioned on the

> grounds that it is necessary to cause environmental degradation to satisfy other basic human rights, the degradation must be tied to an equitable form of compensation that in at least equal measure, benefits the environment of the community or the area of land, air, sea, ecosystem or water that is suffering or would suffer that degradation or risk of degradation.[10]

This earlier draft has formed the basis of Article 1 of the draft GER presented in this chapter. As a foundation it provides the principle that all decision-makers should have a legal obligation towards the environment. Clearly this style of drafting reflects a departure from the standard format of human rights, which traditionally have operated on the basis of an obligation of states towards individuals. However, it can be argued that modern imperatives and a change in the nature and economic influence of non-state actors, requires a different approach if a human rights mechanism is to achieve the levels of protection of the environment that are required.

Therefore, it can be seen that this approach moves beyond the traditional boundaries of human rights in three key respects. First, it does not allow a human right to be constrained by being solely applicable to state actors. Second, though it recognizes state sovereignty relating to the environment and natural resources, it requires that the state is under an obligation to exercise that sovereignty within the constraints appertaining to the draft GER. Third, it directly manifests itself as a duty rather than a right that can be exercised by a victim. This means that it does not require a victim for its mechanisms to be activated.

While the aforementioned draft has been amended slightly, those core features remain. The following draft GER is the culmination of further work that has added a framework that includes more precise responsibilities for each type of actor, details of the potential institutional framework that would be required in the realization of such a right and the framework for the business mechanisms that would be required for it to function in practice.

4.3 Draft Global Environmental Right with commentary

Preamble

The Parties to this treaty,

Recognizing the integral and interdependent nature of the Earth, our home,

Recognizing that no actor whether state or non-state has the inherent right to degrade or pollute the environment,

Recognizing that all actors whether state or non-state have a fundamental duty to protect the environment,

Recognizing that all peoples and communities have a right to a system of national and international governance in which all actors, both state and non-state, have a fundamental duty to protect the environment,

Recognizing that every form of life is unique, warranting respect regardless of its worth to humankind, and, to accord other organisms such recognition, humankind must be guided by a code of action,

Reaffirming the Principles of the United Nations Conference on the Human Environment at Stockholm 1972,

Reaffirming the Principles of the United Nations Conference on Environment and Development at Rio de Janeiro 1992,

Recognizing that sustainable outcomes must be a legal requirement of the decision-making functions of governments, business, trade and industry to protect the environment and to ensure fair and non-discriminatory competition in international trade,

Aware that legal responsibilities of both state and non-state actors should be based on relevant scientific knowledge,

Recognizing that a primary responsibility of all trade organizations whether international or regional is to create trade disciplines that ensure that the environment is protected throughout the processes of production and trade of goods and services,

Recognizing that the operation of business that can impact the environment whether through the medium of a corporation or any other type of business entity, is a privilege that comes with legal responsibilities towards the environment and human rights,

Have agreed as follows:

4.3.1 Article 1 – Statement of Environmental Duties

> *Any decision by a person, group of people, organization or government that brings about or could bring about degradation of the environment, is contrary to the common duty to protect the environment that is part of this global environmental right and as such is fundamentally unlawful. Environmental degradation can be rendered lawful when brought about to satisfy other basic human rights and where other less environmentally degrading alternatives are not viable. In the event that such decisions are sanctioned (on the grounds that it is necessary to cause environmental degradation to satisfy other basic human rights) the degradation must be tied to an equitable form of compensation that in at least equal measure, benefits the environment of the community or the area of land, air, sea, ecosystem or water that is suffering or would suffer that degradation or risk of degradation. It is a human right to be able to challenge decisions affecting the environment throughout the process of decision-making and in courts of law and tribunals.*

As with all statements of rights and duties and with the entire draft GER, there will be questions over definition, meaning and interpretation. For example in this particular article, inevitably there will be questions relating to the meanings of 'degradation to the environment', 'basic human rights' and what would amount to an 'equitable form of compensation'. Rather than attempt at this stage to answer all of the potential issues that could arise in their interpretation, the remainder of the draft GER seeks to show how the duties created in Article 1 could be meaningfully translated into practical, working arrangements for governments, businesses, communities and individuals.

4.3.2 *Article 2 – Integration of Duties*

(a) Each party shall integrate the legislative measures detailed in this treaty into their own domestic law in accordance with the guidance of the Secretariat (Art. 21).

(b) Each party shall report to the Secretariat (Art. 21) and the World Environment Organization (WEO)(Art.13) on the legislative steps that are taken to comply with the treaty.

4.3.3 *Article 3 – Definitions*

'Corporation' – for the avoidance of doubt, where the word 'corporation' is used within the context of this draft, it can also be read to include other types of business entities.

'Operate Internationally' – refers to the activities of any corporation (or other business entity) that buys or sells goods or services in countries other than those in which it is registered, which operates as a parent or subsidiary of a corporation in another jurisdiction or that works as part of a consortium of corporations where any or all are registered in different jurisdictions.

It is not proposed here for the purposes of this draft to provide full details of all of the definitions that would be required. Suffice it to say that key terms would require definition. An exception is made in relation to corporations and other business entities, as the draft GER refers to corporations and businesses entities that 'operate internationally' and therefore this is included to indicate the types of entities that it is envisaged the treaty would be applicable to.

4.3.4 *Article 4 – National Constitutions and Governmental Duties Towards the Environment*

(a) Each party shall amend that part (or parts) of its constitution (and/or if necessary its national legislation) relating to the environment to state that local, regional and national governments are legally obliged not to make any decision/s that ***will*** *or* ***may*** *cause degradation to the environment (whether they be through policies, executive decisions or law making) without following the relevant procedures prescribed in sub-sections (b)–(e) to this article.*

(b) *In the event that a government (whether local, regional or national) finds that it is necessary to make a decision that* ***will*** *cause degradation to the environment in order to satisfy other basic human rights (whether that be through policies, executive decisions or legislation), it shall be obliged, in accordance with equitable principles, to compensate that aspect/those aspects of the environment through the purchase of direct environmental compensatory offsets from a registered supplier (see Art. 10).*

(c) *Each government shall keep a record of any decisions that* ***will*** *cause degradation to the environment (see sub-section (b)) and a corresponding record of the compensation that has been purchased through a registered supplier of direct environmental compensatory offsets thus forming part of its environmental accounts (see Art. 5).*

(d) *In the event that a government (whether local, regional or national) finds that it is necessary to make a decision that* ***may*** *cause degradation to the environment in order to satisfy other basic human rights (whether that be through policies, executive decisions or legislation), it shall be obliged, in accordance with equitable principles, to purchase insurance from a registered supplier (see Art. 11).*

(e) *Each government shall keep a record of any decisions that* ***may*** *cause degradation to the environment (see sub-section (d)) and a corresponding record of the insurance that has been purchased through a registered supplier of environmental insurance thus forming part of its environmental accounts (see Art. 5).*

This article contains two key features. First it includes a legally binding duty upon the state not to make decisions that will cause degradation to the environment except under certain specified circumstances. Second it contains two mechanisms to compensate the environment for degradation caused to it as a result of state decision-making that is taken, where it is necessary to allow actual or potential environmental degradation to satisfy basic human rights.

The first mechanism is one that requires the environment to be compensated in the event that decision-making takes place that *will* cause actual degradation to it. This may appear on the face of it to create an extremely low threshold of tolerance for environmental degradation. However, it is argued that such a measure is necessary if the ongoing insipid degradation to the environment that is taking place internationally, and that affects fundamental human rights, is to be stemmed. Having said that, while traditional thresholds of acceptable degradation to the environment and the principle of sovereignty over natural resources, have often allowed states a wide margin of appreciation in terms of the accommodation of their economic interests,[11] there has been an increasing move in recent years towards a much higher mandatory level of environmental protection. McGillivray for example states that:

> [t]here are elements of an ever increasing aspiration in environmental regulation (I hesitate to call it a trend) to move away from justifying harm to

> the natural environment because of non-environmental gains. Trading natural capital for economic and social capital no longer commands the persuasive force it once had. In its place is an ethos under which natural resources may only be interfered with if functional equivalents are provided. I term this as an 'ecological impact neutrality' approach.[12]

The second mechanism is one that requires insurance to be purchased to ensure that the environment can be compensated if the need arises, in relation to decision-making that *may* cause degradation. These two mechanisms are consistent throughout the draft GER; more is explained about them in later sections. However, one of the main features of this provision is that it provides a direct market mechanism to ensure that the environmental costs are built into decision-making processes. Naturally such an approach requires a credible system of assessment of those environmental impacts and risks. However, contemporary assessment systems of such risks have now developed to very high standards and the question would be one of tailoring them accordingly (see Arts. 15 and 16).[13]

The article is consistent with the necessity to protect the human rights of individuals and communities that are affected as a result of environmental degradation.[14] Additionally, it is consistent with the polluter pays principle as it creates a mechanism to ensure that ultimately those causing degradation to the environment are those that are required to compensate it.[15]

It adopts a precautionary approach,[16] through its special provision for those decisions that *may* cause degradation to the environment. Additionally, as it ties this in with an insurance mechanism to achieve compensation in those cases where degradation occurs, it can be argued that it is consistent with the intent of Principle 13 of the Rio Declaration relating to liability. It is also supportive of inter-generational equity as it provides a mechanism under which future generations would be protected from the loss of quality to the environment as a result of the over consumption of current generations.[17] Above all however, the provision is consistent with Principle 8 of the Rio Declaration that states that, '[t]o achieve sustainable development and a higher quality of life for all people, States should reduce and eliminate unsustainable patterns of production and consumption'.[18]

Incorporating common but differentiated responsibility (CBDR) is a challenge owing to the many different factors that affect the capacity of states to respond technologically to environmental challenges, their economic capacity to resource policies, the specific developmental needs of individual states and the historical attribution of environmental harm caused.[19] However, the provision enables the integration of an equitable approach to the responsibility of a state by incorporating an obligation 'in accordance with equitable principles' to be applied.[20] However, the overall application of the provisions of the draft GER would require transitional arrangements for all types of states and Article 18 would provide the practical manifestation of this aspect.

Clearly there are a number of factors associated with Article 4 that would automatically create issues relating to its potential acceptance by states. First, as has already been noted, states have carefully guarded their sovereign right over their natural resources and this is evidenced in numerous international instruments.[21] Second, within some states there is an inherent reticence to amend their national constitutions or the legislation associated with them. Third, states are also naturally very wary of surrendering sovereignty to any international organization or system unless there are significant advantages in doing so. Therefore states would need to see significant advantages to accept the provisions within Article 4. This point could also be said to apply to the provisions related to corporate law and WTO law in other parts of the draft GER.[22]

However, with the exception of certain nations such as the US,[23] national constitutions are changed and amended with surprising regularity and therefore such integration is not as challenging as may be perceived. As noted above Law and Versteeg highlight the fact that on average national constitution have a 38 per cent chance of being amended in any given year and between 1990 and 2000, over half of the world's nations made major amendments to their constitutions.[24] Additionally, states are prepared to surrender sovereignty to organizations such as the WTO when it is in their interests to do so and many treaties already provide for the cooperative loss of sovereignty related to specific sectors.

It can be argued that the scale of the environmental challenges that are currently faced, requires a comprehensive approach (both nationally and internationally) to decision-making affecting the environment and therefore there is the need to introduce a contemporary global legal architecture that is capable of meeting that challenge. It is argued that such a system could ultimately benefit all states and therefore there are sound reasons for the provisions here to be given careful consideration.

4.3.5 Article 5 – Annual State Environmental Accounting

All states shall, on an annual basis, lodge a copy of their environmental accounts with the World Environmental Organization (WEO) (see Art. 13).

More is discussed in relation to the establishment of a WEO, its role and reporting requirements in subsequent sub-sections.

4.3.6 Article 6 – Duties of Individuals Towards the Environment

(a) *Each party shall amend that part of its constitution relating to the duties of individual citizens towards the environment (whether that be in the national/federal constitutions or state constitutions or the equivalent provisions in legislation) to state that all individuals are legally obliged not to make any decision that would cause degradation to the environment without following the procedure prescribed in sub-section (b) or (c) to this article.*

(b) *In the event that an individual finds that it is necessary to make a decision that* ***will*** *cause degradation to the environment within the confines of the law, he/she shall be obliged, in accordance with equitable principles, to* *compensate that aspect/those aspects of the environment through the purchase of direct environmental compensatory offsets from a registered supplier (see Art. 10).*

(c) *In the event that an individual finds that it is necessary to make a decision that* ***may*** *cause degradation to the environment, he/she shall be obliged, in accordance with equitable principles, to purchase insurance from a registered supplier (see Art. 11).*

(d) *This article does not apply to the purchase of products and foodstuffs (see Art. 9).*

While, for reasons that form the basis of Article 9, it is not practical to expect individuals in the normal course of their lives to have to deal with assessments of the impacts of their purchasing decisions upon the environment, there are two reasons for including this provision. First, there will be occasions when individuals will seek to carry out an extraordinary activity or plan that involves definite or possible environmental degradation, and as such there is a need to ensure that legal mechanisms are in place to address such decision-making. Second, duties need to be extended to individuals in principle, as a means of developing a consistent acceptance of the shared responsibility of all individuals in all places for the protection of the environment.

4.3.7 Article 7 – Corporate Environmental Duty

(a) *Each party shall amend that part of its law relating to 'directors' duties' (or its equivalent within its corporate law) to state that directors are legally obliged not to make any decision that would cause degradation to the environment without following the procedure prescribed in sub-sections (b) and (c) and/or (d) and (e) to this article.*

(b) *In the event that a corporation finds that it is necessary to make a decision that* ***will*** *cause degradation to the environment, whether that be through an industrial project, business activities, procurement or any other type of activity, it shall be obliged, in accordance with equitable principles, to compensate that aspect of the environment, in equal measure to the level of degradation that will be caused, through the purchase of direct environmental compensatory offsets from a registered supplier (see Art. 10).*

(c) *Each corporation shall keep a record of any decisions that* ***will*** *cause harm to the environment and a corresponding record of the compensation that has been carried out or purchased through a registered supplier of direct environmental compensatory offsets. Such records will become part of their environmental accounts (see Art. 8).*

(d) *In the event that a corporation finds that it is necessary to make a decision that* ***may*** *cause degradation to the environment, whether that be through an industrial project, business activities, procurement or any other type* *of activity, it shall be obliged, in accordance with equitable principles, to purchase insurance from a registered supplier (see Art. 11).*

(e) *Each corporation shall keep a record of any decisions that* **may** *cause harm to the environment and a corresponding record of the insurance that has been purchased through a registered supplier of environmental insurance. Such records will become part of their environmental accounts (see Art. 8).*

(f) *The obligations in this article will be extended to all decision-makers in all types of business entities whether they are partnerships, sole-traders, co-operatives or any other form, to ensure that all businesses are subject to the same legal obligations in relation to the environment.*

Traditional approaches to limiting environmental harm from corporations and businesses have relied on external regulation (originally of the 'command and control' type and in recent decades other variants of it) and also market based mechanisms.[25] While such approaches have been effective to an extent, they largely fail to ensure that industry fully compensates for the environmental degradation it causes, they are expensive to operate and they fail to address the underlying legal mechanisms that drive corporations to externalize costs relating to the environment.[26] There have been various critics who have sought reform that would address these inadequacies.[27]

It was noted in Chapter 3 that there have been numerous developments on the international level that have sought to encourage corporations to adopt strategies into their decision-making in order that they are responsible for environmental and human rights considerations. These have included various codes of conduct, guidelines[28] and most recently the work of the United Nation's 'Special Representative of the Secretary General on the issue of human rights and transnational corporations and other business enterprises'.[29] However, it was noted that in this sphere too, these developments make no fundamental change to the 'constitutional' obligations that corporate directors are bound to adhere to.[30]

Therefore, the provisions in this article are designed to respond directly to these deficits by incorporating the duty for decision-makers, which is consistent throughout the draft GER, into corporate law. It would require corporations to be 'constitutionally' bound to follow procedures that are designed to inevitably lead to environmentally sustainable outcomes.

As emphasized previously such reforms have now become common parlance among those seeking to reframe the manner in which corporations operate. For example, Sjåfjell states (in the context of climate change) that:

> [r]eforming core company law seems in short to present itself as a necessary prerequisite to achieving sustainable companies, both to make the external regulation of companies more effective and to realize the potential within each company to make its own independent, creative, and active contribution to the mitigation of climate change.[31]

The provisions of the article are framed to apply to all business entities. Naturally, the practicalities of achieving this are such that, it would be expected that in the early stages they would apply only to corporations and businesses of a certain size. However the precise application would ultimately depend upon the transitional arrangements that would be agreed under Article 18.

4.3.8 Article 8 – Annual Corporate Environmental Accounting

(a) *Each party shall enact legislation to require that all corporations (and any other type of business entity, as stated in Art. 7(f)) shall lodge environmental accounts annually alongside their financial accounts to the same body that receives the annual financial accounts. Such environmental accounts shall include the details pertaining to Art. 7 (c) and 7(e).*

(b) *Each party shall enact legislation to require that all annual environmental accounts shall be available to the public on the same basis as a corporation's financial accounts.*

(c) *The form of each party's corporate environmental accounts shall be consistent with the style agreed and prescribed by the World Environment Organization (WEO) (see Art. 13).*

(d) *All corporations (and all types of business entities to whom this applies as stated in Art 7(f)) shall lodge a copy of its corporate environmental accounts with the WEO (see Art. 13).*

There have already been attempts to encourage corporations to account for certain aspects of their environmental decision-making. Such steps are of course to be welcomed as, to an extent they have affected corporate culture, had an educative effect and increased the overall expectations of the international community towards corporations and especially MNEs. However, such measures have often suffered from two key drawbacks.[32] First, they are frequently voluntary in nature and therefore lack the 'teeth' to provide the kinds of changes to corporate decision-making that are required. Second, reporting is often inconsistent in its content and therefore provides an inconvenient and difficult measurement of indicators for those wishing to make assessments of, or comparisons between, corporations.[33]

Certain NGOs have worked towards the development of consistent standards of non-financial reporting. For example the Global Reporting Initiative, which has worked in conjunction with UNEP and the UN Global Compact, has made progress in the development of consistent reporting standards in the fields of human rights, labour rights, environmental protection, anti-corruption and other corporate citizenship issues.[34] Other NGOs have used provisions within corporate legislation relating to information published in corporate 'business reviews'[35] to bring MNEs under scrutiny for the environmental information that they publish.[36]

Therefore there has been a steady move towards the standardization of the reporting of environmental performance internationally. A good example of an initiative in this area was the announcement made by the UK government at the Rio

+ 20 conference of the introduction of legislation in 2013 requiring all corporations listed on the main London Stock Exchange to provide mandatory GHG emissions reports.[37]

As such the requirements in this article are consistent with other developments that are already taking place on an incremental level worldwide. In this sense they could have the effect of providing the consistency that is required for fair competition between corporations on an international level and the accountability required for the system within the draft GER to function effectively.[38]

It was noted in the previous section that phase in arrangements would potentially be required for corporations and business entities of different sizes. Therefore the precise phase in arrangements for this and other provisions would be determined by the transitional arrangements that could be agreed by the international community under Article 18.

4.3.9 Article 9 – Consumption, Use and Disposal of Goods and Products

(a) Each party shall enact legislation to ensure that prior to the sale to the consumer of goods or products that ***will*** *cause degradation to the environment in their* ***consumption or use****, direct environmental compensatory offsets are purchased which in at least equal measure will compensate the environment of the community or the area of land, air, sea, ecosystem or water that* ***will*** *suffer that degradation.*

(b) Each party shall enact legislation to ensure that prior to the sale to the consumer of goods or products that ***will*** *cause degradation to the environment in their* ***disposal****, direct environmental compensatory offsets are purchased which in at least equal measure will compensate the environment of the community or the area of land, air, sea, ecosystem or water that* ***will*** *suffer that degradation.*

The environmental right that this draft treaty would create is based on the adoption of duties for all decision-makers that make decisions relating to the environment. Therefore it realizes an inherent responsibility for those businesses and industries that produce products that cause harm to the environment in their consumption, use or disposal. This article provides a mechanism to compensate the environment for that harm prior to the sale, consumption, use and disposal of those products.

In terms of the use and consumption of products, the law currently often leaves the responsibility to the discretion of the consumer.[39] For example, currently a consumer of petrol will have a choice as to whether or not he/she takes steps to compensate the environment for degradation related to its consumption. Such an approach does not appear to be consistent with associated principles within the Rio Declaration (i.e. Principles 8,[40] 13,[41]16[42] and in some cases Principle 2[43]).

With the seriousness of the impacts to present and future generations that were detailed in Chapter 2, it can be argued that such an approach is neither practical nor sustainable. It is not practical as it would not be possible for each individual consumer to carry out an assessment of every product that is purchased to make a determination of the environmental (and/or human rights) harm that is associated with it and subsequently compensate the environment for that harm. It is not sustainable as such an approach is ultimately reliant on the choices of the purchasers and consumers who, despite good intentions, will often ultimately make decisions out of commercial or financial pressure, expedience or convenience.[44]

One of the reasons for the adoption of this *laissez faire* reliance on purchaser and consumer choice is due to the disconnect that often exists between the consumption, use and disposal of products and the impacts (detailed in Chapter 2) that take place as a result. For example, there is often very little perceived connection between the consumption of electricity (generated through the combustion of fossil fuels) and the potential impacts in certain parts of the world that may result through a contribution to climate change.

Such an approach is not adopted in other areas of human activity where the impacts upon human rights through consumption, use and disposal are more immediate. For example, where there are inherent immediate dangers to health and safety in the use of certain products, strict health and safety obligations will be built into the product standards to ensure that the safety of individuals and communities is maintained. Health and safety requirements are not left as a choice for purchasers and consumers and yet in terms of the human rights impacts related to environmental degradation, this is often the approach which is taken.

Therefore Article 9 introduces a mechanism that requires states to implement systems to compensate for the harm that will be caused through the consumption, use and disposal of goods and products. As a result it achieves three key objectives. First, it is consistent with the polluter pays principle as it would require the purchaser or consumer to absorb the environmental costs of compensating the environment within the cost of the product.[45] It is also consistent with the requirement under Principle 8 of the Rio Declaration to 'eliminate unsustainable patterns of production and consumption'.[46] Second, business and industry would as a result, be disincentivized to produce goods that would cause degradation to the environment, in their consumption use or disposal.[47] Such a mechanism allows business and industry and the markets to enable the most environmentally friendly goods and products to be at a commercial advantage through their lower production costs. Third, the requirement to purchase direct environmental compensatory offsets means that the degradation caused to the environment within individual sectors could be addressed through the identification and application of the specific offset requirements related to the specific consumption, use and disposal scenarios.

The third and final point is important as it is not always possible to determine the costs to the environment of the consumption, use and disposal of specific goods and products until there is knowledge of how a consumer will use those goods or products. For example, one tonne of coal could cause significant degradation to the environment if burnt within a traditional coal-fired power station. However, within a coal-fired power station that incorporated carbon capture and storage far less degradation may be caused. Therefore it is important that the requirements of the compensatory offsets within this section are appropriate for the type of use involved. This is particularly important to avoid perverse incentives that might encourage less environmentally friendly patterns of consumption, use and disposal.

Law and policy relating to waste will vary from state to state. However, ultimately the primary responsibility will rest with national governments to provide systems for dealing with it.[48] This is due to the disparate nature of the creation of waste following the sale of goods and the location of the consumption, use and ultimate disposal. Increasingly there have been initiatives from governments that require industry to take responsibility for the costs associated with the disposal of goods and products, however so far consistent approaches have not been properly developed.[49]

Therefore Article 9(b) integrates this responsibility into the overall cost of goods and products in order that the associated market mechanism and compensatory response are created. While this approach provides a basis upon which to achieve those objectives, the precise offsets that would be required could be the subject of argument. This is because the actual type of degradation caused to the environment may depend on the manner in which disposal occurs, for example incineration, landfill or other methods.[50] While absolute precision may not be possible, such a mechanism would provide an incentive for manufacturers generally to use the least environmentally harmful components and create recovery schemes for spent goods and products.

4.3.10 Article 10 – Registered Suppliers of Direct Environmental Compensatory Offsets (DECOs)

(a) *Each party will establish a system of registered suppliers of direct environmental compensatory offsets within its own jurisdiction in accordance with the standards agreed by the World Environment Organization (WEO) (see Art. 13).*

(b) *Each party will establish a national office to regulate and oversee the registered suppliers of direct environmental compensatory offsets in accordance with the standards agreed by the WEO (see Art. 13).*

(c) *Each party will require that registered suppliers of direct environmental compensatory offsets produce annual reports of the offsets provided in each accounting year in accordance with standards agreed by the WEO (see Art. 13).*

(d) *Each party shall require that a copy of the annual report provided by the registered suppliers of direct environmental compensatory offsets is delivered to the WEO (see Art. 13).*

(e) *Each party shall ensure that the standards of direct environmental compensatory offsets supplied by their registered suppliers of direct environmental compensatory offsets are consistent with standards established by the WEO (see Art. 13).*

(f) *Each party will facilitate on-site standards inspections by representatives of the WEO of direct environmental compensatory offsets.*

(g) *The WEO will be the ultimate authority on the granting or revocation of the licenses of registered suppliers of direct environmental compensatory offsets and also sanctions for non-compliance with standards.*

The term 'offset' has different meanings depending upon the context in which it is used. Within the field of environmental protection there are different uses and meanings of this term. Therefore it is worth noting these differences prior to clarifying the type of offset that is referred to within the draft GER.

In Western Australia for example the relatively new tool of an 'environmental offset' is described as, 'an offsite action or actions to address significant residual environmental impacts of a development or activity'.[51] In this context environmental offsets may be used following environmental impact assessments to compensate for residual environmental impacts that have caused degradation to the environment.[52] Similarly in other countries this concept has either been adopted or is being considered for adoption as a policy option within specific sectors. In recent years the UK government has been considering adopting a similar approach to compensate for the loss of biodiversity following development projects.[53]

These so-called 'biodiversity offsets' are based on the concept of the trading of losses to biodiversity in one place through biodiversity gains purchased or created in another (often using market mechanisms).[54] Such schemes attempt to design into projects, 'no net loss of biodiversity' and preferably a net gain through practical work to compensate the environment.[55] This type of offset is the most similar in its characteristics to that envisaged within the draft GER.

However, there are other types of offsets that must also be mentioned. For example, within the UNFCCC regime, carbon 'offsets' are provided for in the Clean Development Mechanism (CDM).[56] These are rights to emit GHGs that are granted through the development of projects in developing (non-Annex I) countries that have the effect of reducing GHG emissions in those countries.[57] These types of projects may amount to avoided emissions, for example through the development of clean energy projects such as wind turbines in the place of coal-fired powered stations where there is new demand for energy.

The difference that these types of offsets have to those previously mentioned is that they do not necessarily compensate for the harm to the environment caused by the emissions of the industry, they allow the industry to purchase the right to pollute through the purchase of what are known as a certified emission reductions (CER).[58] It has to be noted that additionally under the UNFCCC, efforts are being made to attempt to develop forestry schemes which would act as sinks for carbon emissions and such schemes could be regarded as 'offsets' that compensate the atmosphere for degradation caused.[59]

Within the context of Article 10 of the draft GER, direct environmental compensatory offsets should compensate the environment in at least equal measure to the degradation that would be caused by any of the actors concerned. Therefore, for any given case of environmental degradation, two steps are required. First, the degradation must be assessed and quantified; this may require an environmental assessment or it may be possible for authorities to calculate the degradation on the basis of a standard criteria. Second, the party responsible for compensating the harm to the environment will purchase the necessary environmental offset from a registered supplier.

Although a comprehensive system of this nature has not been established on national or international levels, the underlying concept is gradually garnering increased support.[60] The approach has been referred to by McGillivray as 'ecological impact neutrality'.[61] While such a system is not completely straightforward owing to the difficulties in replacing certain components of the environment or ecosystems, it provides a logical basis upon which to attempt to achieve sustainability.[62]

The system envisaged would enable those actors who cause pollution, which has transboundary effects or which affects the global commons, to purchase offsets in other jurisdictions, thus potentially making them more economical and potentially providing much needed investment in ecosystem improvement and protection in developing countries. While the precise criteria of the system are not considered here, there is the potential that this mechanism could play a significant role in creating the necessary finance for reforestation, afforestation and the development of agroforestry schemes in developing countries.

4.3.11 Article 11 – Registered Suppliers of Environmental Insurance

(a) *Each party will establish a system of registered suppliers of environmental insurance within its own jurisdiction in accordance with the standards agreed by the WEO.*

(b) *Each party will establish a national office to regulate and oversee the registered suppliers of environmental insurance in accordance with the standards agreed by the WEO.*

(c) *Each party will require that registered suppliers of environmental insurance produce annual reports of all the insurance provided in the preceding accounting year in accordance with the standards agreed by the WEO.*

(d) *Each party will require that a copy of the annual report provided by the registered suppliers of environmental insurance is delivered to the WEO.*

(e) *Each party shall ensure that the standards of environmental insurance supplied by their registered suppliers of environmental insurance are consistent with the standards agreed by the WEO.*

(f) *Each party will facilitate on-site standards inspections by representatives of the WEO of work undertaken by or on behalf of registered suppliers of environmental insurance.*

(g) *The WEO will be the ultimate authority on the granting or revocation of the licenses of registered suppliers of environmental insurance and also on sanctions for non-compliance with standards.*

On both national and international levels specific liability regimes have developed and these have resulted in businesses insuring against certain risks of environmental degradation.[63] However, such schemes are by no means comprehensive and can be limited in both the type of degradation that is covered and the extent to which businesses are required to restore and compensate the environment or the individuals and communities that may become victims.[64]

Over recent decades a catalogue of environmental disasters caused by business and industry (especially in developing countries) have impacted not only on the environment but also on the human rights of individuals and communities. Far too often the legacies of such disasters have been long protracted claims against the industries concerned that frequently have failed to provide adequate redress and sometimes a failure to reach the merits stage owing to the procedural hurdles involved. There are many examples of such instances.[65]

Therefore a universal obligation for businesses to procure comprehensive insurance in relation to their operations would enable claimants to make claims much more easily and directly. It would also enable universal standards agreed by the WEO to apply. This in itself could achieve certain objectives.

Primarily, such a mechanism would internalize the risks associated with business activities and as a result realize the polluter pays principle.[66] On a practical level, it would provide a method of dealing with uncertain risks owing to the analysis and experience of the insurance providers who would be required to operate to agreed international standards in the cover provided.[67] However in addition, comprehensive systems of insurance have the potential of being linked to the provision of rapid response systems for disasters such as oil spills and toxic leaks. There is also the potential for a requirement of insurance providers to invest in stocks of environmental assets such as reforestation projects or marine conservation projects for example, the credits of which could be surrendered in the event of degradation caused to the global commons by an insured business or industry.

The requirement of environmental insurance on an international level would have certain key beneficial effects. It would provide a level competitive playing field for business and industry but equally importantly provide a level playing field in terms of environmental protection for citizens in different parts of the world. Additionally, it would inevitably generate a growth sector within insurance industries worldwide.

4.3.12 Article 12 – International Corporation Registration Body

An International Corporation Registry Body is hereby established. Its functions shall be:

(a) To maintain a register of all corporations (or other business entities) that, 'operate internationally'.

(b) To provide a license for corporations (or other business entities) to 'operate internationally'.

(c) *To provide standardized sanctions for directors, corporations (and other business entities) that fail to comply with the standards agreed and determined by the WEO.*

(d) *To act as the ultimate authority for all parties in relation to the sanctions, including the revocation of licenses to 'operate internationally', for those corporations (and other business entities) that fail to comply with the standards agreed and determined by the WEO.*

As was discussed in Chapter 3, one of the key features of corporations within all jurisdictions is their separate legal personality. This currently provides the capacity for corporations to become MNEs by operating internationally through the use of subsidiaries registered in different jurisdictions. By structuring operations in this way, parent corporations have been able to avoid liability for environmental harm caused by their subsidiaries in jurisdictions with either limited standards of environmental protection or limited enforcement of the standards that are in place.[68]

Muchlinski notes that an MNE can come into being not just through a parent corporation establishing a subsidiary in another country but in a variety of other ways, which include contractual arrangements, equity based groups, joint ventures and informal alliances between corporations.[69] Therefore it is not sufficient simply to rely on provisions amending the duties of corporations internationally and requiring them to account (as stated in Articles 7 and 8). It is necessary that a complete international system is developed which necessitates that those corporations that 'operate internationally' (in any of the above mentioned forms) are subject to comprehensive legal constraint in whichever jurisdiction they are operating and under whatever corporate structure they have adopted. Such a system is required to ensure that they operate to required environmental standards. It can be said that there are two principle reasons why this type of reform should be implemented.

First, as was indicated in Chapter 3, the existing system was designed long before the advent of the levels of international trade and certainly long before the advent of MNEs that are now such influential actors within commerce and trade. It is therefore a system that was designed for a set of circumstances that were prevalent in the nineteenth century and that now often fails to provide adequate accountability within the context of complex transnational business.

Second, there is the question of privilege. Businesses that are incorporated enjoy certain key privileges; the most prominent of these are that the business enterprise itself enjoys 'separate legal personality' and the shareholders normally enjoy the privilege of 'limited liability'. These privileges enable businesses to be run with less risk to investors. However, it follows that along with those privileges should come responsibilities towards those individuals, communities and the environment that are affected by corporations' (or other business entities') activities wherever they take place.[70]

The system that the draft GER introduces would simply require that for corporations (and other types of business entities) to operate internationally, they would have to be registered and licensed. To maintain their registration, their business activities would have to comply with the international standards of this treaty as agreed and elaborated by the WEO.

As has already been mentioned earlier in relation to Articles 7 and 8, the task required for the complete implementation of this type of system is a huge one. Therefore it is anticipated that such arrangements would be phased in according to agreed transitional arrangements under Article 18. This could mean, for example, that only corporations and business entities above a certain size would be subject to these provisions in the early stages.

4.3.13 Article 13 – World Environment Organization

A World Environment Organization is hereby established. Its functions shall be:

(a) Standard Setting

(i) To provide an international authority for environmental standard setting.

(ii) To agree the standards required for direct environmental compensatory offsets (see Art. 10) and to agree the requirements for environmental insurance (see Art. 11).

(b) Governance

(i) To receive and monitor the direct environmental compensatory offset reports (see Art. 10).

(ii) To inspect the quality and adequacy of direct environmental compensatory offsets through a system of international environmental assessors (see Arts. 10 and 16).

(iii) To oversee and license registered suppliers of direct environmental compensatory offsets and registered suppliers of environmental insurance and to revoke their licenses in the event of a failure to provide offsets or insurance that meets the WEO agreed standards (see Arts. 10 and 11).

(c) Transitional Arrangements

(i) To agree the transitional arrangements for both states and non-state actors (see Art. 18).

(d) Dispute Settlement

(i) To provide a dispute settlement body to hear disputes relating to decisions within the ambit of this treaty.

(ii) To provide authoritative advice to the Dispute Settlement Body of the WTO (World Trade Organization) on environmental matters (see Art. 14).

(e) *Compliance*

(i) *To receive reports from each party to this treaty relating to the legislative steps taken to comply with it and advise the Secretariat accordingly (see Art. 2).*

(ii) *To receive copies of each state's environmental accounts and advise the Secretariat accordingly (see Art. 5).*

(iii) *To receive copies of each corporation and business entity's environmental accounts and to advise the International Corporation Registration Body in relation to levels of compliance with the required standards (see Art. 8).*

(iv) *To receive the annual reports from the registered suppliers of direct environmental compensatory offsets (see Art. 10).*

(v) *To receive the annual reports from the registered suppliers of environmental insurance (see Art. 11).*

(vi) *To use the system of environmental assessors (see Art. 16) to assist in ascertaining levels of compliance.*

(vii) *To act as the ultimate authority on the granting or revocation of the licenses of registered suppliers of direct environmental compensatory offsets and also sanctions for non-compliance with standards (see Art. 10).*

(viii) *To act as the ultimate authority on the granting or revocation of the licenses of registered suppliers of environmental insurance and also sanctions for non-compliance with standards (see Art. 11).*

(f) *Corruption*

(i) *To ensure that corporations or other types of business entities are not permitted to influence the decision-making processes of the WEO except through transparent and properly recorded consultation processes open to all sectors of the international community.*

(ii) *To put systems in place to ensure that corrupt practices relating to the environment are eradicated and national authorities prosecute those responsible.*

The concept of a WEO is not new.[71] In fact different versions of the concept have been advocated for several decades. For example proposals for the creation of a WEO have been made by various heads of states, numerous academics and also the representatives and leaders of major international organizations.[72] As Goeteyn and Maes state:

> [f]or over 30 years advocates have tried to convince the international community of the merits of the idea that a more potent environmental organization is needed. So far this has proven to be a fruitless exercise. Indeed, looking

> back, the landscape of International Environmental Governance is littered with failed attempts to break the political deadlock on the creation of a WEO.[73]

One proponent has been Daniel Esty, who in 1994 advocated the institution of a Global Environmental Organization (GEO), in part to counterbalance the influence of the WTO and to provide a specialized authority in relation to environmental issues. It is not claimed that the provision put forward in this book mirrors exactly Esty's vision but there are similarities. He states that:

> [i]n fact, a GEO designed to respond to the collective-action problems plaguing environmental protection efforts and charged with coordinating a comprehensive international response to environmental challenges would do more for the quality of the environment worldwide than any program of 'greening' the GATT could ever accomplish.
>
> Like the GATT, a GEO would provide a bulwark against domestic pressures that undermine long-term thinking and make sensible policies hard to achieve. Such a body could serve as an honest broker in transnational environmental disputes, assessing risks and benefits from environmental threats and allocating costs and cleanup responsibilities. Just as the GATT built on the core concept of nondiscrimination as a means to trade liberalization, a GEO would establish guidelines, centered on the polluter pays principle, to promote international cooperation in addressing environmental matters and the integration of economic policy goals.[74]

It can be argued that a WEO should contain three features to achieve overarching environmental goals. First, it should be part of an integral system that has specified objectives that are common to the whole international community. Second, it should be based on international cooperation between all nations. Third, it should integrate the development of a green economy within its functioning so that business and industry can rely on it to provide the necessary standards required and the basis for a level playing field for international competition.

Within the context of the other parts of the draft GER, the function of the WEO set out here is largely self-explanatory in terms of its role within the provision of an architecture to achieve overall goals. However, there are two other points that must be emphasized. First, for any such organization to operate successfully, legitimacy must be derived through a democratic framework. It is outside the scope of this book to elaborate on the precise make up of such an organization. Second, intrinsic to the legitimacy of such an organization is the need to integrate systems to tackle corruption internationally and the potential of internal corruption through the capture of WEO decision-makers by interested parties.

4.3.14 Article 14 – World Trade Law

> *Each party commits itself to:*
>
> *(a) An amendment to the Charter Establishing the WTO in order that its*

purposes will be changed to include the purpose of being an organization that is required to ensure that goods and services traded do not cause degradation to the environment, in the manner in which they are produced, in their use, or in their disposal, and that where such degradation will be caused, to satisfy basic human rights, the necessary steps are taken in accordance with this treaty to compensate the environment accordingly to ensure that the environment upon which existing and future generations rely is properly protected.

(b) *Amendments to the WTO trade disciplines to ensure that all goods and services traded by states, corporations, other business entities, organizations and individuals are compliant with the environmental duties detailed in this treaty.*

(c) *Amendments to the Agreement Establishing the Dispute Settlement Body (DSB) to ensure that any disputes that involve environmental protection or issues relating to environmental measures will be referred to the relevant organ of the WEO which will investigate and provide advice accordingly (see Art. 13).*

(d) *Amendments to regional trade agreements consistent with the objectives detailed in (a)–(c) above.*

One of the features of the international system of trade, as embodied within the WTO, is that it has largely been regarded as a discrete system within public international law. This has often had the effect of trade lawyers and trade representatives viewing the liberalization of trade as an end in itself rather than as an integrated component within a wider global legal architecture that must have regard to a range of different concerns. Sampson emphasizes this point by stating that:

> [w]hile the WTO takes responsibility for negotiated trade liberalisation, its Members have repeatedly stated that they do not consider the WTO to be responsible for setting and enforcing environmental and social standards. Nor is it the responsibility of the WTO to redistribute the gains from trade in countries that have benefited from trade expansion or to protect those that are adversely affected. This is considered an encroachment on national sovereignty. This argument is buttressed by the fact that at the multilateral level, multilateral agreements outside the WTO are already in place to deal with non-trade concerns such as the environment.[75]

However, certain leading academics in this field take a different view of the relationship between trade and the environment. Esty for example states that:

> [t]he relationship between environmental and trade issues in the context of deepening economic integration is inescapable and multi-layered. Ignoring these linkages threatens to reduce social welfare, limit the gains from trade, and cause unnecessary environmental degradation. Ignoring the environ-

mental implications of trade policymaking poses an acute threat to current and future economic integration efforts, not to mention environmental programs.[76]

Chapter 3 showed that the trade disciplines are very much one component of a global legal architecture that is designed in a manner in which environmental harm can ultimately become an inevitable consequence. The problem of regarding trade law as a discrete system that stands separate from other international regimes is that it can lead to the conclusion that it is not the responsibility of the world trading system to modernize in order that its systems deter rather than contribute to environmental problems.

Chapter 3 showed that the GATT and the WTO were designed upon precepts that did not contemplate the major challenges that the world is currently facing, such as climate change, water shortages, food crises and loss of biodiversity. It is the argument of this book that each and every part of the global legal architecture should be reformed where necessary, so that the side-effects of their operations are not further environmental degradation but true sustainability. Sustainability in this context means that trade and production should cause no net harm to the environment, and if anything, have the side-effect of improving the environment.

For such a shift to occur two changes need to take place. First, it will be necessary to work towards a reformed legal architecture for trade that is designed to achieve sustainability as a properly integrated component of the global legal architecture. Second, it will be necessary for the trade rules themselves to be amended in accordance with the provisions of this article, in order that they become part of the process of environmental protection rather than purely part of a system of 'non-discrimination' and trade liberalization. It is for this reason that Article 13 (a) seeks an amendment to the Agreement Establishing the WTO to provide this as a stated purpose of the organization.

The concept of creating a world trading system that is predisposed to sustainability is not a new one. Newell for example has suggested that reforms could be made to ensure that membership of trade agreements are subject to the condition that specific environmental standards are complied with.[77] (Observers have noted that the WTO is capable of taking on responsibilities that are not purely trade related owing to the development and adoption of TRIPS.)[78] The failures of the Doha round of negotiations have highlighted the tensions and organizational problems that the WTO faces. This has led to debate over how the institution should be reformed.[79] It is argued that the modernization of the organization should include the reforms detailed here.

Article 13 (a) refers to one of the major areas in which the design of the international trading system can be predisposed towards outcomes of environmental degradation, that is 'process and production methods'. Esty has long contended that the trade rules relating to process and production methods are designed in such a manner that they can lead to environmental degradation and asserts that '*how* things are made is just as important as *what* is traded'.[80] This can be particularly important in terms of tackling anthropogenic climate change.

Some states are now looking to impose legal restrictions on manufacturers and operators to ensure that there are limits to the levels of GHGs that are emitted in the production of goods and services, or that appropriate carbon taxes are imposed. To avoid unfair competition, these regulations would be accompanied by the imposition of taxes or countervailing duties on imported goods and services that are not subject to such regulations or taxes in their states of origin. Additionally where carbon taxes are imposed on home state industries there is the question of remitting those taxes on export in order that those industries will not face a competitive disadvantage. This has raised the question of whether or not such measures are consistent with the trade disciplines.[81]

These scenarios, which attract much literature, are indicative of the reason why the trade disciplines need to be reformed. They indicate the potential difficulty that a state could have in attempting to take legislative and policy steps in favour of climate-friendly products. They also indicate that there is no overarching rule within the trade disciplines to ensure that goods and services are 'climate friendly' or at least 'low carbon' in terms of their contribution to the levels of carbon dioxide in the atmosphere.

The provisions of the draft GER look to the reform of trade rules to ensure that membership of the WTO and other trade agreements require that goods and services do not cause harm to the environment in their production. Therefore it envisages that trade rules would reflect and be consistent with the rules that are required of corporations, business entities, banks, financial institutions and states within Articles 1, 4, 5, 7–10, 11–13 and 17 of the draft GER. As such the draft GER looks to streamline obligations towards the environment rather than having certain international rules being diametrically opposed to each other.

This leads on to the final point, which is that one of the problems of the GATT system has been that there have been times when powerful importing states have used environmental standards in a manner that could amount to disguised protectionism. This has produced a catalogue of cases in which the DSB has attempted to determine whether such actions were justified or not, by applying a highly complex set of rules. Therefore the reforms sought within the draft GER include a provision that would require the DSB to refer environmental matters to the WEO. The WEO would provide an international authority on appropriate standards.

Invoking the authority of the WEO to set the benchmark of environmental standards for the international trading regime would provide a mechanism to provide both the stringency and the fairness that is required for all countries. The issue of fairness in this area was especially highlighted at the Rio + 20 Conference in 2012. The report of the conference states that:

> [we] affirm that green economy policies in the context of sustainable development and poverty eradication should…
>
> (h) Not constitute a means of arbitrary or unjustifiable discrimination or a disguised restriction on international trade, avoid unilateral actions to deal with environmental challenges outside the jurisdiction of the importing

country, and ensure that environmental measures addressing transboundary or global environmental problems, as far as possible, are based on an international consensus.[82]

By adopting the approach detailed in the draft GER, it appears that these aspirations could be satisfied.

4.3.15 Article 15 – Environmental Assessments

Each party shall amend its law relating to Environmental Impact Assessments and Strategic Environmental Assessments to ensure that the following apply:

(a) Systems will be developed in accordance with agreed WEO standards to ensure that all aspects of environmental degradation and potential degradation are assessed and addressed, using appropriate methodologies and techniques, in accordance with the provisions of this treaty.

(b) Where an environmental assessment indicates that a decision, arrangement, law, project, plan or policy ***will*** *cause degradation to the environment and no less environmentally degrading alternatives are viable, the assessment will include a report on the quantity and type of direct environmental compensatory offsets (see Art. 10) that will need to be purchased to ensure that the individual, government, business or organization that is seeking to carry it out, knows what is required for compliance with the law.*

(c) Where an environmental assessment indicates that a decision, arrangement, law, project, plan or policy ***may*** *cause degradation to the environment and no less environmentally degrading alternatives are viable, the assessment will include a report on the quantity and type of environmental insurance (see Art. 11) that will need to be purchased to ensure that the individual, government, business or organization that is seeking to carry it out, knows what is required for compliance with the law.*

This provision is self-explanatory and reflects a further development of the system of environmental assessments that has evolved worldwide. There are obvious strengths to environmental impact assessments and strategic environmental assessments, however, they are hampered by the fact that they are not always tied to substantive environmental standards and do not necessarily apply to all types of decision-making that can have negative effects on the environment. Therefore they are currently, by their very nature, procedural and as such do not necessarily lead to decision-making that has an outcome that is positive or even neutral in terms of the environment.[83] Additionally, the methods and assumptions built into an assessment process can have a major negative impact on the final results.[84] In relation to SEAs, Therivel states that:

> [w]hat has also become clear is that SEA practice alone is not leading to more environmentally sound decisions. Much of the recent SEA literature concerns

> the limitations of carrying out rationalist SEAs whose findings must only be 'taken into account' in a non-rationalist, politically driven world. My experience as a consultant bears this out.[85]

Article 15 would make two changes to environmental assessments. The first would be that all aspects of environmental degradation and potential environmental degradation would be addressed. This is a departure from the current system that is common in most countries and international regimes, which relies on a process of screening to determine whether or not the environmental effects that are predicted are 'significant' in nature.[86] In the event that 'significant' negative environmental effects are predicted, an environmental assessment is necessary and the authorities are obliged to take that information into account prior to making decisions.

Article 15 (a) would widen the scope of environmental assessments so that they would go much further than is currently required. Such a step is needed to ensure that all aspects of environmental degradation are compensated and to ensure that the creeping accumulation of environmental harm, which forms a major part of the degradation that was recorded in Chapter 2 and which affects people's human rights, is addressed at source.

In widening the scope of environmental assessments, the responsibilities under Article 15 would encompass not only the responsibilities of those currently carrying out EIAs and SEAs but also the environmental regulators and agencies within each state to ensure that all aspects of environmental degradation are taken into account.

The second change that Article 15 would make, would be to transform environmental assessments from being procedural processes that have to be taken into account by decision-makers, to processes that are tied to substantive standards to ensure that any environmental harm (and potential environmental harm) is compensated for (or insured against) in accordance with the substantive standards of the WEO.

4.3.16 Article 16 – System of International Environmental Assessors

> *The WEO will establish a system of environmental* assessors in accordance with Article 13 (b) *to:*
>
> *(a) Inspect and report on the standards of direct environmental compensatory offsets being provided by registered suppliers of direct environmental compensatory offsets (see Art. 10).*
>
> *(b) Inspect and report on the standards of environmental insurance being provided by registered suppliers of environmental insurance (see Art. 11).*
>
> *(c) Inspect and report on governments, corporations and any other business entities that make decisions that have or could have impacts on the environment to ensure that correct procedures are followed.*

States have traditionally been reticent to accept independent monitoring from international organizations. However, concerted international effort and cooperation to provide level playing fields between states in relation to environmental matters does require not only accountability but also a system that will ensure that all actors are operating to the agreed standards. Such a system would lead to consistent approaches and fairness internationally.

Levels of corruption internationally hamper the protection of the environment and as a result have an impact on the human rights of those that are affected through environmental degradation. It is therefore important that standards are maintained and that fair systems of accountability are developed.

4.3.17 Article 17 – Banks and Financial Institutions

Each party commits itself to:

(a) Amendments to the charters/constitutions of banks and financial institutions to change their purposes to being organizations that will only lend funds to projects that are consistent with the environmental duties detailed in this treaty, at the risk of acting ultra-vires their purposes.

(b) Amendments to the charters/constitutions of banks and financial institutions to change their operational policies and practices to ensure that projects are consistent with the environmental duties detailed in this treaty, at the risk of acting ultra-vires their policies.

In terms of non-state actors, the focus of this book has been on corporations and international trade organizations. Earlier work has focused in more depth on the functioning and impacts of the constitutional rules of multilateral development banks.[87]

While all banks and financial institutions should have systematic procedures that deal with environmental risks, they are not necessarily constitutionally bound to ensure that the projects that they fund, lead to the outcomes that the draft GER puts forward.

As stated previously, for a global legal architecture to function effectively, it is vital that all decision-makers are subject to obligations that lead to the same overall objective. Therefore, it would be problematical if national constitutions, trading organizations and corporations were to have binding obligations that led to sustainable outcomes but that banking and financial institutions were subject to lower standards.

It is important to note that the flow of money into business projects is crucial to the impacts that businesses have upon the environment.[88] Therefore, it is anticipated that all types of investment institutions would be under the same type of obligations as other businesses in relation to their responsibilities towards the environment.[89]

4.3.18 Article 18 – Transitional Arrangements

> *The WEO will coordinate the agreed transitional arrangements, where appropriate, during the incorporation of the system required under this treaty.*

It is outside of the confines of this book to provide details of the transitional arrangements that would be required to phase in the system that is described within the draft GER. However, the transitional arrangements would be of crucial importance for two reasons. First, they would reflect the pace at which the relevant changes would be made. Second, they would need to be designed in a manner that would be fair to both existing and future generations.

The question of transitional arrangements ties in with the issue of CBDR.[90] It is also pertinent to Principle 6 of the Rio Declaration, which relates to the special priorities of developing and least developed countries.[91] Although these principles are integrated into the provisions of a number of multilateral environmental agreements, there is no clear consensus as to their precise meaning or the systems that should be used to achieve the allocation of different responsibilities.[92]

The state-centric approach that is applied through multilateral environmental agreements has led to the categorization of states according to their levels of development. The question of what constitutes a 'developing' country can be a difficult issue. Traditionally, a simple formula has been used that has focused on the GNP per capita.[93] Such an approach does not take into account the diverse capacities of different industrial sectors within a state or other indicators relating to 'well-being' such as levels of literacy, levels of employment and infant mortality.[94]

This book does not advocate a particular technique or method for evaluating or determining the transitional arrangements; this would need to be the subject of separate analysis that carefully took into account the possible methods and criteria that could be used. However, as the draft GER would create obligations for both state and non-state actors, there is potentially a *prima facie* case for applying different transitional arrangements for some non-state actors to those that would be applicable to states themselves.

Whatever transitional arrangements were designed, they would need to be conducive to an organized, clear and equitable transition to the framework under this agreement to ensure that ultimately business and trade could operate on a level playing field and also that the provisions could take effect at the earliest time. However, special care needs to be built into such arrangements to enable communities to develop and maintain access to markets, while treading the transitional path. This could require carefully constructed phase in periods and pre-agreed international institutional and technological support for states in lower stages of development.

4.3.19 Article 19 – Compliance

> *(a) The WEO will have compliance responsibilities in accordance with Art. 13 (e).*
>
> *(b) The International Corporation Registration Body will have compliance responsibilities in accordance with Art. 12 (d).*

Naturally (as discussed in sub-section 3.2.3) compliance within any international treaty regime has traditionally been a sensitive issue owing to the potential impacts upon state sovereignty and national economies. However, equity requires not only a system of compliance but also one that is comprehensive.

4.3.20 Article 20 – Separation of Corporations and the State

> *Each party will enact legislation to ensure that governments only consult business and industry through formal processes of consultation (provided for by government) on decisions relating to the environment. Such processes are to be made available to other interested parties such as NGOs.*

Increasingly it has been recognized that a stumbling block to effective environmental protection in many jurisdictions has been the coercive role of corporations in influencing governments.[95] This would suggest that a duty to protect the environment by any government should be accompanied by systems to ensure that its duty could not be influenced except through properly transparent and democratic channels.

The US is an example of the corporate influence within politics. Speth observes that:

> [t]he failure of U.S. climate policy has more to do with domestic politics than international affairs, and it has everything to do with the forty-year failure of U.S. energy policy. Both failures, are the result of the great political power of the fossil fuel industry, which has prevented any serious U.S. movement to reduce carbon dioxide emissions.[96] The enormous power of Big Oil and Big Coal in American politics is reflected in the fact that at this late date, with all the focus on renewable energy and all the disasters generated by coal, oil, and gas, federal subsidies to fossil fuels between 2002 and 2008 came to $72 billion; those to renewables only $29 billion, with more than half of that going to corn based ethanol.[97] Technological advances that have opened up large supplies of shale oil and gas will make the shift away from fossil fuels even more difficult.[98]

The trend in the US is consistent with the trend that is taking place internationally, and which it can be argued indicates the power of business and industry in influencing the decision-making processes of governments around the globe.[99]

4.3.21 Article 21 – Secretariat

A Secretariat is hereby established. Its functions shall be:

(a) *To organize an annual meeting of the parties.*

(b) *To periodically review the terms of this treaty in order that it can be updated in accordance with the requirements of the parties.*

4.4 Conclusion

This chapter has had the primary objective of putting forward a draft GER that is framed with certain key features. These are that it:

1 primarily creates duties for actors (rather than solely rights for victims);
2 applies ultimately to both state and non-state actors;
3 requires a specific standard of environmental protection to be attained;
4 provides a system that creates long-term certainty for business and industry;
5 provides a clear role for the WTO;
6 provides a business framework for those working within the business of providing direct environmental compensatory offsets and environmental insurance.

Therefore it has provided an overall framework but has still left certain questions to be answered. For example the issue of the transitional arrangements for states would require very careful analysis and agreement, the constitution of a WEO would require careful construction and the application of standards would need international cooperation and expert consultation.

However, probably one of the overriding questions that confronts any international treaty is the question that was raised at the start of this chapter, which is, 'why would states want to adopt it?'. Hathaway has discussed the mechanics of modern-day international law and elaborates on the inevitable process that governments enter into of weighing up the costs and benefits of any proposed treaty.[100] Therefore states need to see not only the environmental advantages of such a system but also the long-term economic and political advantages, especially given the implications that international treaties can have on state sovereignty.

With the pressure that is mounting upon all states to secure an adequate response to global environmental challenges, one important imperative is to establish a system that is practical and workable. As has been noted in the commentary throughout this chapter, many of the features of the provisions within the draft GER are drawn from the suggestions or developments that have been progressing within the field of international environmental governance anyway. This in itself could provide part of the reason why states should consider it as an option. Another part of the answer may lie in the following chapter, which discusses the application of the draft GER to the problem of climate change.

5 The application of the Draft Global Environmental Right to climate change

5.1 Introduction

This chapter discusses how the provisions of the draft GER put forward in Chapter 4 could have direct application to climate change. It highlights the problems with the existing global legal architecture that were identified within Chapter 3, in the context of the international responses to climate change, with specific regard to the UNFCCC regime.[1] It therefore discusses the key features of the current regime and provides an analysis using the framework of the draft GER as a template for comparison.

In carrying this out, the chapter identifies two key features inherent in the UNFCCC system that render it ineffective in achieving its goals. These features are firstly its complete reliance on a traditional Westphalian model and secondly its reliance on the stabilization of GHGs through the commodification of carbon without providing for mechanisms to compensate the environment for the harm caused by the emissions of GHGs that are permitted.

In discussing the features of the existing regime, the chapter illustrates why a different type of approach is needed and considers how the approach put forward in the draft GER could operate effectively without reliance on the traditional Westphalian model or the type of commodification of carbon that is currently used.

Finally the chapter returns to the points made in Chapter 2 to show that not only is an effective system necessary from an economic and environmental standpoint, but that it is very much a human rights issue. It therefore emphasizes the need for a global legal architecture that creates legal duties for all types of actors, to ensure that the environmental goals of the international community can be achieved and that the fundamental rights of individuals and communities can be upheld.

5.2 Deficiencies of the existing regime and the potential remedies through the adoption of the draft GER

Care needs to be taken when discussing the deficiencies of the current regime owing to the complexity of the problem of climate change, the true scale of the challenge and the difficulties of reaching agreements within the global political arena. However, it is necessary to mark the drawbacks of the existing system as those lessons shed light on what is required for the future. Such an approach provides a basis upon which to assess the potential of the legal architecture set out within the draft GER. The following sub-sections provide a break down of key aspects of the existing international climate regime. They do so with a view to identifying underlying flaws within the system or, in other words, the reasons why the system fails to function effectively. Within each of these sub-sections, it then describes how the draft GER could provide the basis of a system that might overcome those flaws with a view to achieving environmental sustainability.

5.2.1 The UNFCCC treaty

The UNFCCC treaty established in 1992 was in itself a remarkable achievement in that it successfully engaged the support of the majority of nations in a multilateral effort to combat anthropogenic climate change. There are now 195 parties to the treaty and it represents the central legal and administrative framework of the international community within the field of climate change mitigation and adaptation.[2] Its declared objective is to 'achieve, in accordance with the relevant provisions of the Convention, stabilization of greenhouse gas concentrations in the atmosphere at a level that would prevent dangerous anthropogenic interference with the climate system'.[3]

Although the treaty did require all parties to take action to mitigate climate change (and cooperate in preparing for adaptation),[4] it did not establish binding emissions limits for specific countries. What it did was to provide an elaborate framework from which more detailed obligations could subsequently be developed. It provided a number of principled bases upon which agreements would be founded, which included CBDR, the precautionary principle, inter and intra-generational equity and the right to development.[5] The treaty provides two annexes that relate to the categories of obligations that different states would assume.

Annex I is mainly comprised of the OECD states and also those with economies in transition (EIT). The Annex I parties under the convention have the responsibility to limit their anthropogenic emissions of GHGs.[6] Annex II is comprised of OECD states but does not include the EIT states. Annex II parties have the responsibility to provide financial assistance to 'Non Annex I' parties (which are generally the developing countries). The obligation for the provision of financial assistance under Annex II was not quantified but was related *inter alia* to assistance with reporting requirements, adaptation to climate change and the transfer of technology.[7]

It has been well documented that while the elaboration of this treaty was an accomplishment in itself, its provisions have resulted in major disagreements between nations and groups of nations as to the precise allocation of obligations between states.

5.2.1.1 Analysis of the deficiencies of the UNFCCC treaty

It is in the very nature of the treaty itself that a fundamental flaw is seen that has undermined its potential for success from that day to this. This is that (like other multilateral environmental agreements) it is based wholly on the traditional

Westphalian system and thus right from the onset, it attempts to create a programme allocating responsibilities between states. Therefore, in a very simple manner, it places the entire responsibility for both mitigation and adaptation on states rather than directly identifying, addressing and resolving the root causes of the problem; it is therefore not surprising that it has not worked.

As was detailed in Chapter 3, one of the key drawbacks with much international environmental law is that it attempts to address the symptoms of problems rather than the legal constructs within the global legal architecture that are predisposed to creating the problems in the first place.

The treaty is framed under traditional public international law, which only recognizes states as subjects. Therefore as public international law does not directly (with certain exceptions) create obligations for non-state actors, the treaty regards states as having the primary responsibility for all activities within their borders.[8] The treaty fails to acknowledge the global legal architecture that has developed since the early 1800s and as such creates a dysfunctional framework within which solutions are sought.

Therefore, the UNFCCC system in failing to create responsibilities for actors other than states, creates two major obstacles that stand in the way of progress. First, it leaves the states themselves with a disproportionate burden for the problems that are occurring. Where there are conflicting pressures upon states to provide a range of services such as education, health, transport infrastructure, energy security, social security infrastructure, military security and administration, the additional burden of providing for climate change mitigation, adaptation and in some cases additional finance, can place a great strain on a nation's treasury. This can be particularly acute if the country is facing other economic pressures, whether they be in the form of widespread poverty, a debt crisis, overpopulation, underdevelopment or any of the other challenges that modern nations face and that place significant financial burdens upon their governments, which are often seeking to reduce their overall financial commitments.

The second problem is that it is a system that creates major inherent conflicts of interest. On the one hand, a state must pursue economic development and create the economic conditions that will stimulate industry to engender competitiveness with other states; this will invariably include creating the conditions for the provision of the cheapest possible energy. On the other hand, states are expected by the international community to reduce the consumption of cheap energy within their borders in order to deal with a global environmental problem. This dysfunctional arrangement has led to major disputes between nations over the precise responsibilities that they should bear. Therefore, it has also led to an integral disincentive for states to take steps to tackle climate change due to the twin fears of the costs involved and of losing economic competitiveness.

These two problems are further reinforced by the traditional notion of state sovereignty over natural resources, which emphasizes the right that states have to exploit their own natural resources pursuant to their own environmental and developmental policies.[9] In practical terms this right, combined with the economic pressures that states are under and an inadequate international climate change regime, has contributed significantly to the very sluggish movement towards the reduction of GHG emissions.

5.2.1.2 Application of the draft GER to the deficiencies of the UNFCCC treaty

The draft GER has the potential to address the problem of multilateral environmental agreements taking the traditional state-centric approach, by creating a generic legal responsibility for all types of actors to protect the environment and compensate it for any environmental degradation that they may cause (Art. 1). Therefore within the context of the UNFCCC, the draft GER overcomes the problem of the traditional state-centric approach in three ways.

First, it reapportions part of the burden of mitigation of anthropogenic climate change away from state actors and directly towards those actors that are actually responsible. It does this primarily by creating the framework for a direct legal responsibility for businesses (generally corporations) to protect the environment, which would provide the basis of a duty not to emit GHGs (except under certain specified circumstances).[10] It reinforces this responsibility with an onus on parties to support the integration of concomitant responsibilities within the WTO.[11]

Second, it creates a legal framework in which businesses that do emit GHGs, would be required to compensate the environment to achieve 'impact neutrality'[12] and sustainability.[13]

Third, it creates these obligations within a globally integrated administrative framework designed to create fair competition[14] and also to achieve CBDR through appropriate transitional arrangements.[15]

5.2.2 The Kyoto Protocol

The Kyoto Protocol established an international agreement in which 37 countries and the EU accepted binding targets to reduce their emissions of GHGs over a commitment period between 2008 and 2012.[16] Over that time they were obliged to reduce their emissions by an average of 5 per cent below 1990 levels. The protocol was agreed in 1997 and finally came into force in 2005. Significantly the US did not ratify the Kyoto Protocol and thus its overall impact was weakened.[17] At the Doha Conference of the Parties in 2012, a second commitment period was agreed which would run from 2012 to 2020.[18] However, this agreement included fewer parties as key nations such as Canada, Japan and Russia indicated that they would not accept emissions limitations under the second commitment period.[19] It has been estimated that during this second period, the Kyoto Protocol will only cover around 15 per cent of global emissions.[20]

Under the protocol each party can decide how it meets its targets. However the protocol provides for three market-based 'flexible mechanisms' that states can use in achieving them. These are Emissions Trading Schemes (ETS),[21] the CDM[22]and Joint Implementation (JI).[23]

Emissions trading allows parties to trade the allowances that are allocated to them under a 'cap and trade' scheme. This type of system is designed to enable efficiency and had previously been used with a certain degree of success by the US in reducing emissions of sulphur dioxide.[24] Cap and trade schemes generally consist of four component parts, which are as follows: first, a government creates a cap on the total volume of GHGs to be emitted and this is divided into allowances; second, those allowances are either given or sold to the emitters; third, those allowances can be traded between the emitters; fourth, the emissions are monitored and at the end of an accounting period, the emitters must surrender allowances to the government equal to the volume of GHGs that they have emitted (any allowances that the emitters have not used can be banked). The rationale of the scheme is that those emitters who are able to reduce their emissions most economically will do so and be able to sell their excess allowances to those emitters for whom it is less economical to make those reductions. This therefore provides greater efficiency for industry as a whole, while maintaining the integrity of the overall cap on emissions.

There are many criticisms of both the concept of carbon trading and also the manner in which it has evolved. (Many of the criticisms relate to the European ETS, which is the largest and best established scheme internationally.) It is not possible within the context of this chapter to provide a comprehensive critique of cap and trade schemes. However, criticisms include the argument that political decision-making relating to the setting of caps suffers from the influence of industry lobbying which means that the caps required for effective mitigation are insufficient,[25] that they have ultimately had little impact on investment patterns and therefore do not drive technological innovation,[26] that they provide a smokescreen for a lack of action and a failure to impose effective 'command and control' regulation,[27] that the extent of the coverage is limited (for example the EU ETS does not cover household use of fuels, most commercial facilities, land transport and agriculture),[28] that there are difficulties in including aviation emissions within a regional scheme such as the EU ETS,[29] that there are difficulties in quantifying and agreeing appropriate emissions limits for individual countries[30] and also that there are practical difficulties in allocating allowances within countries to individual industries.[31]

For all these reasons, it could be argued that carbon trading, despite having the appearance of being 'elegant and efficient', has drawbacks that mean that it has not lived up to the expectations that many have associated with it.[32] Robinson *et al.* observe that, '[t]rading is particularly well-suited where the environmental objective is to reduce emissions to a specific level or achieve a specific level of ambient environmental quality'.[33] As such it is possible to argue that where there is the requirement to reduce emissions by relatively modest amounts, cap and trade schemes may provide an effective mechanism. However, on the basis of the criticisms noted and the failings of the EU ETS, it can be argued that where within an economy there is a requirement to completely convert to different forms of energy generation, cap and trade schemes can be found to be less effective.

One of the principle arguments upon which cap and trade schemes are justified is that they allow industrial sectors to reduce overall emissions by a process of natural selection in which the cheapest emissions reductions are those that are carried out and those industries for which it would be more expensive are able to purchase the right to pollute accordingly. Therefore this approach can only be effective in saving costs where it is necessary for only a certain proportion of the overall emissions to be reduced. Within the existing scenario in which the IPCC now advises that the majority of existing GHG emissions will need to be eradicated (or neutralized), the advantage of the cap and trade system is far less likely to apply.[34] This is because those industries that previously would have sought to continue polluting, on the basis that other industries would be able to reduce their emissions, will have to eradicate (or neutralize) the majority of their emissions anyway and therefore the major advantage of a cap and trade system would be lost.

It certainly is the case that so far, they have not been successful in systematically reducing the levels of emissions of GHGs to the extent required. In a study by the Oxford Institute of Energy Studies, Timmons-Roberts *et al.* state that, 'in the short term, such market-based approaches remain very uncertain tools to address a problem of such magnitude as climate change'.[35]

The CDM is the only one of the flexible mechanisms that enables Non-Annex I states (developing countries) to benefit from the processes of the Kyoto Protocol. It enables industries in Annex I states (developed countries) to invest in projects in developing countries that will result in emissions reductions. The emissions reductions in terms of tonnes of carbon are calculated and credited to the Annex I country industry. The CDM is designed to enable industries in Annex I countries to achieve GHG emission reductions (albeit not in their own geographical region) at more economical costs than if they were made locally. Additionally, the developing countries involved are able to benefit from the investment in the associated projects and also from any relevant transfer of technology.

By 2012 under the CDM scheme, over 1 billion CERs had been issued by the UNFCCC (each one relating to 1 tonne of carbon).[36] This has led to significant transfers of investment to the developing countries involved.[37] Nevertheless, the CDM in practice has been widely criticized for a number of failings that include the facility that they create to disincentivize developed countries from reducing their emissions and developing renewable energy,[38] the high transactions costs,[39] the fact that in certain cases they do not lead to reduced emissions of GHGs[40] and also their application to projects that were destined to proceed regardless of the additional investment afforded to them.[41]

The third flexible mechanism under the protocol is that of JI. This allows developed country parties to earn emission reduction units (ERUs) by investing in emission reduction projects in other developed countries that are parties to the protocol. This has the effect of increasing the allowable emissions for the country investing in the project and lowering the allowable emissions of the country in which the project takes place. This can provide certain industries with more cost-effective means of achieving their reductions if it is cheaper to invest in such projects than reducing emissions in their own countries. There has been much less use of JI than the CDM and as such it has not received the same level of attention as the other flexible mechanisms.

5.2.2.1 Analysis of the deficiencies of the Kyoto Protocol

While the fundamental problem of the UNFCCC is that it relies on an outdated Westphalian model to attempt to tackle something, which requires streamlined commitments and obligations from non-state actors as well as state actors, the Kyoto Protocol, within the context of this analysis, attaches another layer of dysfunction onto the problems that were already systemic within the UNFCCC approach.

This dysfunction has been the reliance on the commodification of carbon through the facilitation of cap and trade schemes without including a system of compensation for the environment. It has to be emphasized that the system is not flawed due to the fact that it has stimulated market mechanisms; it is flawed as it provides polluters with the right to pollute without creating an obligation for them to compensate the environment for the emissions that they are permitted to make. Such an arrangement is not consistent with the 'polluter pays' principle, unless of course the caps under a cap and trade scheme lead to the levels of emission reductions that the IPCC states are required; at this time they do not.

Finally, within this analysis it must be observed that although under a cap and trade scheme (or under a carbon taxation scheme) it is possible for revenue to be generated by the state, which can potentially be used for purposes related to climate change mitigation or adaptation, there is no legal obligation under the international regime for it to be used for those purposes.

5.2.2.2 Application of the draft GER to the deficiencies of the Kyoto Protocol

The provisions of the draft GER would create a system that would place a legal responsibility on all actors (whether state or non-state) to compensate the environment for any degradation caused.[42] Such a mechanism has three effects in the context of climate change. First, it places a burden on emitters of GHGs (often corporations) either to avoid those emissions in the first place or to compensate for them through the purchase of direct environmental compensatory offsets.[43] Such compensation could take place through the provision of additional sinks that would neutralize the harm caused through those emissions. Second, this responsibility would act as a financial disincentive for those actors to make those emissions and provide an integral driver for the transition to a 'green economy'. Third, the provision of such a responsibility would create direct finance for investment in those developing countries that would be able to provide direct environmental compensatory offset services such as the creation of forestry sinks.[44]

The question of the transitional arrangements under which all states and industries or sectors would convert to this system would be governed under Article 18 of the draft GER.

5.2.3 The need for stabilization of GHGs in the atmosphere

In recent years it has been widely recognized that the efforts to combat climate change under the UNFCCC regime have not been adequate.[45] At the UNFCCC

Conference of the Parties (COP) 2010 in Cancun, it was agreed that the international community would aim to ensure that the rise in mean temperatures globally would not be more than 2° Celsius above pre-industrial levels.[46] This benchmark had been established some years previously.[47] The IPCC reported in 2007 that to achieve this (or an estimated global temperature of 2 to 2.4°C above pre-industrial levels) emissions would need to peak before 2015 and thereafter be reduced to 50–85 per cent of 2000 levels by 2050.[48] The existing trajectory of GHG emissions is not adequate to meet this target nor are there currently binding agreements in place to change that path. As such there is a much greater likelihood that the planet will experience significant 'dangerous anthropogenic interference with the climate system'[49] that could lead to the range of potential impacts that were detailed in Chapter 2.[50] Additionally, the IPCC reports that even if GHG concentrations were stabilized at existing levels, anthropogenic warming and sea-level rise could continue for centuries due to the timescales for removal of GHGs from the atmosphere.[52]

Since 2010, UNEP has commissioned scientists to produce reports relating to the gap between the levels of emissions reductions that are being pledged by states and those which the IPCC advises are required to lead to a stabilization of the mean temperature below 2°C.[52] These reports show that the international community is failing to achieve the required emissions reductions by significant margins.[53]

5.2.3.1 Analysis of the need for stabilization of GHGs

The existing cap and trade approach lacks any unequivocal and automatic mechanism that links the caps that are set by governments with the emission levels that the IPCC state are necessary for the required stabilization of levels of GHGs in the atmosphere. As stated above, analysis shows that the reductions in emissions that have been agreed internationally have been significantly lower than the levels that many within the scientific community believe are actually required.[54]

5.2.3.2 Application of the draft GER to the need for stabilization of GHGs

The draft GER provides an integral system that does not rely on state-centred caps and targets for the achievement of the stabilization of GHGs. It would provide a system that created a legal responsibility for all actors (both state and non-state) to ensure that any degradation that they cause to the environment is compensated for.

Therefore the system would require large-scale emitters of GHGs (such as carbon dioxide) to neutralize the harm caused through the purchase of direct environmental compensatory offsets (Art. 10). This could for example be achieved through the creation of areas of forest or the use of technology to remove carbon dioxide from the atmosphere.

The question of stabilization within the 2°C target would be a question of how quickly the new regime could be implemented under the treaty's transitional arrangements (Art. 18).

5.2.4 *The requirement for a global and comprehensive system that addresses the root causes of climate change*

The failure of the UNFCCC system to deliver a regime that can reduce the emissions of GHGs to acceptable levels and provide a balanced system that leads to sustainability in the future, has exacerbated the tendency of states (and also non-state actors) to adopt a range of fragmented approaches to climate mitigation on national and regional levels.[55] For example, some countries or regions such as Japan and the EU have adopted their own cap and trade schemes. Some countries such as New Zealand have implemented carbon taxation. Some countries such as Australia are implementing carbon taxation with a view to moving towards cap and trade schemes. Many developed countries tend to adopt a mixture of market-based and regulatory-based approaches.

Some countries favour border penalties on imported products or services that have high carbon footprints associated with them. (These policies have the potential to create complicated challenges under trade agreements in trade organizations such as the WTO.)[56] It should also be mentioned that on a transnational level a variety of initiatives have developed such as the International Standards Organization (ISO) 14000 environmental management system standards.[57]

In the forestry sector, the failure of the international community to develop comprehensive functioning systems of financing for existing forests, reforestation and afforestation has led to a variety of different schemes and voluntary initiatives with a range of different standard setting bodies.[58]

In addition to these approaches certain NGOs have begun to use litigation in a variety of different ways to pressurize governments and industry to take steps towards lower emissions. In the US, such litigation is relatively common and has in certain cases achieved some significant impacts.[59]

At the COP 18 of the UNFCCC in Doha in 2012 there was still no global agreement that was oriented towards achieving the stabilization of GHGs (although a commitment was established to create a new global agreement by 2015 that would come into effect by 2020).[60]

5.2.4.1 Analysis of the requirement of a global comprehensive system that addresses the root causes of climate change

While the range of different approaches reflects a determination to tackle the issue, the problem with these fragmented approaches being taken internationally is that they are no substitute for a properly functioning and effective global system.[61] The IPCC has indicated the need for massive cuts in the emissions of GHGs and this will only be possible through a comprehensive global system.[62] While some nations, as stated above, have taken certain specific unilateral climate mitigation measures,[63] the general trend is that governments are extremely hesitant to adopt significant mitigation measures that place them at an unfair disadvantage economically *vis à vis* competing nations (whether they be developed or developing countries).[64]

Neuhoff argues that:

> [a]n adequate response to climate change requires action on a global scale. Otherwise it is impossible to achieve the earlier mentioned 2°C target and reduce emissions by at least 50–85 per cent below 2000 levels. Thus, the main driver for global climate co-operation will remain the engagement of all nations in supporting emissions reduction with their domestic efforts.[65]

Therefore the need for a global system, which is capable of the scale of change indicated, calls for concerted action that involves mitigation measures from all major emitters of GHGs.[66] Having said this, there can be a strong relationship between what occurs on the international level and that which occurs on domestic levels. This has been recognized by GLOBE International, which has developed studies of the national climate change legislation of 33 participating states with a view to encouraging a synthesis of approaches.[67] At the first GLOBE Climate Legislation Summit in London in 2013, Christiana Figueres the Executive Secretary of the UNFCCC recognized this importance by emphasizing that, '[d]omestic legislation on climate is the absolutely critical, essential, linchpin between action at the national level and international agreements'.[68]

There has been a range of different suggestions of the type of global system that should be adopted. It is not possible within the scope of this book to summarize all of these. However they have included calls for global carbon taxes or carbon pricing schemes,[69] contraction and convergence schemes on a per capita allowance basis,[70] various different types of cap and trade schemes[71] and sometimes of course a combination of different approaches including traditional regulation.[72]

Ultimately the debates are deeply affected by the economic bottom lines for individual states. These are defined by pressures that include the need for development, the need for energy security, the need for economic stability, the need for financial assistance, the need for technology transfer and in some cases the need for emergency assistance.

The issue of a global comprehensive system leads back, once again, to the analysis that was made in Chapter 3. One of the key problems of the approaches of the international community, not just to the issue of climate change but to many environmental problems, is that the 'root causes' of the problems are not addressed. On the whole the approaches that are taken seek to constrain the symptoms of the problem rather than to redesign the global legal architecture, which in its current form leads to degradation of the atmosphere. While the existing global legal architecture is allowed to continue in its current form, it will inevitably continue to stimulate the conditions that will bring about further degradation of this nature.

5.2.4.2 Application of the draft GER to the requirement to provide a global comprehensive system that addresses the root causes of climate change

In terms of a global approach, the argument of this book is that it is necessary for any global solution to climate change to address the root causes of the problem rather than simply placing caps on emissions. Therefore it is necessary to design a system that ensures that for each unit of production or consumption that takes place, the net outcome for the atmosphere is neutral.[73]

For this to occur, two global reforms would need to take place. The first would be the creation of new obligations for all decision-makers or decision-making systems that can negatively impact the atmosphere. This fundamental legal obligation would be comprised of a duty not to cause harm to the atmosphere without facilitating restorative compensation of it.[74] Second, it would be necessary to design within the global legal architecture administrative systems that ensure that those obligations are streamlined in terms of compliance. As previously discussed, the obligations and administrative frameworks within the draft GER are designed to achieve these objectives.[75]

One of the main fears in the business world is that individual corporations will suffer unfair competitive disadvantage in the event that they are subject to climate change policies that their competitors in other countries are free from. The draft GER establishes an international system of registration for corporations to ensure that they are all treated fairly.[76] The role of the WEO would be key to the functioning of that system, as the international expertise within the organization would enable it to equitably set standards and provide a framework for sanctioning corporations that failed to meet the necessary requirements.[77]

In terms of trade, the draft GER sets out a pathway for the rules of the WTO and other trade organizations to be amended in order that they too would be consistent with the obligations of the other actors within a reformed global legal architecture.[78]

5.2.5 The need for finance

It has been alluded to above that one of the substantial issues facing the international community is the need to finance work relating to the challenges of climate change in terms of mitigation, adaptation and administration.[79] Many developing countries especially need the right kind of financial assistance to help with the process of putting in place the infrastructure to cope with climate change, alongside the introduction of 'green technology'[80] and steps to achieve the MDGs.

Additionally within specific sectors, there is the need to create systems of finance that will enable the realization of specific types of mitigation measures. For example adequate investment in the sector of Land-Use, Land-Use Change and Forestry (LULUCF) is recognized as having a major potential to curb the emission of GHGs. The contribution of deforestation to GHG emissions has been estimated in the IPCC's 2007 report to amount to 18 per cent of all anthropogenic emissions.[81] It was observed in Chapter 2[82] that rates of deforestation are still extremely high. Therefore systematic investment in reforestation, afforestation, avoided deforestation and other aspects of land-use change have huge potential to lead to the avoidance of further GHG emissions and also to the creation of new carbon sinks.

In recent years the emphasis on an international level has been to seek to move towards a 'green economy'; this was a particular focus of the Rio + 20 conference in 2012.[83] As all nations start the process of transition towards economies that are sustainable, the availability of finance will be crucial to the realization of this end.

At the same time, finance and investment needs to be designed in such a way that it does not fall prey to the widespread corruption that is endemic within the administrative frameworks of many countries and their governments.[84]

The UNFCCC treaty includes provisions relating to the transfer of finance. It requires that the developed country parties provide financial assistance to developing countries in order that they can meet their administrative and reporting obligations.[85] It provides that developed countries shall provide financial assistance to meet the adaptation costs of those developing countries that are particularly vulnerable to the adverse effects of climate change.[86] It also states that developed country parties shall take all practicable steps to provide for the transfer of environmentally sound technology to developing country parties.[87] The treaty allows for a financial mechanism to administer these aspects of the treaty.[88]

The original 'operating entity' for the financial mechanism was the Global Environmental Facility (GEF). Since COP 15 at Copenhagen, a new 'operating entity' has been established in 'The Green Climate Fund' (GCF), which is based in Songdo, Republic of Korea.[89] Developed country parties have made a commitment as part of the UNFCCC COP 18 negotiations to mobilize funding to the value of US$100 billion per annum from 2020.[90]

5.2.5.1 Analysis of the need for finance

The debates relating to the establishment of finance under the UNFCCC have been long and arduous.[91] This has been complicated by the changing economic situations of numerous states and the changing understanding of the urgency related to climate change mitigation and adaptation. This is combined with intense practical and political difficulties associated with the transfer of finance and the realization of investment. Therefore, the comment here will be restricted to two points.

First, the existing international system based on the traditional Westphalian model continues to place a significant systemic obstacle that hampers the achievement of the levels of investment that are ultimately required. This stems from the point made above that the entire direct responsibility for resolving climate change is placed on state actors rather than placing appropriate responsibilities on the range of different types of actors that are in fact responsible either through business or through the international regimes that they administer. This creates a major burden on Annex II states to finance the growing costs related to climate change directly from their own treasuries.

Second, by adopting the type of financial mechanism that the UNFCCC has introduced under Article 11, major challenges are immediately apparent, not only in apportioning appropriate contributions from individual countries but also in dealing with the administration and distribution of those funds. The reliance on an 'operating entity' to the financial mechanism that must then disburse the funds to developing countries creates major layers of administration through which transaction costs, administrative costs and potential corruption can weaken the impact of funds that should ideally be allocated directly to dealing with the problems concerned.

5.2.5.2 Application of the draft GER to the need for finance

It is not claimed that the application of the draft GER could resolve all of the issues related to finance, nor is it argued that states should not shoulder a significant responsibility for funding the work related to climate change mitigation and adaptation. However, the application of the draft GER would address the existing problem of the UNFCCC treaty and the Kyoto Protocol failing to create direct responsibilities for actors other than states. It proposes mechanisms whereby corporations and other actors would be required to compensate the damage that they cause to the atmosphere through harmful GHG emissions.

As a result, the system provided within the draft GER would automatically create significant flows of funds towards the registered suppliers of 'direct environmental compensatory offsets'.[92] These flows of funds would result primarily from the legal responsibilities of businesses[93] and states.[94]

This system has the potential to provide an important component in the transition to a 'green economy'. Significantly it has the potential to open up a major funding resource for compensation projects such as afforsestation and reforestation schemes. Whether or not the system could or should be designed to enable the flow of funds towards avoided deforestation is a question that is outside the scope of this initial draft.

One of the advantages of implementing this system is that it would not require the processing of funds through state actors and through the 'operating entity' of the UNFCCC's finance mechanism. This therefore could avoid large-scale transaction costs and the potential problems of corruption when funds are processed through state actors. In terms of governance, the system would rely on the oversight of the WEO assessors and the WEO authorities that would have the responsibility of ensuring the integrity of the direct environmental compensatory offsets and potentially the environmental insurance being purchased.[95]

In summary, the system described would automatically release significant private funds to developing countries, which would be directly invested in mitigation projects without the costs and leakage that are associated with the provision of funds channeled indirectly.

5.2.6 The need to achieve equity

One of the major problems of any climate regime is achieving equity or simply 'fairness'. This single issue is deeply contentious for numerous reasons that include the different historic responsibility of countries for the majority of GHGs currently in the atmosphere, the financial incapacity of many developing countries, the varying levels of development of Non-Annex I (developing) countries, the impacts on individual countries associated with a reduction of reliance on fossil fuels and the varying impacts that climate change has on different countries.

The UNFCCC treaty includes provision for CBDR, which is integrated throughout the text. Much has been written on this subject and it is not possible here to discuss all of the wide-ranging issues.[96] Therefore only specific points relating to the application of the draft GER will be made.

5.2.6.1 Analysis of the need to achieve equity

The failure of the UNFCCC treaty and the Kyoto Protocol to achieve their objectives ultimately means that equity has not been achieved. The onset of many of the impacts of climate change are inherently unfair upon those that face them. Therefore it is of crucial importance to strive towards the adoption of a workable international system that can achieve equitable solutions.

Under the UNFCCC regime it has been very difficult to achieve a consensus relating to the responsibilities of individual states or groups of states. For example the US' refusal to become a party to the Kyoto Protocol was largely based *inter alia* on its argument that major developing state emitters such as China, India and Brazil should also be subject to emissions limitations.

This problem is partly related to the reliance by the UNFCCC on the traditional Westphalian model. Its failure to distribute the burden of costs to the actors (other than state actors) involved in creating emissions has major side-effects. Among these is the resulting pressure on those actors (states) that are subject to the obligations under the existing system. This is exacerbated through the failure of the regime to ensure that either the polluter pays principle is applied or that those polluting are legally required to compensate the environment to ensure that business and industry operate to achieve 'impact neutrality'.[97]

5.2.6.2 Application of the draft GER to the need to achieve equity

The issue of fairness between actors, whether they be state or non-state, will continue to be contentious. However, the provisions within the draft GER arguably make major steps towards a fairer regime for three reasons.

First, there is immediately greater fairness as the system places all actors, rather than just state actors, under obligations to ensure that they do not cause harm to the environment.[98] This would mean that corporations would be under an obligation to ensure that their services and production processes were 'impact neutral'.[99] This in turn decreases the pressure on states who would be able to focus greater attention on adaptation and in the case of developed countries, assistance for developing countries to adapt to the challenges ahead.

Second, the draft GER creates the WEO,[100] which would have the role of standard setting, and also resolving trade-related disputes concerned with the applicable climate related standards of goods and services.

Third, the draft GER provides for transitional arrangements to apply to states in varying stages of development.[101] This would mean that there would be an application of the system in accordance with equitable criteria. Such criteria and such application could be developed within the WEO/UNFCCC, following scientific, economic and social analysis.

5.3 Conclusion

There is a tendency when discussing approaches to reform of the international climate regime to attempt to understand the existing systems (especially cap and trade and carbon pricing systems) with a view to improving them.[102] It is argued that this approach is limited as it does not tackle the root causes of the problem of excess GHGs and it also does not address the problems that are intrinsic to the existing regime. This results in an approach that attempts to superimpose solutions onto a dysfunctional system without addressing the fundamental dysfunctions themselves.

In certain respects this chapter has acted as a case study upon which the draft GER could be tested against the practical challenges of a particular environmental regime. The issue of climate change is a particularly difficult environmental problem to solve owing to the complexity of the threat that it poses and the difficulty in achieving adequate responses to it. In spite of this, the lens of the draft GER has enabled the identification of key deficiencies with the UNFCCC and the Kyoto Protocol regimes.

The chapter has noted that whereas the type of regime that has developed so far may have been appropriate for relatively small reductions in the levels of GHG emissions and relatively modest adaptation measures, the more recent awareness of the potential challenge that is faced means that a more comprehensive, integrated approach is required. Therefore the experiences of recent decades have completely exposed the frailties of the traditional Westaphalian system that the UNFCCC regime is founded upon and also the inadequacies of the cap and trade systems that have evolved from it. To reiterate, the Westphalian system is failing owing to its state-centric nature and its failure to apply responsibilities directly to non-state actors. Cap and trade systems are inadequate as they fail to ensure that industries compensate the environment for the emissions that they are permitted to emit.

Having identified those deficiencies, the chapter has been able to demonstrate that while the draft GER does not contain all of the answers to all of the issues, it does create a more comprehensive and streamlined framework than that which is currently provided for in the UNFCCC treaty. It does this through its distribution of burdens, its consistency with the polluter pays principle, its capacity to generate privately sourced finance for climate investment on a global level and its potential capacity to lead to a system that is entirely predisposed towards environmental sustainability rather than one that is predisposed to unsustainability.

Therefore this chapter has in part, answered the question of why states should consider the legal framework in the draft GER. It provides not just a different type of approach to the traditional Westphalian style used to address environmental problems but also an approach that it is argued, could lay the foundations for a long-term solution to the issue of climate change caused by anthropogenic emissions.

6 Conclusion

The main conclusions of this book are embedded within the different chapters as presented. Therefore they progressively build upon each other and the outcomes of those conclusions are developed into the suggested reforms that would address some of the existing failures of international environmental governance. Those proposals are presented in Chapter 4, which provides a draft framework treaty, the draft GER, and also Chapter 5, which details how that draft treaty could apply to climate change. Therefore this chapter summarizes those conclusions and adds two additional conclusions that flow from the preceding chapters and the overall analysis.

The work of this book has been to take a journey that began with the acknowledgement in Chapter 2 that environmental degradation often leads to impacts on basic human rights such as the right to life and the right to health. The natural question that then emerges from this recognition is whether or not existing human rights mechanisms, whether at the international level or at the national level, are sufficient to respond effectively to those impacts.

The evidence demonstrates that human rights as legal mechanisms have only had limited effectiveness in curtailing these trends. Despite the many benefits of the continued development of procedural environmental rights, they only have a limited impact in affecting decision-making processes owing to the very fact that they are procedural in nature. This is not to decry procedural rights; it is to place them within the wider context of the scale of degradation that is occurring to the environment on a global scale.

Additionally it has been seen that existing substantive rights, which are used for the protection of the environment, only have a limited capacity to respond to environmental degradation. It was shown that where the impacts of environmental degradation on human rights are particularly extreme and localized, substantive human rights mechanisms can be and have been invoked successfully in many cases. However, where the origins of the degradation are more distant, for example with anthropogenic climate change, it is extremely difficult to invoke a human rights mechanism to address the harm that is suffered. As much environmental degradation falls within this latter category, this poses a significant problem.

With these impacts in mind, Chapter 3 sought to analyse the reasons why international environmental law so often fails to lead to positive outcomes for the environment. It particularly sought to analyse the reasons why it fails to respond adequately to the 'root causes' or 'drivers' of decision-making that leads to environmental degradation. It examined the legal reasons why on an international scale, states, business, industry and trade are operating in a manner that often facilitates widespread degradation of the environment, which in turn can have a harmful effect on the human rights of individuals and communities around the planet.

To tackle this question, the chapter made a historical summary of the development of the legal frameworks that in practice govern the decision-making of the major actors whose decisions or systems affect the environment. Therefore it was necessary to track the historical development of the law relating to corporations, trade organizations and also national constitutions.

In highlighting these areas, four fundamental points became clear. These were that first, a global legal architecture has developed that includes but may not be exclusive to corporate law, WTO law and also national constitutional law. The result of the operation of this global legal architecture often means that environmental degradation is an inevitable outcome of decision-making processes. The second point was that the various different component parts of this global legal architecture were designed in this way for very good reasons, but that this design took place long before the modern concern and understanding of the environment that now exists. The third point was that international environmental law has failed to address these 'root causes' or 'drivers' of environmental degradation and has largely focused on the symptoms of the problems and placed the onus on states to respond to those symptoms. The fourth point was that if that global legal architecture was purposefully designed (albeit in ignorance of the environmental consequences to future generations), it can be redesigned to ensure that those harmful side-effects are neutralized in the future.

This led to Chapter 4, which presented a draft GER. This is a framework international treaty that would create the basis for a series of legal obligations for those actors (both state and non-state) whose constitutional frameworks are currently designed in such a manner that environmental degradation is, a possible and sometimes an inevitable, consequence of their functioning. It drew heavily, but not entirely, on many of the reform suggestions that have already been made within different legal disciplines and brought them together to create the framework for a reformed global legal architecture that would operationalize those new legal obligations.

In doing this the draft GER also creates practical mechanisms that have the potential to breathe life into certain principles of international environmental law such as the polluter pays and the precautionary principles. However, it is in the combination of straightforward obligations, mechanisms and administrative frameworks that the draft GER provides a response to the impacts that environmental degradation has upon human rights. It posits that ultimately human rights are best realized not through litigation but through the creation of laws and administrative systems that predispose the relevant actors concerned to make decisions that can only have one outcome. In this case, that outcome is one that is environmentally sustainable and therefore cannot impact upon the human rights of individuals or communities.

The presentation of the draft GER in Chapter 4 provided a format that could be tested against existing legal regimes relating to specific environmental problems that have significant impacts on human rights. This was the subject of Chapter 5. Climate change was chosen owing to the significant impacts that it has upon human rights and the failure of the existing international legal regime to lead to actual solutions to the problem in hand. The features of the draft GER provided a lens through which the existing international regime could be viewed. It highlighted the various different shortcomings of the UNFCCC regime in terms of the legal framework and the mechanisms that it creates. It particularly emphasized the fact that the existing regime is fundamentally flawed because it focuses on the symptoms (i.e. GHG emissions) rather than addressing the root causes of the problem. It was shown that there are numerous flaws with the existing system but that there are two fundamental flaws. These are first, that the current system has adopted the traditional Westphalian model which means that it directly addresses state actors and not non-state actors. Second, it relies heavily on the commodification of carbon without creating a mechanism requiring those actors that are emitting GHGs to neutralize the negative impacts that they cause to the environment. The chapter showed how the application of the draft GER could resolve these fundamental problems. It also showed that it provided a framework for the facilitation of private finance for mitigation purposes internationally and also a process for achieving an equitable transition to the new system.

Therefore the book posits that the key to providing good environmental governance that will protect human rights is through the creation of a comprehensive network of duties for all actors, which is managed and governed on the international level. While the main conclusion of this book manifests itself in the draft GER provided in Chapter 4, it is important to note that it is provided as a draft framework. As noted in the introduction, it is analogous to an architects drawing in the sense that it still leaves many details unanswered and leaves much room for consultation and adjustment.

As such there are important questions that the draft GER leaves outstanding. For example probably the most difficult and contentious area that is not elaborated upon within the draft is the question of the transitional arrangements. In other words the question of the pace at which the provisions would be introduced for specific state and non-state actors would require painstaking economic analysis and negotiation. Another example is that it leaves the question of the constitutions of the WEO and the International Corporation Registration Body to be ascertained. A further example is that it does not provide the detail of the definitions that would be required to make the treaty fully functional. Therefore the complete development of the draft GER would obviously require further significant work and painstaking negotiation in relation to numerous issues.

There are two additional conclusions that stem from the approach that this book has taken. The first additional conclusion is that there is insufficient research in the field of international environmental law and global environmental governance that takes the macro legal analysis approach.[1] There is much more research that takes the micro legal analysis approach. It is argued that there needs to be a better balance of the two. The second additional conclusion is that in addition to the redesign of the global legal architecture it is also necessary to redesign appropriate administrative frameworks. These two additional conclusions will be elaborated upon.

In relation to the first of these additional conclusions, this book has taken a macro legal analysis approach. It has taken a 'problem-solving approach' to the issue of the impacts that environmental degradation have upon human rights. Therefore it has responded to the challenge that has been laid down by various experts who have expressed concern that the international community has not addressed the 'root causes' of environmental degradation and climate change.[2] In terms of scholarship, this has meant that it has been necessary to have regard to a wide range of factors and different areas of law that have included international environmental law, national constitutional law, national and international human rights law, corporate law, trade law and climate change law. This has been necessary to obtain the overview required to gain an understanding of the way that these systems operate together and how the 'global legal architecture' operates in its entirety.

Within this approach has been the recognition that often the different areas of law mentioned above are treated or studied in isolation of each other. It has also been noted that there is often a disconnect between different academic disciplines. This can be unhelpful in finding solutions which ultimately require the integration of scientific, economic, social, political, legal, administrative and technological factors.

This suggests that there is a strong case for seeking to take broader approaches within research relating to international environmental law and global environmental governance. While analysis of specific detail is crucial of course, it is argued that unless such work is accompanied by corresponding analysis that seeks to consider the overall architecture on a global scale, it is possible that we will fail to see overarching deficits within legal frameworks and as a result overlook possible solutions.

The second and related additional conclusion appertains to the way in which a global environmental right could be developed. This book has considered that the 'root causes' of environmental degradation are, at least in part, related to the 'constitutional' legal frameworks that govern state law, corporate law and trade law. It has posited that as such, those legal frameworks should be redesigned by creating legal duties within them, in order that they are consistent with an overarching goal. Those duties were detailed in the draft GER. However, it can be concluded that alongside that drafting process, it is necessary to redesign a workable, administrative framework that would enable those duties to be realized nationally and internationally.

This second additional conclusion is tied in with the observation that has been made, that sometimes international declarations relating to the environment amount to 'wish lists' of outcomes that the international community should be achieving rather than providing the redesign of the legal and administrative frameworks that would be required to achieve those outcomes.[3] Therefore this book suggests that logical redesign is an evolutionary process not just of the law but of the administrative frameworks upon which it operates.

The main conclusion of the book of course is that for the international community to adequately deal with the challenges of environmental degradation and especially those of climate change, the type of global legal architecture that is summarized in the draft GER should be adopted. Such a framework can be seen as evolutionary as it creates a basis to realise the aspiration of sustainable development that has been stated by the international community on many occasions.

While it is tempting not to amend the existing global legal architecture, as it is the system that we are used to, it can be insightful to recall the words of Thomas Jefferson:

> [s]ome men look at constitutions with sanctimonious reverence, and deem them like the arc of the covenant, too sacred to be touched. They ascribe to men of the preceding age a wisdom more than human, and suppose what they did to be beyond amendment. I knew that age well; I belonged to it and labored with it. It deserved well of its country. It was like the present but without the experience of the present; and forty years of experience in government is worth a century of book-reading; and this they would say themselves, were they to rise from the dead. I am certainly not an advocate for frequent and untried changes in laws and constitutions. I think moderate imperfections had better be borne with; because, when once known, we accommodate ourselves to them, and find practical means of correcting their ill effects. But I know also, that laws and institutions must go hand in hand with the progress of the human mind. As that becomes more developed, more enlightened, as new discoveries are made, new truths disclosed, and manners and opinions change, with the change of circumstances, institutions must advance also, and keep pace with the times. We might as well require a man to wear still the coat which fitted him when a boy, as civilized society to remain ever under the regimen of their barbarous ancestors.[4]

It can certainly be said that over the last 50 years there have been many new developments, that we are more enlightened, that new discoveries have been made and that new truths have been disclosed that have changed our opinions and our circumstances in relation to the global environment and climate change. This book has argued that for these reasons, we should take stock of the global legal architecture that is currently in place and the institutions that accompany it, and that they should be reformed accordingly.

Appendix
Draft Global Environmental Right

Preamble

The Parties to this treaty,

Recognizing the integral and interdependent nature of the Earth, our home,

Recognizing that no actor whether state or non-state has the inherent right to degrade or pollute the environment,

Recognizing that all actors whether state or non-state have a fundamental duty to protect the environment,

Recognizing that all peoples and communities have a right to a system of national and international governance in which all actors, both state and non-state, have a fundamental duty to protect the environment,

Recognizing that every form of life is unique, warranting respect regardless of its worth to humankind, and, to accord other organisms such recognition, humankind must be guided by a code of action,

Reaffirming the Principles of the United Nations Conference on the Human Environment at Stockholm 1972,

Reaffirming the Principles of the United Nations Conference on Environment and Development at Rio de Janeiro 1992,

Recognizing that sustainable outcomes must be a legal requirement of the decision-making functions of governments, business, trade and industry to protect the environment and to ensure fair and non-discriminatory competition in international trade,

Aware that legal responsibilities of both state and non-state actors should be based on relevant scientific knowledge,

Recognizing that a primary responsibility of all trade organizations whether international or regional is to create trade disciplines that ensure that the environment is protected throughout the processes of production and trade of goods and services.

Recognizing that the operation of business that can impact the environment whether through the medium of a corporation or any other type of business entity, is a privilege that comes with legal responsibilities towards the environment and human rights,

Have agreed as follows:

Article 1 – Statement of Environmental Duties

Any decision by a person, group of people, organization or government that brings about or could bring about degradation of the environment, is contrary to the common duty to protect the environment that is part of this global environmental right and as such is fundamentally unlawful. Environmental degradation can be rendered lawful when brought about to satisfy other basic human rights and where other less environmentally degrading alternatives are not viable. In the event that such decisions are sanctioned (on the grounds that it is necessary to cause environmental degradation to satisfy other basic human rights) the degradation must be tied to an equitable form of compensation that in at least equal measure, benefits the environment of the community or the area of land, air, sea, ecosystem or water that is suffering or would suffer that degradation or risk of degradation. It is a human right to be able to challenge decisions affecting the environment throughout the process of decision-making and in courts of law and tribunals.

Article 2 – Integration of Duties

(a) Each party shall integrate the legislative measures detailed in this treaty into their own domestic law in accordance with the guidance of the Secretariat (Art. 21).

(b) Each party shall report to the Secretariat (Art. 21) and the World Environment Organization (WEO) (Art.13) on the legislative steps that are taken to comply with the treaty.

Article 3 – Definitions

'Corporation' – For the avoidance of doubt, where the word 'corporation' is used within the context of this draft, it can also be read to include other types of business entities.

'Operate Internationally' – refers to the activities of any corporation (or other business entity) that buys or sells goods or services in countries other than those in which it is registered, that operates as a parent or subsidiary of a corporation in another jurisdiction or that works as part of a consortium of corporations where any or all are registered in different jurisdictions.

Article 4 – National Constitutions and Governmental Duties Towards the Environment

(a) Each party shall amend that part (or parts) of its constitution (and/or if necessary its national legislation) relating to the environment to state that local, regional and national governments are legally obliged not to make any decision/s that **will** or **may** cause degradation to the environment (whether they be through policies, executive decisions or law making) without following the relevant procedures prescribed in sub-sections (b)–(e) to this article.

(b) In the event that a government (whether local, regional or national) finds that it is necessary to make a decision that **will** cause degradation to the environment in order to satisfy other basic human rights (whether that be through policies, executive decisions or legislation), it shall be obliged, in accordance with equitable principles, to compensate that aspect/those aspects of the environment through the purchase of direct environmental compensatory offsets from a registered supplier (see Art. 10).

(c) Each government shall keep a record of any decisions that **will** cause degradation to the environment (see sub-section (b)) and a corresponding record of the compensation that has been purchased through a registered supplier of direct environmental compensatory offsets thus forming part of its environmental accounts (see Art. 5).

(d) In the event that a government (whether local, regional or national) finds that it is necessary to make a decision that **may** cause degradation to the environment in order to satisfy other basic human rights (whether that be through policies, executive decisions or legislation), it shall be obliged, in accordance with equitable principles, to purchase insurance from a registered supplier (see Art. 11).

(e) Each government shall keep a record of any decisions that **may** cause degradation to the environment (see sub-section (d)) and a corresponding record of the insurance that has been purchased through a registered supplier of environmental insurance thus forming part of its environmental accounts (see Art. 5).

Article 5 – Annual State Environmental Accounting

All states shall, on an annual basis, lodge a copy of their environmental accounts with the WEO (see Art. 13).

Article 6 – Duties of Individuals Towards the Environment

(a) Each party shall amend that part of its constitution relating to the duties of individual citizens towards the environment (whether that be in the national/federal constitutions or state constitutions or the equivalent provisions in legislation) to state that all individuals are legally obliged not to make any decision that would cause degradation to the environment without following the procedure prescribed in sub-section (b) or (c) to this article.

(b) In the event that an individual finds that it is necessary to make a decision that **will** cause degradation to the environment within the confines of the law, he/she shall be obliged, in accordance with equitable principles, to compensate that aspect/those aspects of the environment through the purchase of direct environmental compensatory offsets from a registered supplier (see Art. 10).

(c) In the event that an individual finds that it is necessary to make a decision that **may** cause degradation to the environment, he/she shall be obliged, in accordance with equitable principles, to purchase insurance from a registered supplier (see Art. 11).

(d) This article does not apply to the purchase of products and foodstuffs (see Art. 9).

Article 7 – Corporate Environmental Duty

(a) Each party shall amend that part of its law relating to 'directors' duties' (or its equivalent within its corporate law) to state that directors are legally obliged not to make any decision that would cause degradation to the environment without following the procedure prescribed in sub-section (b) and (c) and/or (d) and (e) to this article.

(b) In the event that a corporation finds that it is necessary to make a decision that **will** cause degradation to the environment, whether that be through an industrial project, business activities, procurement or any other type of activity, it shall be obliged, in accordance with equitable principles, to compensate that aspect of the environment, in equal measure to the level of degradation that will be caused, through the purchase of direct environmental compensatory offsets from a registered supplier (see Art. 10).

(c) Each corporation shall keep a record of any decisions that **will** cause harm to the environment and a corresponding record of the compensation that has been carried out or purchased through a registered supplier of direct environmental compensatory offsets. Such records will become part of their environmental accounts (see Art. 8).

(d) In the event that a corporation finds that it is necessary to make a decision that **may** cause degradation to the environment, whether that be through an industrial project, business activities, procurement or any other type of activity, it shall be obliged, in accordance with equitable principles, to purchase insurance from a registered supplier (see Art. 11).

(e) Each corporation shall keep a record of any decisions that **may** cause harm to the environment and a corresponding record of the insurance that has been purchased through a registered supplier of environmental insurance. Such records will become part of their environmental accounts (see Art. 8).

(f) The obligations in this article will be extended to all decision-makers in all types of business entities whether they are partnerships, sole-traders, cooperatives or any other form, to ensure that all businesses are subject to the same legal obligations in relation to the environment.

Article 8 – Annual Corporate Environmental Accounting

(a) Each party shall enact legislation to require that all corporations (and any other type of business entity, as stated in Art. 7(f)) shall lodge environmental accounts, annually alongside their financial accounts to the same body that receives the annual financial accounts. Such environmental accounts shall include the details pertaining to Art. 7(c) and 7(e).

(b) Each party shall enact legislation to require that all annual environmental accounts shall be available to the public on the same basis as a corporation's financial accounts.

(c) The form of each party's corporate environmental accounts shall be consistent with the style agreed and prescribed by the WEO (see Art. 13).

(d) All corporations (and all types of business entities to whom this applies as stated in Art. 7(f)) shall lodge a copy of its corporate environmental accounts with the WEO (see Art. 13).

Article 9 – Consumption, Use and Disposal of Goods and Products

(a) Each party shall enact legislation to ensure that prior to the sale to the consumer of goods or products that **will** cause degradation to the environment in their **consumption or use**, direct environmental compensatory offsets are purchased that in at least equal measure will compensate the environment of the community or the area of land, air, sea, ecosystem or water that **will** suffer that degradation.

(b) Each party shall enact legislation to ensure that prior to the sale to the consumer of goods or products that **will** cause degradation to the environment in their **disposal**, direct environmental compensatory offsets are purchased that in at least equal measure will compensate the environment of the community or the area of land, air, sea, ecosystem or water that **will** suffer that degradation.

Article 10 – Registered Suppliers of Direct Environmental Compensatory Offsets (DECOs)

(a) Each party will establish a system of registered suppliers of direct environmental compensatory offsets within its own jurisdiction in accordance with the standards agreed by the WEO (see Art. 13).

(b) Each party will establish a national office to regulate and oversee the registered suppliers of direct environmental compensatory offsets in accordance with the standards agreed by the WEO (see Art. 13).

(c) Each party will require that registered suppliers of direct environmental compensatory offsets produce annual reports of the offsets provided in each accounting year in accordance with standards agreed by the WEO (see Art. 13).

(d) Each party shall require that a copy of the annual report provided by the registered suppliers of direct environmental compensatory offsets is delivered to the WEO (see Art. 13).

(e) Each party shall ensure that the standards of direct environmental compensatory offsets supplied by their registered suppliers of direct environmental compensatory offsets are consistent with standards established by the WEO (see Art. 13).

(f) Each party will facilitate on-site standards inspections by representatives of the WEO of direct environmental compensatory offsets.

(g) The WEO will be the ultimate authority on the granting or revocation of the licenses of registered suppliers of direct environmental compensatory offsets and also sanctions for non-compliance with standards.

Article 11 – Registered Suppliers of Environmental Insurance

(a) Each party will establish a system of registered suppliers of environmental insurance within its own jurisdiction in accordance with the standards agreed by the WEO.

(b) Each party will establish a national office to regulate and oversee the registered suppliers of environmental insurance in accordance with the standards agreed by the WEO.

(c) Each party will require that registered suppliers of environmental insurance produce annual reports of all the insurance provided in the preceding accounting year in accordance with the standards agreed by the WEO.

(d) Each party will require that a copy of the annual report provided by the registered suppliers of environmental insurance is delivered to the WEO.

(e) Each party shall ensure that the standards of environmental insurance supplied by their registered suppliers of environmental insurance are consistent with the standards agreed by the WEO.

(f) Each party will facilitate on-site standards inspections by representatives of the WEO of work undertaken by or on behalf of registered suppliers of environmental insurance.

(g) The WEO will be the ultimate authority on the granting or revocation of the licenses of registered suppliers of environmental insurance and also on sanctions for non-compliance with standards.

Article 12 – International Corporation Registration Body

An International Corporation Registry Body is hereby established. Its functions shall be:

(a) To maintain a register of all corporations (or other business entities) that, 'operate internationally'.

(b) To provide a license for corporations (or other business entities) to 'operate internationally'.

(c) To provide standardized sanctions for corporations (and other business entities) that fail to comply with the standards agreed and determined by the WEO.

(d) To provide an ultimate authority for all parties in relation to the sanctions, including the revocation of licenses to 'operate internationally', for those corporations (and other business entities) that fail to comply with the standards agreed and determined by the WEO.

Article 13 – World Environment Organization

A World Environment Organization is hereby established. Its functions shall be:

(a) Standard Setting

  (i) To provide an international authority for environmental standard setting.

  (ii) To agree the standards required for direct environmental compensatory offsets (see Art. 10) and to agree the requirements for environmental insurance (see Art. 11).

(b) Governance

  (i) To receive and monitor the direct environmental compensatory offset reports (see Art. 10).

  (ii) To inspect the quality and adequacy of direct environmental compensatory offsets through a system of international environmental assessors (see Arts. 10 and 16).

  (iii) To oversee and license registered suppliers of direct environmental compensatory offsets and registered suppliers of environmental insurance and to revoke their licenses in the event of a failure to provide offsets or insurance that meets the WEO agreed standards (see Arts. 10 and 11).

(c) Transitional Arrangements

  (i) To agree the transitional arrangements for both states and non-state actors (see Art. 18).

(d) Dispute Settlement

  (i) To provide a dispute settlement body to hear disputes relating to decisions within the ambit of this treaty.

(ii) To provide authoritative advice to the Dispute Settlement Body of the World Trade Organization (WTO) on environmental matters (see Art. 14).

(e) Compliance

(i) To receive reports from each party to this treaty relating to the legislative steps taken to comply with it and advise the Secretariat accordingly (see Art. 2).

(ii) To receive copies of each state's environmental accounts and advise the Secretariat accordingly (see Art. 5).

(iii) To receive copies of each corporation and business entity's environmental accounts and to advise the International Corporation Registration Body in relation to levels of compliance with the required standards (see Art. 8).

(iv) To receive the annual reports from the registered suppliers of environmental offsets (see Art. 10).

(v) To receive the annual reports from the registered suppliers of environmental insurance (see Art. 11).

(vi) To use the system of environmental assessors (see Art. 16) to assist in ascertaining levels of compliance.

(vii) To act as the ultimate authority on the granting or revocation of the licenses of registered suppliers of direct environmental compensatory offsets and also sanctions for non-compliance with standards (see Art. 10).

(viii) To act as the ultimate authority on the granting or revocation of the licenses of registered suppliers of environmental insurance and also sanctions for non-compliance with standards (see Art. 11).

(f) Corruption

(i) To ensure that corporations, or other types of business entities, are not permitted to influence the decision-making processes of the WEO except through transparent and properly recorded consultation processes open to all sectors of the international community.

(ii) To put systems in place to ensure that corrupt practices relating to the environment are eradicated and national authorities prosecute those responsible.

Article 14 - World Trade Law

Each party commits itself to:

(a) An amendment to the Charter Establishing the WTO in order that its purposes will be changed to include the purpose of being an organization that is required to ensure that goods and services traded do not cause degradation to the environment in the manner in which they are produced, in their use, or in their disposal, and that where such degradation will be caused, to satisfy basic human rights, the necessary steps are taken in accordance with this treaty to compensate the environment accordingly to ensure that the environment upon which existing and future generations rely is properly protected.

(b) Amendments to the WTO trade disciplines to ensure that all goods and services traded by states, corporations, other business entities, organizations and individuals are compliant with the environmental duties detailed in this treaty.

(c) Amendments to the Agreement Establishing the Dispute Settlement Body (DSB) to ensure that any disputes that involve environmental protection or issues relating to environmental measures will be referred to the relevant organ of the WEO which will investigate and provide advice accordingly (see Art. 13).

(d) Amendments to regional trade agreements consistent with the objectives detailed in (a)–(c) above.

Article 15 – Environmental Assessments

Each party will amend its law relating to Environmental Impact Assessments and Strategic Environmental Assessments to ensure that the following apply:

(a) Systems shall be developed in accordance with agreed WEO standards to ensure that all aspects of environmental degradation and potential degradation are assessed and addressed, using appropriate methodologies and techniques, in accordance with the provisions of this treaty.

(b) Where an environmental assessment indicates that a decision, arrangement, law, project, plan or policy **will** cause degradation to the environment and no less environmentally degrading alternatives are viable, the assessment will include a report on the quantity and type of direct environmental compensatory offsets (see Art. 10) that will need to be purchased to ensure that the individual, government, business or organization that is seeking to carry it out, knows what is required for compliance with the law.

(c) Where an environmental assessment indicates that a decision, arrangement, law, project, plan or policy **may** cause degradation to the environment and no less environmentally degrading alternatives are viable, the assessment will include a report on the quantity and type of environmental insurance (see Art. 11) that will need to be purchased to ensure that the individual, government, business or organization that is seeking to carry it out, knows what is required for compliance with the law.

Article 16 – System of International Environmental Assessors

The WEO will establish a system of environmental assessors in accordance with Article 13(b) to:

(a) Inspect and report on the standards of direct environmental compensatory offsets being provided by registered suppliers of direct environmental compensatory offsets (see Art. 10).

(b) Inspect and report on the standards of environmental insurance being provided by registered suppliers of environmental insurance (see Art. 11).

(c) Inspect and report on governments, corporations and any other business entities that make decisions that have or could have impacts on the environment to ensure that correct procedures are followed.

Article 17 – Banks and Financial Institutions

Each party commits itself to:

(a) Amendments to the charters/constitutions of banks and financial institutions to change their purposes to being organizations that will only lend funds to projects that are consistent with the environmental duties detailed in this treaty, at the risk of acting ultra-vires their purposes.

(b) Amendments to the charters/constitutions of banks and financial institutions to change their operational policies and practices to ensure that projects are consistent with the environmental duties detailed in this treaty, at the risk of acting ultra-vires their policies.

Article 18 – Transitional Arrangements

The WEO will coordinate the agreed transitional arrangements, where appropriate, during the incorporation of the system required under this treaty.

Article 19 – Compliance

(a) The WEO will have compliance responsibilities in accordance with Art. 13(e).

(b) The International Corporation Registration Body will have compliance responsibilities in accordance with Art. 12(d).

Article 20 – Separation of Corporations and the State

Each party will enact legislation to ensure that governments only consult business and industry through formal processes of consultation (provided for by government) on decisions relating to the environment. Such processes are to be made available to other interested parties such as NGOs.

Article 21 – Secretariat

A Secretariat is hereby established. Its functions shall be:

(a) To organize an annual meeting of the parties.

(b) To periodically review the terms of this treaty in order that it can be updated in accordance with the requirements of the parties.

Notes

Preface

1 Anderson and Boyle, eds., *Human Rights Approaches to Environmental Protection.* Oxford: Clarendon Press, 1996.

1 Introduction

1 UNCED, *Declaration on Environment and Development* (Rio de Janeiro), 14 June, UN Doc. A/CONF. 151/5/Rev.1, 31 ILM. 814. 876, 1992.
2 United Nations, *Millenium Development Goals* (New York), 22 September, 2010, accessed 26 January 2013 from: www.un.org/millenniumgoals/index.shtml.
3 United Nations World Summit on Sustainable Development, *Plan of Implementation* (Johannesburg), UN Doc. A/CONF.199/20, Res.2, 2002.
4 United Nations, Rio + 20 conference, *The Future We Want: Rio + 20 Outcome Document* (Rio de Janeiro), June, UN Doc. A/Conf.216/L.1, 2012.
5 Bodansky, D., *The Art and Craft of International Environmental Law.* Harvard MA: Harvard University Press, 2010, p. 10.
6 See Morrow, K.,'Rio+20, the Green Economy and Re-orienting Sustainable Development', *Envtl. L. Rev.*, 14(4), 2012, pp 279, 294–7.
7 United Nations, *Millennium Ecosystem Assessment – Living Beyond Our Means: Natural Assets and Human Well-Being*, 2005, p. 5, accessed 3 February 2013 from: www.unep.org/maweb/documents.429.aspx.pdf.

2 The state of degradation of the planet's environment, the impact upon human rights and the current status of the development of environmental rights

1 United Nations, *The Millennium Ecosystem Assessment, Ecosystems and Human Well-being Synthesis*. Washington, DC: Island Press, 2005.
2 The term emerged in the early 1970s. See Porritt, J., 'Introduction', in E. F. Schumacher, *Small is Beautiful – A Study of Economics as if People Mattered.* Blond and Briggs Ltd (reprinted by Vintage 1993): London, 1973, p. viii.
3 Botkin, D. B. and Keller, E. A., *Environmental Science – Earth as a Living Planet* (7th ed.). New Jersey: John Wiley and Sons, 2010, p. 50.
4 United Nations, *The Millennium Ecosystem Assessment*, p. 1.
5 Ibid.
6 Ibid.
7 Ibid.
8 UNEP, *Towards a Green Economy: Pathways to Sustainable Development and Poverty Eradication – A Synthesis for Policy Makers*, 2011, accessed 2 February 2013 from: www.unep.org/greeneconomy.
9 Dasgupta, P., 'Nature in Economics', *Envtl. & Resource Econ.*, 39 (1), 2008, p. 1.

10 McKinsey and Company, *Charting our Water Future – Economic Frameworks to Inform Decision-Making*, 2009, accessed 2 February 2013 from: www.mckinsey.com/App_Media/Reports/Water/Charting_Our_Water_Future_Exec_percent20Summary_001.pdf.
11 United Nations, *The Millennium Ecosystem Assessment*, p. 12.
12 Ibid., p. 10.
13 WHO/UNICEF Joint Monitoring Programme for Water Supply and Sanitation, *Progress on Sanitation and Drinking Water: 2010 Update*, 2010, pp. 6–7, accessed 2 February 2013 from: www.wssinfo.org/.
14 United Nations, *The Millennium Ecosystem Assessment*, p. 12.
15 United Nations Department of Economic and Social Affairs, *World Economic and Social Survey – The Great Green Technological Transformation*. United Nations: New York, 2011, p. 78.
16 Ibid.
17 United Nations, *The Millennium Ecosystem Assessment*, p. 10.
18 Ibid.
19 United Nations Department of Economic and Social Affairs, *World Economic and Social Survey*, p. 75.
20 Ibid.
21 Ibid., p. 74.
22 United Nations FAO, *Global Forest Resources Assessment 2010 – Forest Paper 163*, 2010, accessed 2 February 2013 from: www.fao.org/forestry/fra/en/.
23 United Nations FAO, *State of the World's Forests*, 2011, accessed 2 February 2013 from: www.fao.org/forestry/sofo/en/.
24 United Nations FAO, *State of the World's Forests*, p. xiii.
25 Ibid., p. 22.
26 Ibid.
27 Ibid.
28 UNEP, *Towards a Green Economy*, p. 8.
29 United Nations, *The Millennium Ecosystem Assessment*, p. 23.
30 IPCC, Summary for Policymakers. In: *Climate Change 2007: The Physical Science Basis. Contribution of Working Group I to the Fourth Assessment Report of the Intergovernmental Panel on Climate Change* (M. Manning, Z. Chen, M. Marquis, K. Averyt, M. Tignor, and H. Miller, Eds). Cambridge: Cambridge University Press, 2007, p. 2.
31 Ibid.
32 Van Vuuren, D. P. and Riahi, K., 'Do Recent Emission Trends Imply Higher Emissions Forever', *Climate Change* 91, 2008, p. 237.
33 IPCC, *Summary for Policymakers*, p. 683.
34 IPCC, *Climate Change 2007: Synthesis Report for Policy Makers*, 2007, p. 2, accessed 2 February 2013 from: www.ipcc.ch/pdf/assessment-report/ar4/syr/ar4_syr_spm.pdf.
35 Ibid., p. 5.
36 United Nations Department of Economic and Social Affairs, *World Economic and Social Survey*, p. 28.
37 Ibid.
38 Ibid.
39 Ibid.
40 IPCC, *Summary for Policymakers*, p. 862.
41 UNFCCC, *Report of the Conference of the Parties on its sixteenth session held in Cancun from 29 November to 10 December 2010*, UN Doc. FCCC/CP/2010/7/Add.1, 2011.
42 United Nations Department of Economic and Social Affairs, *World Economic and Social*, p. 28.
43 Ibid., p. 105: 'The number of climate-related disasters has grown at an accelerating rate

since the 1950s, while geophysical disasters have followed a relatively stable upward trend, as was shown in figure IV.1. As this suggests the existence of a driver of increasing climate-related disaster events, researchers have tried through complex models to quantify to what extent weather shocks are related to climate change. The Intergovernmental Panel on Climate Change (IPCC) (2007a) warns, however, that results are often not conclusive, since climate models are constantly being updated and improved'.

44 Ibid., p. 98.

45 See Lee, B., Preston, F., Kooroshy, J., Bailey, R. and Lahn, G., *Resources Futures*, 2012, accessed 2 February 2013 from: www.chathamhouse.org/sites/default/files/public/Research/Energy,%20Environment%20and%20Development/1212r_resourcesfutures.pdf. See also United Nations Department of Economic and Social Affairs, *World Economic and Social Survey*, p. 75: 'Notably, in this regard, with temperature rises, crop productivity is forecast to increase at mid-high latitudes and decrease at lower latitudes (Intergovernmental Panel on Climate Change, 2007a). For instance, it is estimated that, in Southern Africa, yields could fall by up to 50 per cent between 2000 and 2020 (Intergovernmental Panel on Climate Change, 2007b); and that, by 2080, 600 million additional people could be at risk of hunger as a direct consequence of climate change'.

46 See Conway, D. and Schipper, L. F., 'Adaptation to Climate Change in Africa: Challenges and Opportunities Identified from Ethiopia', *Global Envtl. Change*, 21, 2011, p. 227: 'Agriculture forms the basis of the economy supporting roughly 42 per cent GDP and 85 per cent employment (Byerlee *et al.*, 2007). The nature of Ethiopia's agriculture, primarily rain-fed, means that production is sensitive to fluctuations in rainfall. Chronic food insecurity affects 10 per cent of the population; even in average rainfall years these households cannot meet their food needs and rely partly on food assistance. Drought may result in sharp reductions in agricultural output and reliant employment, and may have additional multiplier effects on the monetary economy (Benson and Clay, 1998). It also has profound social impacts. The greatest loss of life associated with drought in Ethiopia occurred in 1984, 1974 and 1973, while the greatest number of affected people was 14.2 million in 2002 (over 20 per cent of total population; World Bank, 2007)'.

47 United Nations Department of Economic and Social Affairs, *World Economic and Social Survey*, p. 100.

48 Ibid., p. 101.

49 Harries, T. and Penning-Roswell, E., 'Victim pressure, institutional inertia and climate change adaptation: The case of flood risk', *Global Envtl. Change*, 21, 2011, p. 188–9. (The authors refer to: Evans *et al.*, *Foresight. Future Flooding. Scientific Summary: Volume I – Future Risks and their Drivers*. London: Office of Science and Technology, 2004; and Evans *et al.*, *Foresight. Future Flooding. Scientific Summary: Volume II – Managing Future Risks*. London: Office of Science and Technology, 2004.)

50 United Nations, *The Millennium Ecosystem Assessment*, p. 10.

51 Ibid.

52 Boris Worm, Ray Hilborn, Julia K. Baum, Trevor A. Branch, Jeremy S. Collie, Christopher Costello, Michael J. Fogarty, Elizabeth A. Fulton, Jeffrey A. Hutchings, Simon Jennings, Olaf P. Jensen, Heike K. Lotze, Pamela M. Mace, Tim R. McClanahan, Cóilín Minto, Stephen R. Palumbi, Ana M. Parma, Daniel Ricard, Andrew A. Rosenberg, Reg Watson and Dirk Zeller, 'Rebuilding Global Fisheries', *Science*, 325 (2009), p. 578.

53 Ibid.

54 United Nations FAO, *The State of the World Fisheries and Aquaculture*, 2010, accessed 2 February 2013 from: www.fao.org.docrep/013/i/il820e/il820e.pdf.

55 Ibid., p. 3.

56 See generally United Nations, *The Millennium Ecosystem Assessment*, section 18.

57 Ibid.
58 Ibid., p. 10.
59 UNEP/WCMC, *In the Front Line: Shoreline Protection and other Ecosystem Services from Mangroves and Coral Reefs*, 2008, accessed 2 February 2013 from: www.unep.org/publications/search/pub_details_s.asp?ID=3783.
60 Ibid.
61 Ibid., p. 5.
62 Ibid.
63 United Nations, *The Millennium Ecosystem Assessment*, p.15.
64 Ibid.
65 Ibid., p. 21.
66 United Nations Department of Economic and Social Affairs, *World Economic and Social Survey*, p. 78.
67 See Botkin and Keller, *Environmental Science*, p. 267. For example asprin is a derivative of willow bark, while digitalis, which is used for treating heart conditions, is derived from foxglove. Taxol comes from a tree in the South Pacific and has been developed as a cancer fighting drug. In the US, 25 per cent of prescriptions dispensed contain ingredients extracted from vascular plants.
68 Ibid.
69 United Nations Department of Economic and Social Affairs, *World Economic and Social Survey*, p. 17.
70 Ibid., p. 68.
71 Ibid.
72 Botkin and Keller, *Environmental Science*, p. 6.
73 Ibid.
74 United Nations, *The Millennium Ecosystem Assessment*, p.19.
75 See WHO/UNICEF, *Progress on Sanitation and Drinking Water*, p. 7.
76 United Nations, *The Millennium Ecosystem Assessment*, p.19.
77 Yale Center for Environmental Law and Policy, Yale University and Center for International Earth Science Information Network, Columbia University, *Environmental Performance Index and Pilot Trend Environmental Performance Index*, 2012, accessed 2 February 2013 from: http://epi.yale.edu/epi2012/summary.
78 See Botkin and Keller, *Environmental Science*, p. 3.
79 Ibid.
80 Ibid.
81 See generally Anton, D. K. and Shelton, D. L., *Environmental Protection and Human Rights*. Cambridge: Cambridge University Press, 2011. See also Humphreys, S., ed., *Human Rights and Climate Change*. Cambridge: Cambridge University Press, 2010.
82 Humphreys, S., 'Introduction – Human Rights and Climate Change', in Humphreys, S., (ed.), *Human Rights and Climate Change*, Cambridge: Cambridge University Press, 2010, p. 1.
83 International Covenant on Economic, Social and Cultural Rights, 16 December 1966, in force 3 January 1976, Annex to UNGA Res. 2200 (XXI), 6 ILM 360, 780 (1967) (ICESCR).
84 International Covenant on Civil and Political Rights, 16 Dec. 1966, Art. 6, in force 23 March 1976, Annex to UNGA Res. 2200 (XXI), 6 ILM 360 (1967) (ICCPR).
85 Adopted Apr. 30, 1982, UN Doc. HRI/GEN/1/Rev.7.
86 European Convention for the Protection of Human Rights and Fundamental Freedoms (Rome), Art. 2, 4 November 1950, in force 3 September 1953 , 213 UNT.S 221 (ECHR); ICCPR Art. 6; American Convention on Human Rights (San José) Art. 4, 22 November 1969, in force 18 July 1978, 9 ILM 673 (1970) (ACHR); African Charter on Human and Peoples' Rights (Banjul) Art. 4, 27 June 1981, in force 21 October 1986, 21 ILM 59 (1982) (AFCHPR); Convention on the Rights of the Child (New York) Art. 6, 20 November 1989, in force 2 September 1990, 29 ILM 1340 (1990) (CRC).

87 On procedural grounds, the Human Rights Committee of the ICCPR has rejected the majority of the communications that it has received that relate to claims of violations of the right to life as a result of environmental harm. See *Port Hope Environmental Group v Canada*, Communication No. 67/1980, *UN International Covenant of Civil and Political Rights. 2 Selected Decisions of the Human Rights Committee under the Optional Protocol*, 17 to 32 Sess., UN Doc C.C.P.R/C/OP/2, UN Sales No. E.89.XIV.1, 1990; also *Bordes v France,* UN GAOR, II Hum. Rts. Comm., 51 Sess., Supp. No. 40, at 267 (57'Session), UN Doc. A/51/40, 1996. Certain cases in this category have been successfully brought before the commissions and courts of some of the regional human rights treaties. For accounts of these developments see Shelton, D., 'Human Rights and the Environment: Substantive Rights', in Fitzmaurice, M., Ong, D. M. and Merkouris, P., (eds), *Research Handbook on International Envrionmental Law*. Cheltenham: Edward Elgar, 2010, pp. 269–71; Sands, P., Peel, J., Fabra, A. and Mackenzie, R., *Principles of International Environmental Law.* Cambridge: Cambridge University Press, 2012, p. 788; Anton, D. K. and Shelton, D. L., *Environmental Protection and Human Rights.* Cambridge: Cambridge University Press, 2011, pp. 436–57.

88 *Yanomami v Brazil*, Inter-Am. C.H.R., Case 7615, Report No. 12/85, OAS/Ser.L/VII.66, doc. 10 rev.1, 1985.

89 *Oneryildiz v Turkey*, Eur. H.R. Rep. 41, 325, 2004.

90 *Budayeva v Russia* Eur. Ct. H.R. 15339/02, 2008.

91 *Vellore Citizens Welfare Reform v Union of India*, A.I.R. (S.C.) 2715, 1996.

92 *General Secretary, West Pakistan Salt Miners Labor Union Khwra, Khelum v The Director, Industries and Mineral Development, Punjab, Lahora*, Human Rights Case No. 120 of 1993, S.C.M.R. at 2061, 1994.

93 *Carlos Roberto Mejia Chacon v Municipalidad de Santa Ana*, Judgement No. 3705–93 Supreme Court, Constitutional Chamber, 1993.

94 Rajamani, L., 'The Increasing Relevance and Currency of Rights-based Perspectives in the International Negotiations on Climate Change', *J. Envt'l L.*, 22(3), 2010, pp. 391 and 393–4.

95 See United Nations, *The Millennium Ecosystem Assessment*, p.23; Rajamani, L., 'The Increasing Relevance', pp. 393–4.

96 United Nations Department of Economic and Social Affairs, *World Economic and Social Survey*, p. 78.

97 Ibid., pp. 75–6.

98 See United Nations, *The Millennium Ecosystem Assessment*, p.23.

99 Ibid., p. 18.

100 See section 2.2.8.

101 ICESCR Art. 12 (1).

102 AFCHPR Art. 16; CRC Arts. 24 and 25; Additional Protocol to the to the American Convention on Human Rights in the Area of Economic, Social and Cultural Rights (The Protocol of San Salvador) Art. 10, 17 November 1988, in force 16 November 1999, 28 ILM. 161, 1989.

103 Adopted 11 August 2000, UN Doc. E/C.12/2000/4.

104 See Shelton, D., 'Human Rights and the Environment: Substantive Rights', in *Research Handbook on International Environmental Law*, pp. 271–2.

105 The Inter-American Commission on Human Rights has specifically focused on environmental pollution in certain country reports of members of the Organization of American States. In the *Yanomami v Brazil* (1985) complaint to the Commission it was determined *inter alia* that there had been a violation of the right to health. The African Commission on Human and People's Rights has held that the failure to provide basic services such as safe drinking water amounted to a violation of the right to health under Art. 16 of AFCHPR. See the Communications *25/89, 47/90, 56/91* and *100/93* against Zaire. Additionally in *Social and Economic Rights Action Center for Economic and Social Rights v Nigeria*, Decision Regarding Communication 155/96 (27 October

2001), the African Commission on Human and Peoples' Rights held that there had been a violation of the right to health following the Nigerian government's failure to prevent toxic pollution from oil extraction projects that caused ill health in local communities. Additionally there has been a complaint to the European Social Charter as a result of environmental degradation under its right to health provisions in *Marangopulos Foundation for Human Rights (MFHR) v Greece* Complaint No 30/2005, 2005. See Shelton, D., 'Human Rights and the Environment', and Shelton, D., 'Developing Substantive Environmental Rights', *J. Hum. Rts & Envt.*, 1(1), 2010, p. 89 and 112.

106 See for example the cases of *Lopez Ostra v Spain* 303 Eur. Ct. H.R. 38, 1994, in which noxious fumes from a neighbouring industrial plant triggered a breach of the right; also *Di Sarno and others v Italy* App. No. 30765/08 Eur. Ct. H.R., 10 January 2012, in which the failure of the local government to carry out waste collections for a number of months amounted to such a breach.

107 See Rajamani, 'The Increasing Relevance', pp. 393–4.

108 Gabcikovo-Nagymaros (Hungary/Slovakia), 1997, ICJ Reports. Reprinted 37 ILM. 162, 1997, p. 206.

109 For further support for the right to water see, the CRC Art. 24(2)(c); also United Nations Convention on the Elimination of all Forms of Discrimination Against Women, Art. 14 Para. 2, 18 December 1979, in force 3 September 1981, 19 ILM. 33, 1980 (CEDAW).

110 UN Committee on Economic, Social and Cultural Rights, (29 session, 2002) UN Doc. E/C.12/2002/11, 2003.

111 UNGA Res. A/Res/64/292, July 2010.

112 UNGA, Human Rights Council Res. A/HRC/RES/18/1, 28 September 2011.

113 See Kotze, L. J., '"Some for all, forever" – A Southern perspective on poverty, access to water, environmental health and the North-South divide', in L. Westra, C. L. Soskolne and D. W. Spady, (eds), *Human Health and Ecological Integrity*. London: Routledge, 2012, p. 262.

114 See section 2.3.1.

115 ICESCR Art. 11(1).

116 ICESCR Art. 11(2).

117 The right was originally declared in Art. 25(1) of UDHR; the right has been further endorsed in CRC Art. 27.

118 ICESCR Art. 11(1).

119 ICESCR Art. 11(2).

120 UN Committee on Economic, Social and Cultural Rights, UN Doc. E/C.12/1999/5, 12 May 1999.

121 UN Food Assistance Convention (London), 25 April 2012, in force 1 January 2013, accessed 26 January 2013 from: http://treaties.un.org/Pages/ViewDetails.aspx2src=TREATY&mtdsg_no=XIX-48&chapter=19&lang=eng.

122 Caney, S., 'Climate Change, human rights, and moral thresholds', in S. Humphreys (ed.), *Human Rights and Climate Change*. Cambridge: Cambridge University Press, 2010, p. 77.

123 ICESCR Art. 11. The right was originally declared in Art. 25 of the Universal Declaration of Human Rights, G.Res. 217, UN GAOR, 3 Sess., Part 1, at 71, UN Doc. A/810 (1948) (UDHR). It has been further strengthened through CRC Art. 27.

124 UN Committee on Economic, Social and Cultural Rights, UN Doc. E/1992/23, 13 December 1991.

125 UDHR Art. 17; Protocol 1. Art. 1 to ECHR, 20 March 1952, in force 18 May 1954, 213 UNTS 262; ACHR Art. 21.

126 However, in 2005 a community of Inuit petitioned the Inter-American Commission on Human Rights in relation to the responsibility that they claimed the US had (as the major emitter at the time of greenhouse gases) for the impacts that global warming was

having on their human rights. Petition available at: www.inuitcircumpolar.com/files/uploads/icc-files/FINALPetitionICC.pdf. It should be noted that this claim was unsuccessful. The IACHR dismissed the petition the following year on the basis that it failed to establish 'whether the alleged facts would tend to characterize a violation of rights protected by the American Declaration'. See generally Anton and Shelton, *Environmental Protection and Human Rights*, pp. 512–19.

127 See for example *Fredin v Sweden*, Eur. H.R. Rep. 13, 784, 1991.

128 Anton and Shelton, *Environmental Protection and Human Rights*, pp. 512–19.

129 See for example *Awas Tingni Mayagna (Sumo) Indigenous Community v Nicaragua*, Inter-Am C.H.R. Series C, No. 79, 304, 2001; also *Saramaka People v Suriname,* Inter-Am. C.H.R. Series C, No. 172, 28 Novemeber 2007.

130 See Grear, A., 'Human rights, property and the search for "worlds other"', *J. Hum. Rts. & Envt.* 3(2), 2012, p. 173 and 192.

131 Leopold, A., *A Sand County Almanac – and Sketches Here and There.* New York: Oxford University Press, 1949, pp. 203–4.

132 Carson, R., *Silient Spring.* London: Penguin Books, 1962, p. 29. Originally published in the US by Houghton Mifflin.

133 Stone, C. D., *Should Trees Have Standing – Toward Legal Rights for Natural Objects.* California: William Kaufman, 1972.

134 Cassin, R., 'Les Droits de L'Homme', in *IV Recueil des Cours.* Leiden: Sitjhoff, 1974, p. 327: 'Dans les vingt dernière années est née la notion du droit á l'environment, impossible à classer purement et simplement comme droit politique ou économique et dont il vous sera sûrement parlé'.

135 Gormley, W. P., *Human Rights and the Environment: The Need for International Cooperation.* Leiden: Sitjhoff, 1976, p. 1.

136 Razzaque, J., 'Human Rights to a Clean Environment: Procedural Rights', in M. Fitzmaurice, D. M. Ong and P. Merkouris (eds), *Research Handbook on International Environmental Law.* Cheltenham: Edward Elgar, 2010, p. 284.

137 See UDHR. Art. 19 *inter alia* relating to the right to receive information; Art. 21 (1) relating to the right to take part in government; Art. 8 relating to the right to an effective remedy.

138 UNCED, *Declaration on Environment and Development* (Rio de Janeiro), 14 June 1992, UN Doc. A/CONF. 151/5/Rev.1, 31 ILM. 814. 876.

139 See for example the work in this field of the International Labour Organisation (ILO) and the United Nations Committee on Economic and Social and Cultural Rights (UNCESCR).

140 For example the Convention on Biological Diversity (Rio de Janeiro) Art. 14(1), 5 June 1992, in force 29 December 1993, 31, ILM 822 (CBD); United Nations Framework Convention on Climate Change (Rio de Janeiro) Art. 14(i), 9 May 1992, in force 24 March 1994, 31, ILM 849 (UNFCCC); North American Agreement on Environmental Co-operation (Washington DC) Art. 21, 14 September 1993, in force 1 January 1994, 32, ILM 1480 (NAAEC); Convention on Cooperation and Sustainable Development of the Waters of the Danube (Sofia) Art. 14, 29 June 1994, in force 22 October 1999.

141 The United Nations Economic Commission for Europe (UNECE), Convention on Access to Information, Public Participation and Decision-Making and Access to Justice in Environmental Matters, Ministerial Conference (Aarhus), 25 June 1998, in force 30 October 2001, UN Doc, ECE/CEP43, 1998. Adopted at the 4[t] UNECE, UN Doc 30C/INF.11, 24 September 1999.

142 The treaty is open to accession by non-UNECE members upon 'approval' by a Meeting of the Parties. See Dellinger, M., 'Ten Years of the Aarhus Convention: How Procedural Democracy is Paving the Way for Substantive Change in National and International Enviornmental Law', *Colo. J. Int'l Envtl. L. & Pol'y*, 23(2), 2012, p. 309 and 358.

143 Art. 15
144 See Sands, P. and Peel, J. with Fabra, A. and Mackenzie, R., *Principles of International Environmental Law*, 2012, p. 140.
145 *Pulp Mills on the River Uruguay (Argentina v Uruguay)* (Judgement) I.C.J. 2010, General List No. 135, Para. 240, 20 April.
146 Boyd, D. R., *The Environmental Rights Revolution – A Global Study of Constitutions, Human Rights, and the Environment.* Vancouver: UBC Press, 2012, p. 66.
147 Ibid.
148 Razzaque, J., 'Human Rights to a Clean Environment: Procedural Rights', pp. 291–3; Turner, S. J., *A Substantive Environmental Right – An examination of the legal obligations of decision-makers towards the environment.* Leiden: Wolters Kluwer, 2009, pp. 100–1.
149 See for example, *The Director, Mineral Development Guateng Region and Saol Mining (pty) Ltd v SAVE the Vaal Environment and others* 2 S.A. 709 (SCA), 1999; see further Kotze, L. J., 'The Judiciary, the Environmental Right and the Quest for Sustainability in South Africa: A Critical Reflection', *Rev. Eur. Community & Int'l Envt'l L.*, 16(3), 2007, p. 291 and 298.
150 Tromans, S., *Environmental Impact Assessment* (2nd ed.). London: Bloomsbury Professional, 2012.
151 Therivel, R., *Strategic Environmental Assessment in Action.* London: Earthscan, 2010.
152 See for example s.12 World Bank Operational Policy BP 4.01 (1999) (updated April 2012) relating to environmental assessment. It states *inter alia* that special attention must be given to the consultation processes with affected groups and local NGOs.
153 United Nations Conference on the Human Environment (UNCHE), *Declaration of the United Nations Conference on the Human Environment* (Stockholm) Principle 1, 16 June 1972, UN Doc. A/Conf.48/14/Rev.1, adopted in G.A. Res. 2997. UN GAOR, 27 Sess., Supp. No. 30 at 43, at UN Doc. A/8901, 1972.
154 World Commission on Environment and Development (WCED), *Our Common Future.* Oxford: Oxford University Press, 1987; World Commission on Environment and Development (WCED), *Report of the World Commission on Environment and Development,* UNGA Res. 42/187, UN Doc. A/Res/42/187, 11 December 1987.
155 *See* Shelton, D., 'What Happened in Rio to Human Rights?', *Y.B. Int'l Envtl L.*, 3, 1992, p. 75.
156 UNCED, *Declaration on Environment and Development* (Rio de Janeiro), Principle 1.
157 The World Summit on Sustainable Development (WSSD), *The Johannesburg Declaration on Sustainable Development (Johannesburg), 4 September 2002*, UN Doc. A/CONF.199/20 (2002).
158 United Nations Conference on Sustainable Development (Rio + 20), *The Future We Want: Rio + 20 Outcome Document* (Rio de Janeiro), 24 July 2012, UN Doc. A/Conf.216/16.
159 Ibid.
160 28 ILM. 156 (1989). Art. 11 states that, 'everyone shall have the right to live in a healthy environment and to have access to basic public services'. It also states that, '[t]he state parties shall promote the protection, preservation and improvement of the environment'.
161 O.A.U. Doc CAB/LEG/67/3/Rev. 5, effective October 1996. 21 ILM.59.
162 The Inter-American Commission of Human Rights and the Inter-American Court of Human Rights.
163 Shelton, D., *Environmental Issues and Human Rights in Multilateral Treaties Adopted Between 1991 and 2001* (14–16 January 2002), accessed 31 May 2012 from: http://www2.ohchr.org/english/issues/environment/environ/bp1.htm.
164 *Center for Minority Rights Development on behalf of Endorois Community v Kenya,* Communication 276/2003 Afr. Ct. Hum. Rts (4 February 2010) the court affirmed the Commission holding that a pastoralist community in Kenya had customary rights to

land from which they had been dispossessed resulting in a violation the rights to property (Article 14); culture (Article 17(2) and (3)); religion (Article 8); natural resources (Article 21); and development (Article 22).

165 Nelson Enonchong, 'The African Charter on Human and Peoples Rights: Effective Remedies in Domestic Law?', *J. Afr. L.* 46(2), 2002, p. 197; See also J. Oloka-Onyango, 'Reinforcing Marginalized Rights in an Age of Globalization: International Mechanisms, Non-State Actors, and the Struggle for Peoples' Rights in Africa', *Am. U. Int'l L. Rev.* 18(4), 2003, p. 851 and 859.

166 *Social and Economic Rights Action Centre/Centre for Economic and Social Rights v Nigeria,* Communication 155/96, Case No. ACHPR/ COMM/A044/1, Afr, Comm'n Hum. Rts. (27 May 2002).

167 See League of Arab States, Arab Charter on Human Rights, 22 May 2004, in force 15 March 2008, reprinted in *Int'l Hum. Rts. Rep.* 12, 2005, p. 893.

168 See Gabičkovo-Nagymaros (Hungary/Slovakia) ICJ Reports. Reprinted 37 ILM. 162 (1997), p. 206. It appears that Judge Weeramantry's view strengthens the case for an expanded interpretation of the 'right to life' and the 'right to health' rather than the declaration of a new substantive environmental right on the international level.

169 See Boyd, *The Environmental Rights Revolution*, p. 47. Different adjectives are used in different consitutions to describe the quality of environment that should be provided. These adjectives include among others, 'safe', 'healthy', 'clean' and 'ecologically balanced'.

170 Ibid., p. 77.

171 Fleiner, T. and Fleiner, L. R., *Constitutional Democracy in a Multicultural and Globalised World.* Berlin: Springer, 2009, p. 652.

172 Law, D. S. and Versteeg, M., 'The Declining Influence of the United States Constitution', *N.Y.U. L. Rev.* 87(3), 2012, p. 762 and 807; Law, D. S. and Versteeg, M., 'The Evolution and Ideology of Global Constitutionalism', *Cal. L. Rev.* 99, 2011, p. 1163 and 1168.

173 Law and Versteeg, 'The Declining Influence', p. 807; Law and Versteeg, 'The Evolution and Ideology', p. 1168.

174 Anton & Shelton, *Environmental Protection and Human Rights*, p. 522; Shelton, D., 'Environmental Rights in the State Constitutions of the United States', in I. Larmuseau (ed.), *Constitutional Rights to an Ecologically Balanced Environment.* Gent: V.V.O.R., 2007, p. 106ff.

175 Although the Charter of Fundamental Rights of the European Union (2000) does not contain an environmental right as such, it does refer to the promotion of 'balanced and sustainable development' in its preamble. Also Article 37 states that, '[a] high level of environmental protection and improvement of the quality of the environment must be integrated into the policies of the Union and ensured in accordance with the principle of sustainable development'. See Charter of Fundamental Rights of the European Union, 18 December 2000, OJ (C 364) 20 (2000).

176 Kramer, L., *EU Environmental Law.* London: Sweet and Maxwell, 7th edn., 2011.

177 Government of Ecuador, *Constitution of Ecuador*, Title II, Chapter 7, Rights of Nature, 2008, accessed 9 August 2012 from: http://pdba.georgetown.edu/Constitutions/Ecuador/english08.html.

178 Government of Bolivia, *Ley de derechos de la Madre Tierra*, Law 071 of the Plurinacional State, 2010, accessed 9 August 2012 from: www.scribd.com/Gobernabilidad/d/44900268-Ley-deDerechos-de-la-Madre-Tierra-Estado-Plurinacional-deBolivia.

179 Rio + 20, *The Future We Want*, paras. 39–40.

180 See section 2.3.1.

181 *Montana Environmental Information Center v Department of Environmental Quality* 988 P.2d 1236 (1999).

182 *Beatriz Silvia Mendoza and others v National Government and others in regard to damages suffered* 2008, M. 1569 (8 July 2008).

183 *Colegio de Abogados del Santa*, Exp. No. 0018-2001-AI/TC (2001).
184 *A. Cederstav and others v National Technical Secretary for the Environment, Municipality of Santa Cruz and others*, Exp. 05-002756-0007-C), Res. No. 2008007549 (Constituional Chamber of the Supreme Court) (30 April 2008).
185 *Minors Oposa v Factoran, Jr., Secretary of the Department of the Enviornment and Natural Resources* , 224 SCRA 792 (1993).
186 *K.B. Shresta v HMG, Department of Transportation and others*, Writ No. 3109 (Supreme Court) (1999).
187 Decision No. U-I-30/95. Official Gazette RS, No. 3/96, Doc, No. AN01045 (Constitutional Court) (21 December 1995).
188 *Taskin v Turkey* (46117/99) 42 E.H.R.R. 50 (2006); see Pedersen, O. W., 'A Bill of Rights, Environmental Rights and the UK Constitution', *Public Law*, 2, 2011, p. 577 and 587.
189 See generally Razzaque, J., *Public Interest Environmental Litigation in India, Pakistan and Bangladesh.* Leiden: Kluwer Law International, 2004.
190 See Boyd, *The Environmental Rights Revolution*; Larmuseau, I. (ed.), *Constitutional Rights to an Ecologically Balanced Environment.* Gent: V.V.O.R., 2007; Razzaque, *Public Interest Environmental Litigation*; Fabra, A. and Arnal, E., *Background Paper No. 6 for the Joint UNEP-OHCHR Expert Seminar on Human Rights and the Environment, Review of Jurisprudence on Human Rights and the Environment in Latin America* (14–16 January 2002), accessed 7 August 2012 from: www2.ohchr.org/english/issues/environment/environ/bp6.htm.
191 *Narmada Bachao Andolan v Union of India and others*, Supp. 4 S.C.R. 94 (2000); Cullet, P., *The Sardar Sarovar Dam Project* . Aldershot: Ashgate, 2007, pp. 1–40.
192 *Sandro Chávez Vasquez and Channels Lopez v Provincial Municipal Council of Pisco*, Exp. No. 0021-2003-AI/TC (2003); also for discussion see Turner, *A Substantive Environmental Right*, pp. 36–8.
193 Although a claim based upon environmental rights managed to delay construction of the project for a time, the decision was subsequently overturned. Information at the time of writing from the Minority Rights Group for the Office of the United Nations High Commissioner for Refugees (UNHCR), see Minority Rights Group International, *State of the World's Minorities and Indigenous Peoples 2012 – Case study: Belo Monte Dam: Drowning out indigenous protests in the Brazilian Amazon*, (28 June 2012), accessed 7 August 2012 from: www.unhcr.org/refworld/docid/4fedb3e45.html .
194 See Boyd, *The Environmental Rights Revolution*, p. 244.
195 *M M Levy Associacion Ecologista Limonese v Ministerio del Ambiente y Energia*, Decision 2001-13295, Expediente 00-007280-0007-CO (21 December 2001).
196 An examples is the review of prospective legislation in Hungary in *Magyar Közlöny (The Protected Forests Case)* case 1994/no. 55, p. 1919 (20 May 1994); see also Boyd, *The Environmental Rights Revolution*, p. 244.
197 They were first recognized in a declaration by the General Assembly in 1968, G.A. Res. 2398 (XXII), UN GAOR, 23 Sess., Supp No. 18, at 3, UN Doc A/L. 533 & Add. 1–4 (1968).
198 See generally Anton, D. K. and Shelton, D. L., *Environmental Protection and Human Rights*; Shelton, D., 'Human Rights Bodies: Decisions and Actions', *Envtl. Pol'y & L.*34(2), 2004.
199 See section 2.3.2.
200 United Nations, Economic and Social Council, *Human Rights and the Environment: Preliminary Report*, UN Doc. E/CN.4/ Sub.2/1991/8 (2 August 1992); *First Progress Report*, UN Doc. E/CN.4/Sub.2/1992/7, 2 July 1992; *Second Progress Report*, UN Doc. E/CN.4/Sub.2/1993/7, 26 July 1993; see A. F. Aguila and N. A. Popovic, 'Lawmaking in the United Nations: The UN Study on Human Rights and the Environment', *Rev. Eur. Community Int'l Envtl. L.* 3(4), 1994, p. 197; Caroline Dommen, 'Claiming Environmental Rights: Some Possibilities Offered by the United

Nations' Human Rights Mechanisms', *Geo. Int'l Envtl. L. Rev.* 11, 1998, p. 1 and 32.

201 United Nations, Economic and Social Council, *Review of Further Developments in Fields with Which the Sub-Commission has been concerned. Human Rights and the Environment*, UN Doc. E/CN.4/Sub.2/1994/9 (6 July 1994).

202 See UNGA Res. 63 Sess. GA/10823 A/63/L.69 (22 April 2009).

203 UNHRC, *Human Rights and Climate*, UN Doc. A/HRC/Res/18/22 (30 September 2011); See Cameron, E. and Limon, M., 'Restoring the Climate by Realizing Rights: The Role of the International Human Rights System', *Rev. Eur. Community & Int'l Envtl. L.*, 21(3), 2012, pp. 204–19.

204 UNHRC, *Human Rights and the Environment,* G.A. Res. 19/22, UN Doc. A/HRC/Res/19/10 (22 March 2012).

205 See Turner, *A Substantive Environmental Right*, pp. 46–8.

206 See Sueli Giorgetta, 'The Right to a Healthy Environment', in Nico Schrijver and Friedl Weiss, eds, *International Law and Sustainable Development – Principles and Practice*, 2004, p. 379 and 391; W. Paul Gormley asserted the existence of a right to a 'pure, healthful, or decent environment' in 1976. See W. Paul Gormley, *Human Rights and the Environment*, p. 41; John Lee states that 'the right to a healthy environment has achieved the status of a rule of regional customary international law in Latin America'. John Lee, 'The Underlying Legal Theory to Support a Well-Defined Human Right to a Healthy Environment as a Principle of Customary International Law', *Colum. J. Envtl. L.* 25, 2000, p. 283 and 339.

207 See Boyle, A., 'Human Rights and the Environment: Where Next?', *Eur. J. Int'l L.*, 23(3), 2012, p. 613 and 626.

208 See section 2.3.1.

3 Global environmental governance, the global legal architecture and the root causes of environmental degradation

1 Bodansky, D., *The Art and Craft of International Environmental Law.* Harvard University Press, 2010, p. 24; Birnie, P., Boyle, A. and Redgewell, C., *International Law and the Environment*, 3rd edn. Oxford: Oxford University Press, 2009.

2 United Nations Conference on the Human Environment (UNCHE), *Declaration of the United Nations Conference on the Human Environment* (Stockholm) 16 June 1972, UN Doc. A/Conf.48/14/Rev.1, adopted in G.A. Res. 2997. UN GAOR, 27 Sess., Supp. No. 30 at 43, at UN Doc. A/8901 (1972).

3 United Nations Conference on Environment and Development (UNCED), *Declaration on Environment and Development* (Rio de Janeiro) 14th June 1992, UN Doc. A/CONF. 151/5/Rev.1, 31 ILM. 814. 876 (1992).

4 Protocol on Substances that deplete the Ozone Layer (Montreal) 16 September 1987, in force 1 January 1989, 26 ILM 154 (1987).

5 Bodansky, *The Art and Craft of International Environmental Law*, p. 22.

6 Lauterpacht, H., *International Law and Human Rights.* London: Stevens and Sons, 1950, pp. 6–26.

7 Sands, P., Peel, J., Fabra, A. and Mackenzie, R., *Principles of International Environmental Law.* Cambridge: Cambridge University Press, 2012, p. 92.

8 Ibid.

9 Peel, J., 'Environmental Protection in the Twenty-first century: The Role of International Law' in R. S. Axelrod, S. D. Vandeveer and D. L. Downie, eds., *The Global Environment – Institutions, Law and Policy.* Washington DC: CQ Press, 2011, p. 50.

10 For general discussion of these issues see: Bodansky, *The Art and Craft of International Environmental Law*, pp. 15–16; Birnie, Boyle and Redgewell, *International Law and the Environment*, p. 37; Shelton, D., 'Law, Non-Law and the Problem of "Soft Law"', in D. Shelton, (ed.), *Commitment and Compliance.* Oxford: Oxford University Press, 2000, pp. 1–18.

11 UNEP, *Register of International Treaties and other Agreements in the Field of the Environment,* UNEP/Env.Law/2005/3, Division of Policy Development and Law. Nairobi: UNEP (2005).
12 Jeßberger, C., *Multilateral Agreements up to 2050: Are they Sustainable Enough?*. Inst. Econ. Research at the Univ. Munich. Working Paper No. 98 (February 2011) p. 6, accessed 16 August 2012 from: http://papers.ssrn.com/sol3/papers.cfm?abstract_id=2004241.
13 See Anton, D., *'Treaty Congestion' in Contemporary International Environmental Law*, Australian Nat. Univ. SSRN. Legal Scholarship Network. ANU College of Law Research Paper No. 12–05 (2012), accessed 16 August 2012 from: http://ssrn.com/abstract=1988579.
14 See Bodansky, *The Art and Craft of International Environmental Law*, p. 35; Leary, D. and Pisupati, B. (eds) *The Future of International Environmental Law.* New York: United Nations University Press, 2010, p. 292; Powers, A., 'Climate Change and Pollution: Addressing intersecting threats to oceans, coasts and small island developing states', in D. Leary and B. Pisupati (eds) *The Future of International Environmental Law.* New York: United Nations University Press, 2010, p.19; Breitmeier, H., *The Legitimacy of International Regimes.* London: Ashgate, 2008, p. 8; Mrema, E. M., 'Cross Cutting Issues Related to Ensuring Compliance with MEAs' in U. Beyerlin, P. T. Stoll and R. Wolfram (eds) *Ensuring Compliance with Multilateral Environmental Agreements – A Dialogue Between Practitioners and Academics.* Leiden: Martinus Nijhoff, 2006, p. 205.
15 Sands *et al.*, *Principles of International Environmental Law*, pp. 135–83; Brunnée, J., Doelle, M. and Rajamani, L. (eds) *Promoting Compliance in an Evolving Climate Regime.* Cambridge: Cambridge University Press, 2012; Mackenzie, C. P., 'Lessons from Forestry for International Environmental Law', *Rev. Eur. Community & Int'l Envtl. L.*, 21(2), 2012, pp. 114 and 119–26; Bodansky, *The Art and Craft of International Environmental Law*, pp. 225–51; Birnie, Boyle and Redgewell, *International Law and the Environment*, pp. 237–50; Fitzmaurice, M., 'Compliance with Multilateral Environmental Agreements', *Hague YB Int'l L.* 20, 2007, pp. 19–51; Beyerlin, U., Stoll, P. T. and Wolfrum, R. (eds) *Ensuring Compliance with Multilateral Environmental Agreements.* Leiden: Martinus Nijhoff, 2006; Shelton, D. (ed.) *Commitment and Compliance.* Oxford: Oxford University Press, 2000; Chayes, A. and Chayes, A. H., *The New Sovereignty: Compliance with International Regulatory Agreements.* Cambridge, Massachusetts: Harvard University Press, 1995.
16 See Hathaway, O. and Shapiro, S. J., 'Outcasting: Enforcement in Domestic and International Law'. *Yale L. J.*, 121(2), 2011, pp. 252–349.
17 Bothe, M., 'Ensuring Compliance with Multilateral Environmental Agreements – Systems of Inspection and External Monitoring' in Beyerlin, Stoll and Wolfrum (eds) *Ensuring Compliance*, p. 249.
18 Beyerlin, Stoll and Wolfrum, *Ensuring Compliance.*
19 See Goeteyn, N. and Maes, F., 'The Quest for a World Environment Organization: Reflections on a failing debate as an input for future improvement', in P. Martin, L. Zhiping, Q. Tianbao, A. D. Plessis, Y. L. Bouthillier and A. Williams (eds), *Environmental Governance and Sustainability.* Cheltenham: IUCN Academy of Environmental Law Series;Edward Elgar, 2012; Charnovitz, S., 'Towards a World Environment Organization: Reflections upon a Vital Debate', in F. Biermann and S. Bauer (eds), *A World Environment Organization: Solution or Threat to Effective International Environmental Governance?.* Aldershot: Ashgate, 2005; Esty, D. C., 'The Case for a Global Environmental Organization', in P. Kenen (ed.) *Managing the World Economy: Fifty Years After Bretton Woods.* Washington DC: Institute for International Economics, 1994; Esty, D. C., *Greening the GATT – Trade, Environment, and the Future.* Washington DC: Institute for International Economics, 1994, pp. 78–98.
20 UNCSD, *UN Needs to Establish World Environment Organisation* (22 June 2012),

accessed 17 August 2012 from: www.uncsd2012.org/index.php?page=view&nr=138&type=230&menu=238.

21 Najam, A., 'Neither Necessary, Nor Sufficient: Why Organizational Tinkering Will Not Improve Environmental Governance', in Biermann and Bauer, *A World Environment Organization*, pp. 235–56; Moltke, K. V., 'Clustering International Environmental Agreements as an Alternative to a World Environment Organization', in Biermann and Bauer, *A World Environment Organization*, pp. 175–204.

22 Peel, 'Environmental Protection in the Twenty-first century', p. 65.

23 Sands et. al., *Principles of International Environmental Law*, p. 92.

24 Bodansky, *The Art and Craft of International Environmental Law*, p. 10.

25 Sutherland, H., *Fraser & Stewart: Company Law of Canada*, Toronto: Carswell Legal Publications, 6th edn., 1993, p. 3.

26 Gower, L. (1979). *Principles of Modern Company Law.* London: Stevens and Sons, 4th edn., 1979, p. 22.

27 Garvin, S., Frisby, S. and Hudson, A., *Charlesworth's Company Law.* London: Sweet and Maxwell, 18th edn., 2010, p. 7..

28 Carr, C. T. (ed.) *Select Charters of Trading Companies AD 1530–1707.* London: Selden Society, 1913, p. xi.

29 Sutherland, *Fraser & Stewart: Company Law of Canada*, p. 3.

30 Gower, *Principles of Modern Company Law*, p.24.

31 Ibid.

32 Ibid., p. 23.

33 Brokers Act, 8 & 9 Wm. 3, c. 32 (1696).

34 Blackstone, W., *Commentaries on the Laws of England*, Clarendon Press, 1st edn., 1765, p. 455.

35 Bubble Act, 6 Geo. 1, c. 18 (1720).

36 Henn, H. G. and Alexander, J. R., *Laws of Corporations.* West Publishing Co., 3rd edn., 1983, p. 25.

37 Ibid.

38 In many instances, corporate creditors could sue shareholders directly for debts. Additionally, the management of corporations were able to raise funds by way of a form of levy upon shareholders in the event that money was required to pay creditors. Individual states in America were eager to attract businesses to incorporate and locate within their jurisdictions. This in part led to new approaches to the issue of liability. Therefore in the state of New York a different form of liability was included within its general incorporation statute of 1811. Under this new legislation, shareholders were subject to 'double liability'. This meant that in the event that a corporation could not pay its debts, shareholders could be required to pay an amount equal to that which they had already paid for their shares in the business. Although this meant that there was no total guarantee that the interest of creditors would be protected, it did mean that shareholders could invest with a clear understanding of their potential liability. This mechanism also provided an additional incentive for investors to play an oversight role over the management of a company. However, despite the apparent fair balance of the 'double liability' system, certain states soon began to legislate for the general incorporation of completely limited liability corporations.

39 It can be noted that in Britain in the early nineteenth century statutorily created corporations with special privileges had been created for certain specific new enterprises such as railway companies.

40 Joint Stock Companies Act, 7 & 8 Vict. c. 110 & 111 (1844).

41 Limited Liability Act, 18 & 19 Vict. c. 133 (1855).

42 See French, D., Mayson, S. and Ryan, C., *Company Law.* Oxford: Oxford University Press, 27th edn., 2010, p. 75.

43 See Sjåfjell, B., 'Regulating Companies as if the World Matters – Reflections from the Ongoing Sustainable Companies Project', *Wake Forest L. Rev.*, 47, 2012, p. 113 and 124.

44 French, Mayson and Ryan, *Company Law*, p. 471.
45 Gower, L., *Principles of Modern Company Law*. London: Stevens and Sons, 4th edn., 1979, p. 575.
46 Ibid., p. 576. It should be noted that the UK Companies Act 2006 codified and amended directors' duties in the UK. However, it is useful to examine the basic law prior to those amendments as it reflects not just the basis upon which the majority of the existing law is founded but also the basic principles that apply in many other jurisdictions.
47 See Taylor, C. R., *United States Company Law as it Impacts Corporate Environmental Behaviour, with Emphasis on Climate Change*, Univ. Oslo. Fac. L. Research. Paper No. 2012-31, 10 October 2012, p. 4, accessed 19 January 2013 from: http://papers.ssrn.com/sol3/papers.cfm?abstract_id=2159659.
48 Backer, L. C., *Comparative Corporate Law – United States, European Union, China and Japan – Cases and Materials*. Durham: Carolina Academic Press, 2002, p. 1129.
49 Henderson, G. E., *A Fiduciary Duty to Minimize the Corporation's Environmental Impact*, SSRN (2011), accessed 22 October 2012 from: http://papers.ssrn.com/sol3/papers.cfm?abstract_id=1932032; Villiers, C., *Directors' Duties and the company's internal structures under the UK Companies Act 2006: Obstacles for Sustainable Development*, SSRN (2010), accessed 22 October 2012 from: http://papers.ssrn.com/sol3/papers.cfm?abstract_id=1712791; Speth, J. G., *The Bridge at the End of the World – Capitalism, the Environment, and Crossing from Crisis to Sustainability*. New Haven: Yale University Press, 2008, p. 246–7.
50 See Tully, S. (ed.), *International Corporate Legal Responsibility*. Leiden: Wolters Kluwer, 2012, pp.140–4; also Kerr, M., Janda, R. and Pitts, C., *Corporate Social Responsibility*. Markham: LexisNexis, 2009, pp. 109–45.
51 For example in the UK s. 168 Companies Act 2006, states that a director can be removed by way of an ordinary resolution of the shareholders (in other words a vote of the majority of the shareholders). This right stands notwithstanding any provisions that may have been inserted in the company's articles of association.
52 Gesetz betreffend die Gesellschaften mit beschränkter Haftung (GmbHG).
53 GmbHG para. 43(1); see Andenas, M. and Woolridge, F., *European Comparative Company Law*. Cambridge: Cambridge University Press, 2009, p. 301.
54 The rights of dismissal may be limited under the company's articles; see Andenas and Woolridge, *European Comparative Company Law*, p. 300.
55 GmbHG para. 85.
56 Hopt, K., 'Comparative Company Law', in M. Reimann and R. Zimmerman (eds), *The Oxford Handbook of Comparative Law*. Oxford: Oxford University Press, 2006, p. 1164.
57 See Andenas and Woolridge, *European Comparative Company Law*, p. 283.
58 French Commercial Code. Art. L. 223-18. Where the statutes are silent, the duties are as stated in Art L. 221-4 i.e. 'the manager may carry out all managerial acts in the interest of the partnership'.
59 French Commercial Code, Art. L223–18. (This may be subject to variation under the articles of the company.)
60 French Commercial Code, Art. L223–22.
61 See Andenas & Woolridge, *European Comparative Company Law*, p. 285.
62 Kanda, H. and Milhaupt, C. J., 'Re-examining Legal Transplants: The Director's Fiduciary Duty in Japanese Corporate Law', *Am. J. Comp. L.* 51, 2003, p. 887.
63 Kanda and Milhaupt, 'Re-examining Legal Transplants', p. 887.
64 McAlinn, G., *Japanese Business Law*. Leiden: Kluwer Law International, 2007, p. 109.
65 International Business Publications, *Peru – Business Law Handbook*. Washington DC: International Business Publications, 2011, p. 120 (emphasis added).
66 Ley General De Sociedades (1997). Ley No 26887. (Nov. 19. 1997). Article 180 states, '[t]he directors cannot adopt agreements which do not protect the interests of the

company, its owners or related parties, nor can they use for their own benefit or for the benefit of third parties the commercial or business opportunities that they have knowledge of through their position. They cannot participate in activities that compete with the company without its express consent. The director that in whatever way has an interest which is contrary to that of the company must declare it and abstain from participating in the deliberation and resolution of the issue concerned. The director that contravenes the provisions of this article is responsible for the damage and losses caused to the company and can be removed by the board or by the general membership at the proposal of either a shareholder or a director'.

67 Ibid.

68 Company Law of the People's Republic of China (Revised in 2005). (Adopted at the Fifth Session of the Standing Committee of the Eighth National People's Congress on December 29, 1993. Revised for the first time on December 25, 1999 in accordance with the Decision of the Thirteenth Session of the Standing Committee of the Ninth People's Congress on Amending the Company Law of the People's Republic of China. Revised for the second time on August 28, 2004 in accordance with the Decision of the 11th Session of the Standing Committee of the 10th National People's Congress of the People's Republic of China on Amending the Company Law of the People's Republic of China. Revised for the third time at the 18th Session of the 10th National People's Congress of the People's Republic of China on October 27, 2005.)

69 Ibid., Art. 148.

70 Ibid., Art. 149.

71 Ibid., Art. 150.

72 Ibid., Art. 153.

73 See Villiers, C., 'Directors' Duties and the company's internal structures under the UK Companies Act 2006: Obstacles for Sustainable Development', *Int'l Comp. Corp. L. J.* 8, 2011, p. 47.

74 S.172 Companies Act 2006 provides as follows: Duty to promote the success of the company

(1) A director of a company must act in the way he considers, in good faith, would be most likely to promote the success of the company for the benefit of its members as a whole, and in doing so have regard (amongst other matters) to—
   (a) the likely consequences of any decision in the long term,
   (b) the interests of the company's employees,
   (c) the need to foster the company's business relationships with suppliers, customers and others,
   (d) the impact of the company's operations on the community and the environment,
   (e) the desirability of the company maintaining a reputation for high standards of business conduct, and
   (f) the need to act fairly as between members of the company.

(2) Where or to the extent that the purposes of the company consist of or include purposes other than the benefit of its members, subsection (1) has effect as if the reference to promoting the success of the company for the benefit of its members were to achieving those purposes.

(3) The duty imposed by this section has effect subject to any enactment or rule of law requiring directors, in certain circumstances, to consider or act in the interests of creditors of the company.

75 See Ho, J. K., '"Director's Duty to Promote the Success of the Company": Should Hong Kong Implement a Similar Provision?', *J. Corp. L. Stud.*, 10 (1), 2010, p. 17; also Havercroft, I. and Reisberg, A., *Directors' Duties under the UK Companies Act 2006 and the impact of the Company's Operations on the Environment,* SSRN (15 December 2010), accessed 4 February 2013 from: http://papers.ssrn.com/sol3/paperscfm?abstract_id=1274567

76 Williams, C. W., 'Corporate Social Responsibility in an Era of Economic Globalization', *U.C. Davis L. Rev.*, 35(2), 2002, p. 705 and 735.
77 Speth, J. G., *America the Possible – Manifesto for a New Economy*. New Haven: Yale University Press, 2012, p. 64.
78 Tienhaara, K., Orsini, A. and Falkner, R., 'Global Corporations', in F. Biermann and P. Pattberg (eds) *Global Environmental Governance Reconsidered*. Cambridge, Massachusetts: The MIT Press, 2012, p. 56.
79 Gower, *Principles of Modern Company Law*, p. 22.
80 See Muchlinski, P. T., *Multinational Enterprises and the Law*. Oxford: Oxford University Press, 2nd edn., 2007, pp. 45–79; also Wallace, C. D., *Multinational Enterprise and Legal Control – Host State Sovereignty in an Era of Economic Globalization*. The Hague: Kluwer Law International, 2002, p. 11.
81 Augenstein, D., *Study of the Legal Framework on Human Rights and the Environment Applicable to European Enterprises Operating Outside the European Union*, Study by the University of Edinburgh for the European Commission (2011), accessed 22 October 2012 from: http://ec.europa.eu/enterprise/policies/sustainable-business/files/business-human-rights/101025_ec_study_final_report_en.pdf .
82 Dine, J., 'Jurisdictional arbitrage by multinational companies: a national law solution?', *J. Hum. Rts. & Env.*, 3(1), 2012, p. 44 and 47.
83 See Turner, S. J., *A Substantive Environmental Right – An examination of the legal obligations of decision-makers towards the environment*. Leiden, The Netherlands: Wolters Kluwer, 2009, pp. 124–7.
84 *Re Union Carbide Gas Plant Disaster at Bhopal India Opinion and Order*, 12 May 1986: 634 F. Supp. 842 (SDNY 1986), 25 ILM 771 (1986); aff'd as modified 809 F.2d 195 (USCA 2d Cir), 26 ILM 1008 (1987); cert. Den. 108 S. Ct. 199 (1987).
85 See Government of Madhya Pradesh, *Bhopal Gas Tragedy Relief and Rehabilitation Department*, accessed 6 February 2013 from: www.mp.gov.uk/bgtrrdmp/relief.htm.
86 See Jain, S. and Mishra, N., *Health Effects of the Toxic Gas Leak from the Union Carbide Methyl Isocynate Plant in Bhopal Technical Report on Population Based Long Term Epidemiological Studies (Report of Period: 1985–1994)*, accessed 6 February 2013 from: http://icmr.nic.in/final/synopsis_tech_rep_clinical.pdf.
87 Muchlinski, *Multinational Enterprises and the Law*, p. 491.
88 For further analysis Muchlinski, P. T., 'The Bhopal Case: Controlling Ultrahazardous Industrial Activities undertaken by Foreign Investors', *Mod. L. Rev.*, 50, 1987, p. 545.
89 See generally, Blowfield, M. and Murray, A., *Corporate Responsibility*. Oxford: Oxford University Press, 2011; Kerr, Janda and Pitts, *Corporate Social Responsibility*, 2009; Dine, J., *Companies, International Trade and Human Rights*. Cambridge: Cambridge University Press, 2005; Kinley, D. and Tadaki, J., 'From Walk to Talk: The Emergence of Human Rights Responsibilities for Corporations at International Law', *Va. J. Int'l L.* 4, 2004, p. 931.
90 CERES (2013), accessed 13 January 2013 from: www.ceres.org.
91 Santer, A. L., 'A Soft Law Mechanism for Corporate Responsibility: How the Updated OECD Guidelines for Multinational Enterprises Promote Business for the Future', *Geo. Wash. Int'l L. Rev.*, 43, 2011, p. 375 and 378.
92 See Sjåfjell, B., 'Regulating Companies as if the World Matters – Reflections from the Ongoing Sustainable Companies Project', *Wake Forest L. Rev.*, 47, 2012, p. 113 and 126.
93 Kingsmith, A., *Greenwashing: The Corporate Exaggeration of Environmental Consciousness*, The International (2012), accessed 13 January 2013: www.the international.org/articles/275-greenwashing-the-corporate-exaggeration.
94 See Morgera, E., *Corporate Accountability in International Environmental Law*. Oxford: Oxford University Press, 2009.
95 Erskine, D., *The Companies Act 2006: Directors' Duties Guidance*. Corporate Responsibility, 2007, p. 2, accessed 13 January 2013 from: http://corporate-responsibility.org/wp-content/uploads/2009/09/directors_guidance_final.pdf.

96 OECD, *OECD Guidelines for Multinational Enterprises* (2011), accesseed 6 February 2013 from: www.oecd.org/daf/internationalinvestment/guidelinesformultinational enterprises/48004323.pdf.

97 Ibid.

98 United Nations, *Global Compact*, accessed 6 February 2013 from: www.unglobal-compact.org/.

99 United Nations Sub-Commission on the Promotion and Protection of Human Rights, *Norms on the Responsibilities of Transnational Corporations and other Business Enterprises with regards to Human Rights* (Draft Norms), UN Doc. E/CN.4/Sub.2/2003/12/Rev.2 (2003).

100 United Nations Human Rights Council, *Promotion and Protection of all human rights, civil, political, economic, social and cultural rights, including the right to development,* UN Doc. A/HRC/17/31 (2011).

101 Mares, R., 'Preface', in R. Mares (ed.) *The UN Guiding Principles to Business and Human Rights – Foundations and Implementation.* Leiden: Martinus Nijhoff Publishers, 2012.

102 United Nations Office of the High Commissioner for Human Rights, *Special Representative of Secretary-General on Human Rights and Transnational Corporations and other Business Enterprises.* accessed 6 February 2013 from: www.ohchr.org/EN/Issues/Business/Pages/SRSGTransCorpIndex.aspx.

103 This approach in itself has been seen to have weaknesses. See Harrison, J., *An Evaluation of the Institutionalisation of Corporate Human Rights Due Diligence*, SSRN, 27 July 2012, accessed 21 Ocotober 2012 from: http://papers.ssrn.com/sol3/papers.cfm?abstract_id=2117924.

104 Parker, C. and Howe, J. 'Ruggie's Diplomatic Project and Its Missing Regulatory Infrastructure', in R. Mares (ed.), *The UN Guiding Principles on Business and Human Rights – Foundations and Implementation.* Leiden: Martinus Nijhoff Publishers, 2012, pp. 273–301.

105 Ruggie, J., 'Reconstituting the Global Public Domain – Issues, Actors, and Practices', *European Journal of International Relations*, 10(4), 204, p. 518 as quoted in Mares, R., 'Business and Human Rights After Ruggie: Foundations, the Art of Simplification and the Imperative of Cumulative Progress', in R. Mares (ed.), *The UN Guiding Principles on Business and Human Rights – Foundations and Implementation.* Leiden: Martinus Nijhoff, 2012, p. 29.

106 UNEP Division of Technology, Industry and Economics & The International Institute of Sustainable Development, *Environment and Trade – A Handbook*, 2nd edn. Winnipeg, Manitoba, Canada: International Institute for Sustainable Development, 2005; Matsushita, M., Schoenbaum, T. J. and Marvoidis, P. C., *The World Trade Organization: Law Practice and Policy*, 2nd edn. Oxford: Oxford University Press, 2006, pp. 290–3; Sampson, G., *The WTO and Sustainable Development.* Tokyo: The United Nations University Press, 2005, p. 58; Neumayer, Eric, *Greening Trade and Investment: Environmental Protection without Protectionism.* London: Earthscan, 2005; Vaughan, S. and Nordstrom, H., *Trade and Environment – Special Studies 4*, WTO (1999), accessed 6 February 2013 from: www.wto.org/english/res_e/booksp_e/special_study_4_e.pdf.

107 See Sampson, *The WTO and Sustainable Development*, p.58; Schoenbaum, T., 'Free International Trade and Protection of the Environment', *Am. J. Int'l L.* 86, 1992, p. 700 and 702.

108 Neumayer, E., *Greening Trade and Investment,* p. 41ff.

109 Related to this is the issue of pollution transfer in which high polluting goods and services that are prohibited in the exporting state are exported to other states with lower environmental standards. See Iturregui, P. and Dutschke, M., *Liberalisation of Environmental Goods and Services and Climate Change*, HWWA Discussion Paper 335 (2005, August), accessed 2 Febraury 2013 from: http://papers.ssrn.com/sol3/papers.cfm?abstract_id=872504.

110 Kleeman, L. and Abdulai, A., 'The Impact of Trade and Economic Growth on the Environment: Revisiting the Cross-Country Evidence', *Journal of International Development*, 25(2), 2013, pp. 180–205.
111 Cavlovic T. A, B. K., 'A meta-analysis of environmental Kuznets curve studies', *Agricultural and Resource Economics Review*, 29(1), 2000, pp. 32–42.
112 See Matsushita *et al.*, *The World Trade Organization*, pp. 290–3.
113 Kleeman and Abdulai, 'The Impact of Trade and Economic Growth on the Environment', pp. 180–205.
114 Frankel, J., 'Environmental Effects of International Trade', Expert Report No 31 to Sweden's Globalisation Council. Stockholm: Sweden's Globalisation Council, 2011, p. 17; Kleeman and Abdulai, 'The Impact of Trade and Economic Growth on the Environment'.
115 Frankel, *Environmental Effects of International Trade*, p.7.
116 Ibid., p. 17; Neumayer, E., *Greening Trade and Investment*, p. 107; See also Yale Center for Environmental Law and Policy, Yale University and Center for International Earth Science Information Network, Columbia University, *Environmental Performance Index and Pilot Trend Environmental Performance Index*.
117 Sutherland, *Fraser & Stewart: Company Law of Canada*, p. 3.
118 Irwin, D. A., *Against the Tide – An Intellectual History of Free Trade*. Princeton NJ: Princeton University Press, 1996, p. 11.
119 Ibid, p. 18.
120 Ibid.
121 Landes, D. S., *The Wealth and Poverty of Nations – Why Some are so Rich and Some are so Poor*. London: W. W. Norton and Co, 1998, p. 55.
122 Ibid., p. 56.
123 Ibid., p. 56.
124 Irwin, *Against the Tide*, p. 22.
125 Ibid., p. 30.
126 Ibid., p. 34.
127 Smith, A., *An Inquiry into the Nature and Causes of the Wealth of Nations*. (K. Sutherland, ed.) Oxford: Oxford University Press, 1776 (reprinted 1993).
128 Ibid., pp. 292–3.
129 Irwin, *Against the Tide*, p. 219.
130 David Ricardo, *Principles of Political Economy and Taxation* (1817).
131 Macmillan, F., *WTO and the Environment*. London: Sweet and Maxwell, 2001, p. 226.
132 Landes, *The Wealth and Poverty of Nations*, p. 448.
133 Pomeranz, K. and Topik, S., *The World that Trade Created – Society, Culture, and the World Economy, 1400 – the Present*. New York: M. E. Sharpe Inc., 2nd edn., 2006.
134 Zeiler, T. W., *Free Trade Free World – The Advent of GATT*. North Carolina: The University of North Carolina Press, 1999, p. 8.
135 Kooper, C., 'New Perspectives on the 1931 banking crisis in Germany and Central Europe', *Business History* 53(2), 2011, p. 216 and 229.
136 Zeiler, *Free Trade Free World*, p. 1.
137 Ibid., p. 25.
138 Lowenfeld, A. F., *International Economic Law*. Oxford: Oxford University Press, 2nd edn., 2002, p. 502.
139 Ibid., p. 22.
140 Ibid., p. 24.
141 Art. XI General Elimination of Quantitative Restrictions.
142 Art. X Publication and Administration of Trade Regulations.
143 Art. XI(2)(c).
144 Art. XXVIII.
145 Art. XIX.
146 Art. XXXV.

147 Art. XXI.
148 Lowenfeld, *International Economic Law*, p. 32.
149 Ibid., p. 31. As an example, this allowed Britain to maintain the preferential arrangements that it had developed with countries in the Commonwealth
150 Art. XXIV.
151 The European Economic Community.
152 The North American Free Trade Agreement.
153 Zeiler, *Free Trade Free World*, p. 196.
154 The Marrakesh Agreement Establishing the World Trade Organization, 15 April 1994, in force 1 January 1995, 33 ILM. 1143.
155 The Dispute Settlement Understanding, 15 April 1994, Marrakesh Agreement Establishing the World Trade Organization, Annex 2.
156 The General Agreement on Trade in Services, 15 April 1994, Marrakesh Agreement Establishing the World Trade Organization, Annex 1B. 33 ILM 1167 (1994) (GATS).
157 Agreement on Trade Related Aspects of Intellectual Property Rights, 15 April 1994, Marrakesh Agreement Establishing the World Trade Organization, Annex 1C. 33 ILM 1197 (1994).
158 Agreement on Technical Barriers to Trade (1994).
159 Agreement on the Application of Sanitary and Phytosanitary Measures, 15 April 1994, Marrakesh Agreement Establishing the World Trade Organization, Annex 1A.
160 General Agreement on Tariffs and Trade (Geneva) 30 October 1947, not yet in force: 55 UNTS 194 (in force provisionally since 1 January 1948 under the 1947 Protocol of Application, 55 UNTS 308); Article XX

General Exceptions

Subject to the requirement that such measures are not applied in a manner which would constitute a means of arbitrary or unjustifiable discrimination between countries where the same conditions prevail, or a disguised restriction on international trade, nothing in this Agreement shall be construed to prevent the adoption or enforcement by any contracting party of measures:

(*a*) necessary to protect public morals;
(*b*) necessary to protect human, animal or plant life or health;
(*c*) relating to the importations or exportations of gold or silver;
(*d*) necessary to secure compliance with laws or regulations which are not inconsistent with the provisions of this Agreement, including those relating to customs enforcement, the enforcement of monopolies operated under paragraph 4 of Article II and Article XVII, the protection of patents, trade marks and copyrights, and the prevention of deceptive practices;
(*e*) relating to the products of prison labour;
(*f*) imposed for the protection of national treasures of artistic, historic or archaeological value;
(*g*) relating to the conservation of exhaustible natural resources if such measures are made effective in conjunction with restrictions on domestic production or consumption;
(*h*) undertaken in pursuance of obligations under any intergovernmental commodity agreement which conforms to criteria submitted to the CONTRACTING PARTIES and not disapproved by them or which is itself so submitted and not so disapproved;*
(*i*) involving restrictions on exports of domestic materials necessary to ensure essential quantities of such materials to a domestic processing industry during periods when the domestic price of such materials is held below the world price as part of a governmental stabilization plan; *Provided* that such restrictions shall not operate to increase the exports of or the protection afforded to such domestic industry, and shall not depart from the provisions of this Agreement relating to non-discrimination;

(*j*) essential to the acquisition or distribution of products in general or local short supply; *Provided* that any such measures shall be consistent with the principle that all contracting parties are entitled to an equitable share of the international supply of such products, and that any such measures, which are inconsistent with the other provisions of the Agreement shall be discontinued as soon as the conditions giving rise to them have ceased to exist. The CONTRACTING PARTIES shall review the need for this sub-paragraph not later than 30 June 1960

161 General Agreement on Tariffs and Trade (Geneva) 30 October 1947, not yet in force: 55 UNTS 194 (in force provisionally since 1 January 1948 under the 1947 Protocol of Application, 55 UNTS 308).

162 GATS, Marrakesh Agreement Establishing the World Trade Organization, Annex 1B. 33 ILM 1167 (1994). Article XIV.

163 For example Gomula, J., 'Environmental Disputes in the WTO', in M. Fitzmaurice, D. M. Ong and P. Merkouris, *Research Handbook on International Environmental Law*. Cheltenham: Edward Elgar, 2010, pp. 401–25; Turner, *A Substantive Environmental Right*, pp. 193–206; Pauwelyn, J., *Conflicts of Norms in Public International Law – How WTO Law Relates to other Rules of International Law*. Cambridge: Cambridge University Press, 2003.

164 The Marrakesh Agreement Establishing the World Trade Organization, 15 April 1994 in force 1 January 1995, 33 ILM. 1143 at 1144.

165 See Gomula, 'Environmental Disputes in the WTO', pp. 401–25.

166 Esty, D. C., *Greening the GATT-- Trade, Environment, and the Future*. Washington DC: Institute for International Economics, 1994.

167 Neumayer, E., *Greening Trade and Investment*, pp. 230–1.

168 See Esty, *Greening the GATT*, pp. 25–7; also Neumayer, *Greening Trade and Investment*, pp. 15–17; Kawara, F. and Kwa, A., *Behind the Scenes at the WTO*. Zed Books, 2003; Stiglitz, J. E., *Globalization and its Discontents*. New York: Norton and Company, 2001, p. 74; Dine, *Companies, International Trade and Human Rights*, p.76; Esty, D. C., 'The World Trade Organization's Legitimacy Crisis', *World Trade Review* 1(1), 2002, p. 7 and 9.

169 See Esty, *Greening the GATT*, pp. 25–7; Neumayer, *Greening Trade and Investment*, pp. 15–17.

170 Elkins, Z., Ginsburg, T. and Melton, J., *The Endurance of National Constitutions*. Cambridge: Cambridge University Press, 2009, p. 38.

171 Maddex, R. L., *Constitutions of the World*. Washington DC: CQ Press, 3rd edn., 2008.

172 Elkins *et al.*, *The Endurance of National Constitutions*, p. 41.

173 Adserà, A. and Boix, C., 'Constitutions and Democratic Breakdowns', in J. M. Sánchez-Cuenca (ed.), *Controlling Governments – Voters, Institutions, and Accountability*. Cambridge: Cambridge University Press, 2008, p. 247.

174 Fleiner, T. and Fleiner, L. R., *Constitutional Democracy in a Multicultural and Globalised World*. Berlin: Springer, 3rd edn., 2009, p. 651.

175 McIlwain, C. H., *Constitutionalism – Ancient and Modern*. New York: Ithaca, 1947, p. 25.

176 Thornhill, C., *A Sociology of Constitutions – Constitutions and State Legitimacy in Historical-Sociological Perspective*. Cambridge: Cambridge University Press, 2011, p. 153.

177 Fleiner & Fleiner, *Constitutional Democracy*, p. 657

178 Elkins *et al.*, *The Endurance of National Constitutions*, p. 41.

179 Greene, J. P., 'Law and the Origins of the American Revolution', in M. Grossberg and C. Tomlins (eds), *The Cambridge History of Law in America – Vol I: Early America (1580–1815)*. Cambridge: Cambridge University Press, 2008, p. 447.

180 Elkins *et al.*, *The Endurance of National Constitutions*, p. 6.

181 Law, D. S. and Versteeg, M., 'The Evolution and Ideology of Global Constitutionalism', *Cal. L. Rev.* 99, 2011, p. 1163 and 1175.

182 Elkins *et al.*, *The Endurance of National Constitutions*, p. 41.
183 Fleiner & Fleiner, *Constitutional Democracy*, p. 652.
184 Sands *et al.*, *Principles of International Environmental Law*, p. 191.
185 There are various United Nations resolutions referring to this principle. For example UNGA Res. 523 (VI) (1950); UNGA Res. 1803 (XVII) (1962). Additionally the Stockholm Declaration UN (1972), *The United Nations Conference on the Human Environment.* G.A. Res. 2997. UN GAOR, 27th Sess., Supp. No. 30, At 43, UN Doc. A/8901 and the Rio Declaration UN (1992) *Declaration on Environment and Development*, United Nations Conference on the Environment and Development, 31 ILM 814, UN Doc. A/Conf.151/5/Rev.1 both provide for this right in principles 21 and 2 respectively; also numerous multilateral environmental agreements such as the preamble of the United Nations Framework Convention of Climate Change (UNFCCC) (9 May, 1992) in force 24 March 1994, 1771 UNTS 107.
186 See section 2.4.2.
187 See section 2.4.1.
188 See Boyd, D. R., *The Environmental Rights Revolution – A Global Study of Constitutions, Human Rights, and the Environment.* Vancouver: UBC Press, 2012, pp. 53–7.
189 See section 2.4.2.
190 See Turner, *A Substantive Environmental Right*, p. 73.
191 Government of South Africa, *Constitution of South Africa* (1996) Art. 24, accessed 20 August 2012 from: www.info.gov.za/documents/constitution/1996/96cons2.htm.
192 See Glasewski, J., *Environmental Law in South Africa.* Durban: Lexis Nexis Butterworths, 2005, p. 75.
193 Government of Norway, *Constitution of Norway* (1814 including amendments up to 2012) §110(b), accessed 20 August 2012 from: www.servat.unibe.ch/icl/no00000_.html
194 See Anker, H. T., Olsen, B. E. and Ronne, A., 'Wind Energy and the Law: A Comparative Analysis'. *J. Energy and Nat. Resources L.* 27, 2009, p.145 and 158.
195 Government of Chile, *Constitution of Chile* (1980 with amendments up to 2011). Art. 19(8), accessed 20 August 2012 from: http://pdba.georgetown.edu/Constituions/Chile/vigente.html.
196 See for example the Constitution of the Kingdom of Thailand, which states that 'The right of a person to participate with State and communities in the preservation and exploitation of natural resources and biological diversity and in the protection, promotion and conservation of the quality of the environment for usual and consistent survival in the environment which is not hazardous to his health and sanitary condition, welfare or quality of life, shall be protected appropriately'. Government of Thailand, *Constitution of the Kingdom of Thailand,* s.67 (2007), accessed 21 August 2012 from: www.asianlii.org/th/legis/const/2007/1.html#C05P08. Also the Constitution of Spain, which refers to the, 'right to enjoy an environment suitable for the development of the person'. Government of Spain, *Constitution of Spain,* Art. 45(1), (1978 modified 1992), accessed 21 August 21 2012 from: www.senado.es/constitu_i/indices/consti_ing.pdf. Also the Constitution of Peru, which states that every individual has the right to, 'peace, tranquility, enjoyment of leisure time and rest, as well as to a balanced and suitable environment within which he may conduct his life'. Government of Peru, Constitution of Peru, Art. 2(22) (1993), accessed 21 August 2012 from: www.congreso.gob.pe/_inlges/CONSTITUTION_29_08_08.pdf. Also generally Boyd, *The Environmental Rights Revolution*; Turner, *A Substantive Environmental Right*, pp. 82–7.
197 Government of the Kingdom of Bhutan, Constitution of the Kingdom of Bhutan, Art. 5(3) (2008), accessed 21 August 2012 from: www.constitution.bt/TsaThrim%20Eng%20(A5).pdf.
198 Government of Kenya, Constitution of Kenya, Art. 69(b) (2010), accessed 21 August 2012 from: www.kenyaembassy.com/pdfs/The%20Constitution%20of%20Kenya.pdf.
199 The Constitution of India states that, '[t]he State shall strive to promote the welfare of

the people by securing and protecting as effectively as it may a social order in which justice, social, economic and political, shall inform all the institutions of the national life'. Government of India, Constitution of India, Art. 38, (1949), accessed 21 August 2012 from: www.india.gov.in/govt/constitutions_india.php.

200 The Constitution of Ghana states that, '[t]he State shall take all necessary action to ensure that the national economy is managed in such a manner as to maximize the rate of economic development and to secure the maximum welfare, freedom and happiness of every person in Ghana and to provide adequate means of livelihood and suitable employment and public assistance to the needy'. Government of Ghana, Constitution of the Republic of Ghana, Art. 36(1), (1992), accessed 21 August 2012 from: www.politicsresources.net/docs/ghanaconst.pdf.

201 The Constitution of the People's Republic of China states that, 'The state economy is the sector of socialist economy under ownership by the whole people; it is the leading force in the national economy. The state ensures the consolidation and growth of the state economy'. Government of the People's Republic of China, Constitution of the People's Republic of China, Art. 7 (1982), accessed 21 August 2012 from: http://english.people.com.cn/constitution/constitution.html.

202 The Constitution of the Republic of Government of the Republic of Ecuador states that, '[t]he economic policy shall have the following objectives: 1. To ensure an adequate distribution of the country's revenues and wealth. 2. To encourage national production, systemic productivity and competitiveness, the accumulation of scientific and technological knowledge, strategic insertion into the world economy, and complementary productive activities within regional integration. 3. To ensure food and energy sovereignty. 4. To promote the incorporation of added value with maximum efficiency, within the biophysical limits of nature, and respect for life and cultures. 5. To achieve a balanced development of the national territory, integration among regions, in the rural sector, and between the countryside and the city, in economic, social and cultural terms. 6. To foster full employment and value all forms of work, with respect for labor rights. 7. To uphold economic buoyancy, understood as the maximum sustainable level of production and employment over time. 8. To foster the fair and complementary exchange of goods and services on transparent, efficient markets. 9. To encourage socially and environmentally responsible consumption'. Government of the Republic of Ecuador, Constitution of the Republic of Ecuador, Art. 284 (2008 with amendments up to 2011), accessed 21 August 2012 from: http://pdba.georgetown.edu/Consitutions/Ecuador/english08.html.

203 See Speth, J. G., *America the Possible – Manifesto for a New Economy.* New Haven: Yale University Press, 2012, p. 4.

204 Turner, *A Substantive Environmental Right*, p. 27–40.

205 Each corporation is subject to the individual corporate law of the jurisdiction within which it is operating.

206 See Turner, *A Substantive Environmental Right.*

207 Elkins *et al.*, *The Endurance of National Constitutions*, p. 38.

4 A Global Environmental Right: Draft with commentary

1 See Hathaway, O. A., 'Why Do Countries Commit to Human Rights Treaties?' *J. Conflict Resol.* 51, 2007, p. 588. Hathaway observes that 'states take into account the likely costs and benefits of complying with a treaty (as determined primarily by legal enforcement and collateral consequences) when they decide whether to commit to a treaty'; See also Posner, E. A. and Weisbach, D., *Climate Change Justice.* Princeton: Princeton University Press, 2010, p.170.

2 See Anton, D. K. and Shelton, D. L., *Environmental Protection and Human Rights.* Cambridge: Cambridge University Press, 2011; Shelton, D., 'Developing Substantive Environmental Rights', *Journal of Human Rights and the Environment*, 1(1), 2010, pp.

89–120; Shelton, D., 'Human Rights Bodies: Decisions and Actions', *Envtl. Pol'y & L.* 34(2), 2004, pp. 66–72; Shelton, D., 'Environmental Rights', in P. Alston (ed.), *Peoples' Rights.* Oxford: Oxford University Press, 2001; Shelton, D., 'Environmental Protection and the Right to Food', in A. A. Trindade (ed.), *Derechos Humanos Desarollo Sustenable y Medio Ambiente.* San Josė: Instituto Interamericano de Derechos Humanos, 1995; Shelton, D., 'What Happened in Rio to Human Rights?', *Y.B. Int'l Envtl L.* 3, 1992), p. 75; Shelton, D., 'Human Rights, Environmental Rights and the Right to Environment', *Stan J. Int'l L.* 28, 1991, p. 103.

3 See for example Razzaque, J., 'Human Rights to a Clean Environment – Procedural Rights', in M. Fitzmaurice, D. M. Ong and P. Merkouris (eds), *Research Handbook on International Environmental Law.* Cheltenham: Edward Elgar, 2010, p. 284.

4 See for example Humphreys, S. (ed.), *Human Rights and Climate Change.* Cambridge: Cambridge University Press, 2009; Rajamani, L., 'The Increasing Relevance and Currency of Rights-based perspectives in the International Negotiations on Climate Change', *J. Envt'l L.*, 22(3), 2010, pp. 391–423.

5 See for example Narain, V., 'Water as a Fundamental Right: A Perspective from India', *Vt. L. Rev.*, 34, 2010, p. 917; Hiskes, R. P., 'Missing the Green: Golf Course Ecology, Environmental Justice, and Local "Fulfillment" of the Human Right to Water', *Hum. Rts. Q.*, 32, 2010, p. 326; McCaffrey, S. C. and Neville, K. J., 'Small Capacity and Big Responsibilities: Financial and Legal Implications of a Human Right to Water for Developing Countries', *Geo. Int'l Envtl L. Rev.*, 21, 2009, p. 679; Huang, L.Y., 'Not just another drop in the Human Rights Bucket: The Legal Significance of a Codified Human Right to Water', *Fla. J. Int'l L.*, 20, 2008, p. 353.

6 See Sands, P., 'The Environment, Community and International Law', *Harv. Int'l L. J.* 30, 1989, p. 393 and 398. Sands states that, 'Unlike national society, which treats each of these actors as participants endowed with legal rights, international society exists in a quasi-feudal state in which the sovereign (the state) is vested with all rights and powers'.

7 See section 3.7.1; see also Anton, D. K. and Shelton, D. L., *Environmental Protection and Human Rights.* pp. 863–976.

8 Humphreys, S., 'Introduction – Human Rights and Climate Change', in S. Humphreys (ed.), *Human Rights and Climate Change.* Cambridge: Cambridge University Press, 2009, p.3.

9 See Turner, S. J., *A Substantive Environmental Right – An examination of the legal obligations of decision-makers towards the environment.* Leiden: Wolters Kluwer, 2009.

10 Ibid., p. 73.

11 See generally Kysar, D. A., *Regulating from Nowhere.* New Haven: Yale University Press, 2010.

12 McGillivray, D., 'Compensating Biodiversity Loss: The EU Commission's Approach to Compensation under Article 6 of the Habitats Directive', *J. Env. L.*, 24(3), 2012, p. 417 and 418. The author makes this comment in relation to the approach of the European Union towards developments that can have a negative impact on areas of land that form part of the Natura 2000 network under the Habitiats Directive (Council Directive 92/43/EEC of 21 May 1992 on the conservation of natural habitats and of wild fauna and flora [1992] OJ 1206/7).

13 See Tromans, S., *Environmental Impact Assessment.* London: Bloomsbury Professional, 2nd edn., 2012; also Therivel, R., *Strategic Environmental Assessment in Action.* London: Earthscan, 2010.

14 See chapter 2.

15 In other words it is consistent with Principle 16 of the Rio Declaration as it provides a mechanism for the internalization of environmental costs. United Nations Conference on Environment and Development (UNCED), *Declaration on Environment and Development* (Rio de Janeiro) 14 June 1992, UN Doc. A/CONF. 151/5/Rev.1, 31 ILM. 814. 876. (Rio Declaration).

16 Principle 15, Rio Declaration.

17 While the precise status of the concept of 'intergenerational equity' under international law is unclear, reference to the responsibility of existing generations to preserve the environment for future generations is one that has been included in international instruments such as Principle 1 of the Stockholm Declaration; additionally a version is included in Prinicple 4 of the Rio Declaration.

18 Principle 8, Rio Declaration.

19 Sands, P., Peel, J., Fabra, A. and Mackenzie, R., *Principles of International Environmental Law.* Cambridge: Cambridge University Press, 2012, pp. 234–6; Cullet, P., 'Common but differentiated responsibilities', in D. M. Malgosia Fitzmaurice and P. Merkouris (eds), *Research Handbook on International Environmental Law.* Cheltenham: Edward Elgar, 2010, pp. 161–81; Birnie, P., Boyle, A. and Redgewell, C., *International Law and the Environment.* Oxford: Oxford University Press, 3rd edn., 2009, pp. 132–3; Cullet, P., *Differential Treatment in International Environmental Law.* Aldershot: Ashgate, 1993.

20 See sub-sections (b) and (d).

21 See section 3.3.3.2.

22 See Kysar, *Regulating from Nowhere*, pp. 245–6.

23 Ibid.

24 Law, D. S. and Versteeg, M., 'The Evolution and Ideology of Global Constitutionalism', *Cal. L. Rev.*, 99, 2011, p. 1163 and 1168.

25 Macrory, R., *Regulation,* Enforcement *and Governance in Environmental Law.* London: Cameron May, 2008, pp. 159–61.

26 Henderson, G. E., *A Fiduciary Duty to Minimize the Corporation's Environmental Impact*, SSRN (2011), accessed 22 October 2012 from: http://papers.ssrn.com/sol3/papers.cfm?abstract_id=1932032.

27 See Villiers, C., *Directors' Duties and the company's internal structures under the UK Companies Act 2006: Obstacles for Sustainable Development.* SSRN (2010), accessed 22 October 2012 from: http://papers.ssrn.com/sol3/papers.cfm?abstract_id=1712791; Hoo, S. D. and Olaerts, M., *Sustainable Development and the Need for Sustainable Oriented Corporate Law and Regulation.* SSRN (2011), accessed 22 October 2012 from: http://papers.ssrn.com/sol3/papers.cfm?abstract_id=1926065; Henderson, G. E., *A Fiduciary Duty to Minimize the Corporation's Environmental Impact*, SSRN (2011), accessed 22 October 2012 from: http://papers.ssrn.com/sol3/papers.cfm?abstract_id=1932032.

28 See Morgera, E., *Corporate Accountability in International Environmental Law.* Oxford: Oxford University Press, 2009.

29 See section 3.3.1.7.4.

30 Taylor, C. R., *United States Company Law as it Impacts Corporate Environmental Behaviour, with Emphasis on Climate Change*, University of Oslo Faculty of Law Research Paper No 2012-31, SSRN (2010), accessed 19 January 2013 from: http://papers.ssrn.com/sol3/papers.cfm?abstract_id=2159659; Villiers, *Directors' Duties*; Henderson, *A Fiduciary Duty*; Hoo and Olaerts, *Sustainable Development*; Dine, J., *Companies, International Trade and Human Rights.* Cambridge: Cambridge University Press, 2005, p. 269.

31 Sjåfjell, B., 'Regulating Companies as if the World Matters – Reflections from the Ongoing Sustainable Companies Project', *Wake Forest L. Rev.*, 47, 2012, p. 113 and 132.

32 Tully, S. (ed.), *International Corporate Legal Responsibility.* Leiden: Wolters Kluwer, 2012, pp. 140–5.

33 See Marquis, C. and Toffel, M. W., *When do Firms Greenwash? Corporate Visibility, Civil Society Scrutiny, and Environmental Discolosure*, Working Paper 11-115, Harvard Business School (2012), accessed 19 January 2013 from: www.hbs.edu/faculty/Publication%20Files/11-115_af40ca36-f8fa-4542-b211-0ef0ebc64da3.pdf; see

also Lancaster, K. A., Strand, C. A. and Carr, J., 'An Evaluation of the Usefulness of Web-based Financial and Environmental Performance Information Provided by Oil and gas Companies', *Oil & Gas Energy Q.* 50, 2001–2002, pp. 591 and 601.

34 Global Reporting Initiative, accessed 22 October 2012 from: https://www.globalreporting.org/pages/default.aspx.

35 s.417 of the UK Companies Act 2006 requires large companies to produce 'business reviews' that provide a report on the manner in which the company directors have taken non-financial considerations into account in their decision-making.

36 See Lord, R., Goldberg, S., Rajamani, L. and Brunnee, J. (eds)., *Climate Change Liability – Transnatioanal Law and Practice.* Cambridge: Cambridge University Press, 2012, p. 43. See Client Earth, *Referral to the Financial Review Panel. Re: The Rio Tinto Annual Report and Accounts* (2008), accessed, 22 October 2012 from: www.clientearth.org/reports/clientearth-submission-to-frrp-re-rio-tinto-annual-report-2008.pdf; also Client Earth, *Client Earth – Referral to the Financial Reporting Review Panel. Re: The BP Annual Report and Accounts* (2009), accessed 22 October 2012 from: http://clientearth.org/reports/clientearth-referral-to-the-frrp-to-the-bp-annual-report-and-accounts-2009.pdf.

37 At the time of writing the relevant legislation had not been passed and was still in the consultative stage. See UK Government, *The Greenhouse Gas Emissions (Directors' Report) Regulations 2013* (2012), accessed 22 October 2012 from: www.defra.gov.uk/consult/files/consult-ghg-regulations-20131.pdf.

38 Sjåfjell, 'Regulating Companies as if the World Matters', p.126.

39 This is especially true of the use of goods and products that have detrimental environmental impacts upon the global commons such as the atmosphere.

40 Principle 8 states that, '[t]o achieve sustainable development and a higher quality of life for all people, *States should reduce and eliminate unsustainable patterns of production and consumption* and promote appropriate demographic policies' (emphasis added).

41 Principle 13 states that, '[s]tates shall develop national law regarding liability and compensation for the victims of pollution and other environmental damage. States shall also cooperate in an expeditious and more determined manner to develop further international law regarding liability and compensation for adverse effects of environmental damage caused by activities within their jurisdiction or control to areas beyond their jurisdiction'.

42 Principle 16 states that, '[n]ational authorities should endeavour to promote the internalization of environmental costs and the use of economic instruments, taking into account the approach that the polluter should, in principle, bear the cost of pollution, with due regard to the public interest and without distorting international trade and investment'.

43 Principle 2 states that, [s]tates have, in accordance with the Charter of the United Nations and the principles of international law, the sovereign right to exploit their own resources pursuant to their own environmental and developmental policies , and the responsibility to ensure that activities within their jurisdiction or control do not cause damage to the environment of other States or of areas beyond the limits of national jurisdiction'.

44 Associated with this approach has been the development of 'eco-labeling' to both encourage consumers to purchase more environmentally friendly products and to place a greater imperative upon producers to minimize the environmental harm associated with their products. See Tully, *International Corporate Legal Responsibility*, pp. 145–6; Bell, S. and McGillivray, D., *Environmental Law.* Oxford: Oxford University Press, 7th edn., 2008, pp. 308–9; also Eritja, M. C. (ed.), *Sustainability Labelling and Certification.* Madrid: Marcial Pons, 2004; De Boer, J., 'Sustainability Labelling Schemes: The Logic of their claims and their functions for stakeholders', *Bus. Strat. Env.* 12, 2003, pp. 254–64.

45 Principle 16, Rio Declaration.
46 Principle 8, Rio Declaration.
47 This is entirely consistent with standard approaches to dealing with waste. For example the use of the cornerstone 'waste hierarchy' requires 'prevention' of waste to be the primary objective in dealing with a nations waste. This would then be followed by 'recycling and reuse' which in turn is followed by 'proper management and disposal' in that order of preference. See for example Bell and McGillivray, *Environmental Law*, p. 638.
48 See for example in the United Kingdom, Wolf, S. and Stanley, N., *Wolf and Stanley on Environmental Law*, Abingdon: Routledge, 2011, pp. 200–88; Holder, J. and Lee, M., *Environmental Protection Law and Policy.* Cambridge: Cambridge University Press, 2007, pp. 451–7.
49 For example within the EU there are specific directives, which impose producer responsibility for waste products that are inherent following the use of specific products. See for example the Waste Electrical and Electronic Equipment Directive (2002/96/EC) and also the End of Life Vehicles Directive (2000/53/EC).
50 See Bell and McGillivray, *Environmental Law*, p. 638.
51 Government of Western Australia, *Western Australia Environmental Offset Policy* (26 September 2011), accessed 11 November 2012 from: www.epa.wa.gov.au/EPADocLib/WAEnvOffsetPolicy-270911.pdf p.1.
52 Ibid.
53 See Reid, C. T., 'The Privatisation of Biodiversity? Possible New Approaches to Nature Conservation Law in the UK', *J. Envt'l L.*, 23(2), 2011, pp. 203–1.
54 Ibid., p. 215.
55 Ibid.
56 See McNish, T., 'Carbon Offsets are a Bridge too Far in the Tradable Property Rights Revolution', *Harv. Envtl. L. Rev.*, 36, 2012, pp. 387–443.
57 Ibid.
58 Ibid., p. 389.
59 Ibid.
60 For example in the EU the Environmental Liability Directive (2004/35/EEC) requires that where certain types of environmental degradation have occurred, remediation must take place and if that does not fully restore the site then further remediation must take place either on the site or elsewhere to compensate. Also the EU's Habitats and Species Directive (92/43/EEC) art. 4(4) requires that if a Member State is satisfied that there are no alternatives to a project for which there is an overriding public interest which will cause harm to a site protected under EU law, it must take compensatory measures to ensure that the overall coherence of Natura 2000 is preserved.
61 McGillivray, 'Compensating Biodiversity Loss', p. 417.
62 Ibid., pp. 424–31.
63 On an international level see Sands *et al.*, *Principles of International Environmental Law*, pp. 700–72; on a national level see for example the EU Environmental Liability Directive (2004/35/EEC).
64 See for example Kazimova, R., 'Insurance as a Risk Management Tool', in S. Leader and D. Ong (eds), *Global Project Finance, Human Rights and Sustainable Development.* Cambridge: Cambridge University Press, 2011, p. 269.
65 For further analysis see Turner, *A Substantive Environmental Right*, pp. 122–7. Prominent examples include the following: the Bhopal disaster referred to in Chapter 3; *Social and Economic Rights Action Centre/Centre for Economic and Social Rights v Nigeria*, Communication 155/96, Case No. ACHPR/ COMM/A044/1, Afr, Comm'n Hum. Rts. (27 May 2002); *Flores v Southern Peru Copper Corporation*, 28 U.S.C 1350, United States Court of Appeals 2nd Circuit (2003).
66 See Principle 16, UNCED, *Declaration on Environment and Development* (Rio Declaration); see also Porrini, D., *Law and Economics of Environmental Insurance*

(Editorial), The International Association for the Study of Insurance Economics, (2008), accessed 12 November 2012 from: www.genevaassociation.org/PDF/Geneva_papers_on_Risk_and_Insurance/GA2008_GP33(2)_Porrini.pdf.

67 Traditionally industry has often exposed individuals and the environment to potential risk without adequate insurance having been perceived. For a modern case example see Popovsky, M., 'Nanotechnology and Environmental Insurance', *Colum. J. Envt'l L.*, 36(1), 2011, p. 125.

68 See Muchlinski, P. T., *Multinational Enterprises and the Law.* Oxford: Oxford University Press, 2007, pp. 5–7; Wallace, C. D., *Multinational Enterprise and Legal Control – Host State Sovereignty in an Era of Economic Globalization.* The Hague: Kluwer Law International, 2002. pp. 9–11.

69 Muchlinski, P. T., *Multinational Enterprises and the Law*, pp. 51–79.

70 Steinhardt, R. G., 'Corporate Responsibility and the International Law of Human Rights: The New Lex Mercatoria', in P. Alston (ed.), *Non-State Actors and Human Rights.* Oxford: Oxford University Press, 2005, p. 215.

71 See Goeteyn, N. and Maes, F., 'The Quest for a World Environment Organization: Reflections on a failing debate as an input for future improvement', in P. Martin, L. Zhiping, Q. Tianbao, A. D. Plessis, Y. L. Bouthillier and A. Williams (eds), *Environmental Governance and Sustainability.* Cheltenham: IUCN Academy of Environmental Law Series – Edward Elgar, 2012; Charnovitz, S., 'Towards a World Environment Organization: Reflections upon a Vital Debate', in F. Biermann and S. Bauer (eds), *A World Environment Organization: Solution or Threat to Effective International Environmental Governance?.* Aldershot: Ashgate, 2005; Esty, D. C., 'The Case for a Global Environmental Organization', in P. Kenen (ed.), *Managing the World Economy: Fifty Years After Bretton Woods.* Washington D.C.: Institute for International Economics, 1994, p. 287; Esty, *Greening the GATT.*

72 Charnovitz, S., *A World Environment Organization* (February 2002), accessed 23 December 2012 from: http://archive.unu.edu/inter-linkages/docs/IEG/Charnovitz.pdf.

73 Goeteyn and Maes, 'The Quest for a World Environment Organization', p. 243.

74 Esty, *Greening the GATT*, p. 230.

75 Sampson, G. P, *UNEP – First Preparatory Meeting of the World Congress on Justice, Governance and Sustainability*, UNEP (12–13 October 2011), accessed 9 November 2012 from: www.unep.org/delc/Portals/24151/GreenEconomyInternationalEG.pdf .

76 See Esty, D. C., 'Economic Integration and Environmental Protection', in R. S. Axelrod, S. D. Vandeveer and D. L. Downie, eds., *The Global Environment – Institutions, Law and Policy.* Washington DC: CQ Press, 2011, p. 168.

77 Newell, P., 'Climate Change, Human Rights and Corporate Accountability', in S. Humphreys (ed.), *Climate Change and Human Rights.* Cambridge: Cambridge University Press, 2010, p. 152.

78 The Agreement on Trade-Related Aspects of Intellectual Property Rights 1994, 33 ILM. 1197 (1994). See Annan, K., 'Laying the Foundations of a Fair and Free World Trade System', in G. Sampson (ed.), *The Role of the World Trade Organization in Global Governance.* Tokyo: United Nations University Press, 2001, p. 27.

79 Petersmann, E.U., 'The Future of the WTO: From Authoritarian "Mercantilism" to Multilevel Governance for the Benefit of Citizens', *Asian J. WTO & Int'l Health L. & Pol'y*, 6, 2011, p. 45; Hoekman, B., 'Proposals for WTO Reform: A Synthesis Assessment', *Minn. J. Int'l L.*, 20(2), 2011, pp. 324–64; Deere-Birkbeck, C., *Reinvigorating Debate on WTO Reform: The Contours of a Functional and Normative Approach to Analyzing the WTO System*, SSRN (2009), accessed 19 November 2012 from: http://papers.ssrn.com/sol/papers.cfm?abstract_id=1436593.

80 Esty, 'Economic Integration and Environmental Protection', p.167.

81 See Meltzer, J., 'Climate Change and Trade – The EU Aviation Directive and the WTO', *J. Int'l Econ. L.*, 15(1), 2012, pp. 111–56; Low, P., Marceau, G. and Reinaud, J., *The Interface Between the Trade and Climate Change Regimes: Scoping the*

Issues, The WTO (12 January 2011), accessed 19 November 2012 from: www.wto/english/res_e/reser_e/ersd201101_e.pdf; Condon, B., 'Climate Change and Unresolved issues in WTO Law', *J. Envtl. L.*, 12(4), 2009, pp. 895–926; Veel, P. E. 'Carbon Tarrifs and the WTO: An Evaluation of Feasible Policies', *J. Int'l Econ. L.*, 12(3), 2009, pp. 749–800.

82 Para. 58(h), United Nations Conference on Sustainable Development (Rio + 20), *The Future We Want: Rio + 20 Outcome Document* (Rio de Janeiro), 24 July 2012, UN Doc. A/Conf.216/16.

83 Tromans, *Environmental Impact Assessment*, pp. 99–174.

84 See Kysar, *Regulating from Nowhere*, pp. 71–98.

85 Therivel, R., *Strategic Environmental Assessment in Action*. London: Earthscan, 2010, p. 6.

86 See for example: United Nations Convention on the Law of the Sea (Montego Bay) Arts. 205 and 206, 10 December 1982, in force 16 November 1994, 21 ILM 1261 (1982); Convention on Enviornmental Impact Assessment in a Transboundary Context (Espoo) Art. 2, 25 February 1991, in force 10 September 1997, 30 ILM 802 (1991); SEA Directive 2001/42/EC on the assessment of the effects of certain plans and programmes on the environment, L197 21.7.2001; EIA Directive 85/337/EEC on the assessment of the effects of certain public and private projects on the environment. L175 5.7.1985; World Bank – Operational Policy – Environmental Assessment OP 4.01 para. 8, The World Bank Operational Manual – 1999; Inter-American Development Bank – Environmental and Safeguards Compliance Policy B.3. para. 4.17 – 19 January 2006; Asian Development Bank – para. 6 Operations Manual Operations Procedures – 29 October 2003; African Development Bank – 3 B. para. 3.7 Environmental and Social Assessment Procedures for African Development Bank's Public Sector Operations – June 2001; European Bank of Reconstruction and Development – Sec. III para. 16. Environmental Policy – July 2003.

87 Turner, *A Substantive Environmental Right*, pp. 149–83.

88 See section 4.3.21.

89 See Art. 7, section 4.3.7.

90 Principle 7, Rio Declaration states that: '[s]tates shall co-operate in a spirit of global partnership to conserve, protect and restore the health and integrity of the Earth's ecosystem. In view of the different contributions to global environmental degradation, states have common but differentiated responsibilities. The developed countries acknowledge the responsibility that they bear in the international pursuit of sustainable development in view of the pressures their societies place on the global environment and of the technologies and financial resources they command'.

91 Principle 6, Rio Declaration states that, '[t]he special situation and needs of developing countries, particularly the least developed and those most environmentally vulnerable, shall be given special priority. International actions in the field of environment and development should also address the interests and needs of all countries'.

92 See Honkonen, T., *The Common but Differentiated Responsibility Principle in Multilateral Environmental Agreements*. Leiden: Wolters Kluwer, 2009; Rajamani, L., *Differential Treatment in International Environmental Law*. Oxford: Oxford University Press, 2006; Cullet, P., 'Common but differentiated responsibilities', M. Fitzmaurice; D. M. Ong and P. Merkouris (eds), *Research Handbook on International Environmental Law*. Cheltenham: Edward Elgar, 2010; French, D., 'Developing States and International Environmental Law: The Importance of Differentiated Responsibilities', *Int'l & Comp. L. Q.*, 49, 2000, p. 35.

93 Cullet, P., *Differential Treatment in International Environmental Law*. Aldershot: Ashgate, 2003, p. 11.

94 See for example Jeni Klugman, *Human Development Report – Sustainability and Equity. A Better Future for All*, UNDP (2011), accessed 26 November 2012 from: http://hdr.undp.org/en/reports/global/hdr2011.

95 Speth, J. G., *America the Possible – Manifesto for a New Economy*, New Haven: Yale University Press, 2012, pp. 160–2.
96 See for example, J. Goodell, *Big Coal: The Dirty Secret Behind America's Energy Future*. New York: Houghton Mifflin, 2007.
97 Environmental Law Institute, 'Energy Subsidies Black, Not Green', press release, 18 September 2009, accessed from: www.eli.org/pdf/Energy_Subsidies_Black_Not_Green.pdf.
98 Speth, *America the Possible*, p. 64.
99 Rubini, L., 'Ain't Wastin' Time No More: Subsidies for Renewable Energy, The SCM Agreement, Policy Space and Law Reform', *J. Int'l Econ. L.*, 15(2), 2012, p. 525 and 527; Chestney, N. and Vukmanovic, O., *Door to 2 degree temperature limit is closing – IEA*, Reuters (16 May 2012), accessed 22 December 2012 from: www.reuters.com/article/2012/05/16/US-energy-summit-iea-idUSBRE84F0Z820120516.
100 Hathaway, 'Why Do Countries Commit to Human Rights Treaties?' p. 588; also Posner and Weisbach, *Climate Change Justice*, p. 170.

5 Climate change

1 United Nations Framework Convention on Climate Change (Rio de Janeiro), 9 May 1992, in force 24 March 1994, 31 ILM 849 (UNFCCC).
2 See Redgwell, C., 'Climate Change and International Environmental Law', in R. Rayfuse and S. V. Scott (eds), *International Law in the Era of Climate Change*. Cheltenham: Edward Elgar, 2012, p. 118ff.
3 Art. 2 UNFCCC.
4 Art. 4.1
5 Art. 3.
6 Art. 4.2
7 Arts. 4.3–4.5
8 Additionally, it can be noted that the concept of state sovereignty is mentioned in the preamble to the UNFCCC. Here it recognizes state sovereignty over natural resources by stating that, '[s]tates have, in accordance with the Charter of the United Nations and the principles of international law, the sovereign right to exploit their own resources pursuant to their own environmental and developmental policies, and the responsibility to ensure that activities within their jurisdiction or control do not cause damage to the environment of other States or of areas beyond the limits of national jurisdiction'.
9 Ibid.
10 Art. 7.
11 Arts. 14 and 17.
12 See section 4.3.10
13 Arts. 7, 8, 10 and 11.
14 Arts. 8–17.
15 Art. 18.
16 The Kyoto Protocol to the United Nations Framework Convention on Climate Change (Kyoto), 11 December 1997, in force 16 February 2005, UN Doc. FCCC/CP/1997/7/Add.1, 37 ILM 22 (1998).
17 UNFCCC, *Status of Ratification of the Kyoto Protocol* (2012), accessed 28 December 2012 from: http://unfccc.int/kyoto_protocol/status_of_ratification/items/2613.php.
18 UNFCCC, Conference of the Parties serving as the Meeting of the Parties to the Kyoto Protocol 8 Sess., *Report of the Ad Hoc Working Group on Further Commitments for Annex I Parties under the Kyoto Protocol*, UN Doc. FCCC/KP/CMP/2012/L.9 (8 December 2012).
19 Ibid.

20 Recio, E., *On the Road to Doha: Will the Bell Toll for the Kyoto Protocol*, IISD (9 October 2012), accessed 28 December 2012 from: http://climate-l.iisd.org/policy-updates/on-the-road-to-doha-will-the-bell-toll-for-the-kyoto-protocol/.
21 Art. 17.
22 Art. 12.
23 Art. 6.
24 Neuhoff, K., *Climate Policy after Copenhagen – The Role of Carbon Pricing*. Cambridge: Cambridge University Press, 2011, pp. 58–61.
25 See Martin, R., Muûls, M. and Wagner, U., *Europe's Emission Trading Scheme: Taxpayers versus the industry lobby*, Centre for Economic Performance – London School of Economics (2010), accessed 7 January 2013 from: http://cep.lse.ac.uk/pubs/download/cp311.pdf.
26 Spassov, Y., Krustev, A. and Nikolovska, V., 'Lowest-Cost Abatement in Light of the EU ETS and Renewable Feed in Tarrifs in the Electricity Sector in Bulgaria', *J. Energy & Nat. Resources. L.*, 29(2), 2011, p. 281 and 289.
27 See generally Clifton, S. J., *A Dangerous Obsession – The Evidence Against Carbon Trading and for Real Solutions to Avoid a Climate Crunch*, Friends of the Earth (M. Cullen, ed.) (2009), accessed 7 January 2013 from: www.foe.co.uk/resourc/reports/dangerous_obsession.pdf.
28 Weisbach, D., 'Carbon Taxation in the EU: Expanding the EU Carbon Price', *J. Envtl. L.*, 24(2), 2012, p. 183.
29 See Meltzer, J., 'Climate Change and Trade – The EU Aviation Directive and the WTO', *J. Int'l Econ. L.*, 15(1), 2012, p. 111.
30 Neuhoff, K., *Climate Policy after Copenhagen – The Role of Carbon Pricing*. Cambridge: Cambridge University Press, 2011, p. 64.
31 Ellerman, D., 'The EU Emission Trading Scheme: A prototype global system?' in J. E. Aldy and R. N. Stavins (eds), *Post-Kyoto International Climate Policy – Implementing Architectures for Agreement*. Cambridge: Cambridge University Press, 2010, p. 93.
32 Winter, G., 'The Climate is no Commodity: Taking Stock of the Emissions Trading System, *J. Envtl. L.*, 22(1), 2009, p. 1 and 16.
33 Robinson, J., Barton, J., Dodwell, C., Heydon, M. and Milton, L., *Climate Change Law – Emissions Trading in the EU and the UK*. London: Cameron May, 2007, p. 44.
34 IPCC, *Climate Change 2007: Mitigation of Climate Change – Contribution of Working Group III to the Fourth Assessment Report* (B. Metz, O. Davidson, P. Bosch, R. Dave and L. Mayer, eds.). Cambridge: Cambridge University Press, 2007, p.15 Table SPM.5. See also Stern, N., 'Changing Economics', in F. Dodds, A. Higham and R. Sherman (eds), *Climate Change and Energy Security*. London: Earthscan, 2009, pp. 83–4.
35 Timmons-Roberts, J., Starr, K., Jones, T., & Abdel-Fattah, D., *The Reality of Official Climate Aid,* The Oxford Institute of Energy Studies (2008, Nov.) p.2. Retrieved January 9th, 2013 from Oxford Institute for Energy Studies: www.oxfordenergy.org/2008/11/the-reality-of-official-climate-aid/ .
36 UNFCCC, *News Release: Kyoto Protocol's CDM passes one billionth CER milestone* (12 September 2012), accessed 28 December 2012 from: https://cdm.unfccc.int/CDMNews/issues/Issues/I_POQZOFWYYKFKOSAZ5GYH2250DRQK/viewnewsitem.html.
37 See Boyd, E., Boykoff, M. and Newell, P., 'The "New" Carbon Economy: Whats New?', in P. Newell, M. Boykoff and E. Boyd (eds), *The New Carbon Economy – Constitution, Governance and Contestation*. Hoboken, NJ: Wiley – Blackwell, 2012, p. 1.
38 Neuhoff, *Climate Policy after Copenhagen*, pp. 224–6; Winter, 'The Climate is no Commodity' p. 18.
39 Winter, 'The Climate is no Commodity', p. 20.
40 Gutiérrez, M., 'Making Markets out of Thin Air', in P. Newell *et al.*, *The New Carbon Economy*, p. 45. See Sindico, F., 'Post-2012 compliance and carbon markets', in J. Brunee, M. Doelle and L. Rajamani (eds), *Promoting Compliance in an Evolving*

Climate Regime. Cambridge: Cambridge University Press, 2012, pp. 250–4; Humphreys, S., 'Competing Claims: Human Rights and Climate Harms', in S. Humphreys (ed.), *Human Rights and Climate Change.* Cambridge: Cambridge University Press, 2009, p. 63.

41 McNish, T., 'Carbon Offsets are a Bridge too far in the Tradable Property Rights Revolution', *Harv. Envtl. L. Rev.*, 36, 2012, p. 387 and 418.

42 These provisions are found in Arts 1, 4, 6, 7, 14 and 17 of Chapter 4.

43 See Art. 10 (Chapter 4).

44 See Arts 10 and 11 (Chapter 4).

45 See for example: Brunée, J., Goldberg, S., Lord, R. and Rajamani, L., 'Policy Considerations', in J. Brunée, S. Goldberg, R. Lord andL. Rajamani (eds), *Climate Change Liability.* Cambridge: Cambridge University Press, 2012, p. 53; Weisbach, 'Carbon Taxation in the EU': Expanding the EU', p. 183; Larragan, J. D., *Distributional Choices in EU Climate Change Law and Policy – Towards a Principled Approach?.* Leiden: Wolters Kluwer, 2011, pp. 25–8; Neuhoff, *Climate Policy after Copenhagen*; Aldy, J. E. and Stavins, R. N. (eds), *Post Kyoto International Climate Policy – Implementing Architectures for Agreement.* Cambridge: Cambridge University Press, 2010; Winter, 'The Climate is no Commodity', pp. 9–15.

46 UNFCCC, Conference of the Parties, *Report of the Conference of the Parties on its sixteenth session held in Cancun from 29 November to 10 December 2010*, UN Doc. FCCC/CP/2010/7/Add.1 (15 March 2011).

47 Department of Environment Food and Rural Affairs (DEFRA) – The International Scientific Steering Committee, *Avoiding Dangerous Climate Change* (May 2005), accessed 23 December 2012 from: www.eeg.tuwien.ac.at/eeg.tuwien.ac.at_pages/publications/pdf.NAK_BOO_2006_01_summary.pdf.

48 IPCC, *Climate Change 2007: Mitigation of Climate Change – Contribution of Working Group III*, p. 15 Table SPM.5; Stern, N., 'Changing Economics', in F. Dodds, A. Higham and R. Sherman (eds), *Climate Change and Energy Security.* London: Earthscan, 2009, pp. 83–4.

49 Art. 2 UNFCCC.

50 See section 2.2.5.

51 See IPCC, 'Summary for Policymakers', in: *Climate Change 2007: The Physical Science Basis. Contribution of Working Group I to the Fourth Assessment Report of the Intergovernmental Panel on Climate Change* (M. Manning, Z. Chen, M. Marquis, K. Averyt, M. Tignor and H. Miller, eds.). Cambridge, United Kingdom and New York, NY: Cambridge University Press, 2007.

52 UNEP, *The Emissions Gap Report 2012 – A Synthesis Report* (2012), accessed 24 December 2012 from: www.unep.org/publications/ebooks/emissionsgap2012/.

53 Ibid.

54 Ibid.

55 See Scott, J. and Rajamani, L., 'EU Climate Change Unilateralism', *Eur. J. Int'l L.* 23(2), 2012, p. 469 and 470.

56 Meltzer, J., 'Climate Change and Trade', pp. 111–56.; Rubini, L., 'Ain't Wastin' Time No More'; Frankel, J., Global environment and trade policy, in J. E. Aldy and R. N. Stavins (eds), *Post-Kyoto International Climate Policy – Implementing Architectures for Agreement.* Cambridge: Cambridge University Press, 2010, p. 493; Condon, B., 'Climate Change and Unresolved issues in WTO Law', *J. Envtl. L.*, 12(4), 2009, p. 895.

57 Quirico, O., 'Disentangling Climate Change Governance: A Legal Perspective', *Rev. Eur. Community & Int'l Envtl. L.*, 21(2), 2012, p. 92 and 93.

58 Srivastava, N., 'Changing Dynamics of Forest Regulation: Coming Full Circle?', *Rev. Eur. Community & Int'l Envtl. L.*, 20 (2), 2011, p. 113. Generally, see Streck, C., O'Sullivan, R., Janson-Smith, T. and Tarasofsky, R. (eds), *Climate Change and Forests – Emerging Policy and Market Opportunities.* Washington DC: Brookings Institute Press, 2008.

59 See Lord *et al.*, *Climate Change Liability*.
60 UNEP, *Doha Climate Conference Opens Gateway to Greater Ambition and Action on Climate Change*, UNEP (9 December 2012), accessed 29 December 2012 from: www.unep/newscentre/default.aspx?DocumentID=2700&ArticleID=9353.
61 See Quirico, 'Disentangling Climate Change Governance', p. 100.
62 Although opinions differ on the type of system that should be adopted, numerous experts concur that the resolution to the problem requires a central or global authority to be instituted. See for example Lee, B., Preston, F., Kooroshy, J., Bailey, R. and Lahn, G., *Resources Futures (Executive Summary)*, Royal Institute of International Affairs, accessed 2 February 2013 from: www.chathamhouse.org/sites/default/files/public/Research/Energy,%20Environment%20and%20Development/1212r_resourcesfutures.pdf, p. xiv; Ellerman, D, 'The EU Emission Trading Scheme: a prototype global system?' in J. E. Aldy and R. N. Stavins (eds), *Post-Kyoto International Climate Policy – Implementing Architectures for Agreement*. Cambridge: Cambridge University Press, 2010, p. 99; Cao, J., 'Reconciling Human Development and Climate Protection – A Multistage Hybrid Climate Policy Architecture', in J. E. Aldy and R. N. Stavins (eds), *Post-Kyoto International Climate Policy – Implementing Architectures for Agreement*. Cambridge: Cambridge University Press, 2010, p. 569.
63 See for example, the UK passed the Climate Change Act (2008), which binds the government to adopt measures that will lead to an 80 per cent reduction in GHG emissions by 2050.
64 See Weil, G., 'Subnational Climate Mitigation Policy: A Framework for Analysis', *Col. J. Env. L. & Pol'y*, 23(2), 2012, p. 285 and 286; also Shelton, D., 'Equitable Utilization of the atmosphere: A rights-based approach to climate change?', in *Human Rights and Climate Change*. Cambridge: Cambridge University Press, 2010, p. 114.
65 Neuhoff, *Climate Policy after Copenhagen*, p. 10.
66 Soltau, F., *Fairness in International Climate Change Law and Policy*. Cambridge: Cambridge University Press, 2009, p. 265.
67 GLOBE International, accessed 2 February 2013 from: www.globeinternational.org/.
68 Figueres, C., *GLOBE International – World Summit of Legislators*, GLOBE International (14 January 2013), accessed 2 February 2013 from: www.globeinternational.org/index.php/christiana-figueres-unfccc.
69 Weil, 'Subnational Climate Mitigation Policy', p. 289; Weisbach, 'Carbon Taxation in the EU', p. 185; Neuhoff, *Climate Policy after Copenhagen*; Cooper, R. N., 'The case for charges on greenhouse gas emissions', in J. E. Aldy and R. N. Stavins (eds), *Post Kyoto International Climate Policy – Implementing Architectures for Agreement*. Cambridge: Cambridge University Press, 2010, p. 151.
70 For details see Humphreys, S., 'Introduction – Human Rights and Climate Change' in S. Humphreys (ed.), *Human Rights and Climate Change*. Cambridge: Cambridge University Press, 2009; see also Soltau, F., *Fairness in International Climate Change Law and Policy*. Cambridge: Cambridge University Press, 2009.
71 See for example Jaffe, J. and Stavins, R. N., 'Linkage of tradable permit systems in international climate policy architecture', in J. E. Aldy and R. N. Stavins (eds), *Post-Kyoto International Climate Policy – Implementing Architectures for Agreement*. Cambridge: Cambridge University Press, 2010, p. 119; Tickell, O., *Kyoto 2 – How to Manage the Global Greenhouse*. London: Zed Books, 2008.
72 Condon, B., 'Climate Change and Unresolved issues in WTO Law', *J. Envtl. L.*, 12(4), 2009, p. 895 and 896.
73 See section 4.3.10 i.e. the concept of 'impact neutrality' referred to by Donald McGillivray.
74 See Arts 1, 4, 6, 7, 9, 14 and 17 (Chapter 4).
75 See Arts 5, 8, 10–13, 15 and 16–20 (Chapter 4).
76 See Art. 12 (Chapter 4).
77 See Art. 13 (Chapter 4).

78 Art. 14 (Chapter 4).
79 See Ban, Ki-Moon, *Foreword*, Report of the Secretary-General High Level Advisory Group on Climate Financing, accessed 2 February 2013 from: www.un.org/wcm/webadv/site/climatechange/shared/Documents/AGF_reports/AGF%20Report.pdf.
80 Burns, M., 'A Sustainable Framework for International Green Technology Transfer', *Colo. J. Int'l Envtl. L. & Pol'y*, 23(2), 2012, pp. 405–32.
81 Denman, K., Brasseur, G., Chidthaisong, A., Ciais, P., Cox, P., Dickinson, R., *et al.* 'Couplings Between Changes in the Climate System and Biogeochemistry', in S. Solomon, D. Qin, M. Manning, Z. Chen, M. Marquis, K. B. Averyt *et al.* (eds), *Climate Change 2007: The Physical Science Basis – Contribution of Working Group I to the Fourth Assessment Report of the IPCC.* Cambridge UK & New York USA: Cambridge University Press, 2007, pp. 499–587.
82 See section 2.2.4.
83 United Nations Conference on Sustainable Development (Rio + 20), *The Future We Want: Rio + 20 Outcome Document* (Rio de Janeiro), 24 July 2012, UN Doc. A/Conf.216/16.
84 Transparency International, *Global Corruption Report: Climate Change.* London & Wasington DC: Earthscan, 2011; See also Standing, A., *Corruption and REDD+: Identifying risks amid complexity* U4 Anti-Corruption Resource Centre: CHR Michelsen Institute(2011, May), accessed 3 January 2013 from: www.u4.no/.
85 UNFCCC Art. 4(3).
86 Ibid., Art. 4(4).
87 Ibid., Art. 4(5).
88 Ibid., Art. 11.
89 See The Green Climate Fund website, accessed 3 January 2012 from: http://gcfund.net/home.html.
90 UNEP Doha Climate Conference Opens Gateway to Greater Ambition and Action on Climate Change (9 December 2012), accessed 29 December from: www.unep/newscentre/default.aspx?DocumentID=2700&ArticleID=9353.
91 Gomez-Echeverri, L. and Müller, B., *The Financial Mechanism of the UNFCCC – A Brief History*, The European Capacity Building Initiative (2009, April), accessed 3 January 2013 from: www.oxfordclimatepolicy.org/publications.
92 Art. 10.
93 Art. 7
94 Art. 4
95 Arts 10, 11, 13 and 16.
96 See generally Posner and Weisbach, *Climate Change Justice*; Humphreys (ed.), *Human Rights and Climate Change*; Rajamani, L., 'The Increasing Currency and Relevance of Rights-Based Perspectives in the International Negotiations on Climate Change', *J. Env. L.*, 22(3), 2010, p. 391; Soltau, *Fairness in International Climate Change Law and Policy*.
97 See section 4.3.10.
98 Arts. 1, 4, 6, 7, 14 and 17.
99 See section 4.3.10.
100 Art. 13.
101 Art. 18.
102 Winter, 'The Climate is no Commodity', p. 21.

6 Conclusion

1 There is evidence that this may be changing. See for example, Weston. B. and Bollier, D., *Green Governance: Ecological Survival, Human Rights, and the Law of the Commons.* Cambridge University Press, 2013.

2 See Bodansky, D., *The Art and Craft of International Environmental Law.* Harvard University Press, 2010, p. 10.
3 See Morrow, K., 'Rio+20, the Green Economy and Re-orienting Sustainable Development', *Envtl. L. Rev.*, 14(4), 2012, p. 279 and 295.
4 Excerpt from Thomas Jefferson's letter to Samuel Kercheval, 12 July 1816 in Jefferson, T., *Jefferson: Political Writings.* (J. Appleby and T. Ball, eds.). Cambridge: Cambridge University Press, 1999, pp. 210–18.

Bibliography

Adserà, A. and Boix, C. (2008). Constitutions and Democratic Breakdowns. In J. M. Sanchez-Cuenca, *Controlling Governments – Voters, Institutions, and Accountability*. Cambridge: Cambridge University Press.

Aldy, J. E. and Stavins, R. N. (eds) (2010). *Post Kyoto International Climate Policy – Implementing Architectures for Agreement*. Cambridge: Cambridge University Press.

Alfredsson, G. (2010). Human Rights and the Environment. In D. Leary and B. Pisupati (eds), *The Future of International Environmental Law*. New York: United Nations University Press.

Andenas, M. and Woolridge, F. (2009). *European Comparative Company Law*. Cambridge: Cambridge University Press.

Anker, H. T., Olsen, B. E. and Ronne, A. (2009). Wind Energy and the Law: A Comparative Analysis. *J. Energy and Nat. Resources L.*, *27*, 145.

Annan, K. (2001). Laying the Foundations of a Fair and Free World Trade System. In G. P. Sampson (ed.), *The Role of the World Trade Organization in Global Governance*. Tokyo: United Nations University Press.

Anton, D. K. and Shelton, D. L. (2011). *Environmental Protection and Human Rights*. Cambridge: Cambridge University Press.

Anton, D. (2012). *'Treaty Congestion' in Contemporary International Environmental Law*. Retrieved 16 August 2012 from The Australian National University. Social Science Research Network. Legal Scholarship Network. ANU College of Law Research Paper No. 12–05: http://ssrn.com/abstract=1988579

Augenstein, D. (2011). *Study of the Legal Framework on Human Rights and the Environment Applicable to European Enterprises Operating Outside the European Union*. Retrieved 22 October 2012 from University of Edinburgh: http://ec.europa.eu/enterprise/policies/sustainable–business/files/business–human–rights/101025_ec_study_final_report_en.pdf

Axelrod, R. S., Vandeveer, S. D. and Downie, D. L. (eds) (2011). *The Global Environment – Institutions, Law and Policy*. Washington DC: CQ Press.

Backer, L. C. (2002). *Comparative Corporate Law – United States, European Union, China and Japan – Cases and Materials*. Durham: Carolina Academic Press.

Ban, K-M. (2010). *Foreword*. Retrieved 2 February 2013 from United Nations – Report of the Secretary-General High-Level Advisory Group on Climate Financing: www.un.org/wcm/webadv/site/climatechange/shared/Documents/AGF_reports/AGF%20Report.pdf

Bell, S. and McGillivray, D. (2008). *Environmental Law*, 7th edn. Oxford: Oxford University Press.

Beyerlin, U., Stoll, P. T. and Wolfrum, R. (eds) (2006). *Ensuring Compliance with Multilateral Environmental Agreements*. Leiden: Martinus Nijhoff.

Biermann, F. and Bauer, S. (eds) (2005). *A World Environment Orgnanization: Solution or Threat to Effective International Environmental Governance?* Aldershot: Ashgate.

Biermann, F. and Pattburg, P. (eds) (2012). *Global Environmental Governance Reconsidered*. Cambridge, Massachusetts: The MIT Press.

Birnie, P., Boyle, A. and Redgewell, C. (2009). *International Law and the Environment*. (3rd, ed.) Oxford: Oxford University Press.

Blackstone, W. (1765). *Commentaries on the Laws of England* (1st ed.). Clarendon Press.

Blowfield, M. and Murray, A. (2011). *Corporate Responsibility*. Oxford: Oxford University Press.

Bodansky, D. (2010). *The Art and Craft of International Environmental Law*. Harvard University Press.

Bothe, M. (2006). Ensuring Compliance with Multilateral Environmental Agreements – Systems of Inspection and External Monitoring. In U. Beyerlin, P.-T. Stoll and R. Wolfrum (eds), *Ensuring Compliance with Multilateral Environmental Agreements – A Dialogue between Practitioners and Academia*. Leiden: Martinus Nijhoff.

Botkin, D. B. and Keller, E. A. (2010). *Environmental Science – Earth as a Living Planet*, 7th edn. New Jersey: John Wiley and Sons, Inc.

Boyd, D. R. (2012). *The Environmental Rights Revolution – A Global Study of Constitutions, Human Rights, and the Environment*. Vancouver: UBC Press.

Boyd, E., Boykoff, M. and Newell, P. (2012). The 'New' Carbon Economy: What's New? In P. Newell, M. Boykoff and E. Boyd (eds), *The New Carbon Economy – Constitution, Governance and Contestation*. Hoboken (NJ): Wiley Blackwell.

Boyle, A. (2012). Human Rights and the Environment: Where Next? *Eur. J. Int'l L., 23* (3), 613.

Boyle, A. and Anderson, M. A. (eds) (1996). *Human Rights Approaches to Enviornmental Protection*. Oxford: Oxford University Press.

Breitmeier, H. (2008). *The Legitimacy of International Regimes*. London: Ashgate.

Brunee, J., Goldberg, S., Lord, R. and Rajamani, L. (2012). Policy Considerations. In J. Brunée, S. Goldberg, R. Lord and L. Rajamani (eds), *Climate Change Liability*. Cambridge: Cambridge University Press.

Brunnee, J., Doelle, M. and Rajamani, L. (eds). (2012). *Promoting Compliance in an Evolving Climate Regime*. Cambridge: Cambridge University Press.

Burns, M. (2012). A Sustainable Framework for International Green Technology Transfer. *Colo. J. Int'l Envtl. L. & Pol'y, 23* (2), 405–32.

Cameron, E. and Limon, M. (2012). Restoring the Climate by Realizing Rights: The Role of the International Human Rights System. *Rev. Eur. Community & Int'l Envtl. L., 21* (3), 204–19.

Cameron, J. and Mackenzie, R. (1996). Access to Environmental Justice and Procedural Rights in International Institutions. In A. Boyle and M. Anderson (eds), *Human Rights Approaches to Environmental Protection*. Oxford: Oxford University Press.

Caney, S. (2010). Climate Change, Human Rights, and Moral Thresholds. In S. Humphreys (ed.), *Human Rights and Climate Change*. Cambridge: Cambridge University Press.

Cao, J. (2010). Reconciling Human Development and Climate Protection – A Multistage Hybrid Climate Policy Architecture. In J. E. Aldy and R. N. Stavins (eds), *Post-Kyoto International Climate Policy – Implementing Architectures for Agreement*. Cambridge: Cambridge University Press.

Carr, C. T. (ed.) (1913). *Select Charters of Trading Companies AD 1530–1707*. London: Selden Society.

Carson, R. (1962). *Silient Spring*. London: Penguin Books (Originally published in the US by Houghton Mifflin).

Cassin, R. (1974). Les Droits de L'Homme. In *IV Recueil des Cours*. Leiden: Sitjhoff.

Cavlovic TA, B. K. (2000). A meta-analysis of environmental Kuznets curve studies. *Agricultural and Resource Economics Review, 29* (1), 32–42.

Charnovitz, S. (2002 February). *A World Environment Organization*. Retrieved 23 December 2012 from http://archive.unu.edu/inter–linkages/docs/IEG/Charnovitz.pdf

Charnovitz, S. (2005). Towards a World Environment Organization: Reflections upon a Vital

Debate. In F. Biermann and S. Bauer (eds), *A World Environment Organization: Solution or Threat to Effective International Environmental Governance?* Aldershot: Ashgate.

Chayes, A. and Chayes, A. H. (1995). *The New Sovereignty: Compliance with International Regulatory Agreements*. Cambridge, Massachusetts: Harvard University Press.

Chestney, N. and Vukmanovic, O. (16 May2012). *Door to 2 degree temperature limit is closing: IEA*. Retrieved 22 December 2012 from Reuters: www.reuters.com/article/2012/05/16/US–energy–summit–iea–idUSBRE84F0Z820120516

Client Earth (2008). *Referral to the Financial Review Panel. Re: The Rio Tinto Annual Report and Accounts 2008*. Retrieved 22 October 2012 from Client Earth: www.clientearth.org/reports/clientearth–submission–to–frrp–re–rio–tinto–annual–report–2008.pdf

Client Earth (2009). *Client Earth – Referral to the Financial Reporting Review Panel. Re: The BP Annual Report and Accounts 2009*. Retrieved 22 October 2012 from Client Earth: http://clientearth.org/reports/clientearth–referral–to–the–frrp–to–the–bp–annual–report–and–accounts–2009.pdf

Clifton, S.–J. (2009 November). *A Dangerous Obsession – The Evidence Against Carbon Trading and for Real Solutions to Avoid a Climate Crunch*. (M. Cullen, ed.) Retrieved 7 January 2013 from Friends of the Earth: www.foe.co.uk/resourc/reports/dangerous_obsession.pdf

Condon, B. (2009). Climate Change and Unresolved issues in WTO Law. *J. Envtl. L., 12* (4), 895–926.

Conway, D. and Schipper, L. F. (2011). Adaptation to Climate Change in Africa: Challenges and Opportunities Identified from Ethiopia. *Global Environmental Change, 21*, 227.

Cooper, R. N. (2010). The case for charges on greenhouse gas emissions. In J. E. Aldy and R. N. Stavins (eds), *Post Kyoto International Climate Policy – Implementing Architectures for Agreement*. Cambridge: Cambridge University Press.

Cullet, P. (2010). Common but differentiated responsibilities. In M. Fitzmaurice, D. M. Ong and P. Merkouris (eds), *Research Handbook on International Environmental Law*. Cheltenham: Edward Elgar.

Cullet, P. (2003). *Differential Treatment in International Environmental Law*. Aldershot: Ashgate.

Cullet, P. (2007). *The Sardar Sarovar Dam Project*. Aldershot: Ashgate.

Dasgupta, P. (2008). Nature in Economics. *Environmental and Resource Economics, 39*, 1–7.

De Boer, J. (2003). Sustainability Labelling Schemes: The Logic of their claims and their functions for stakeholders. *Bus. Strat. Env., 12*, 254–264.

Deere-Birkbeck, C. (2009). *Reinvigorating Debate on WTO Reform: The Contours of a Functional and Normative Approach to Analyzing the WTO System*. Retrieved 19 November 2012 from Social Sciences Research Network: http://papers.ssrn.com/sol/papers.cfm?abstract_id=1436593

DEFRA – The International Scientific Steering Committee (May2005). *Avoiding Dangerous Climate Change*. Retrieved 23 December 2012 from www.eeg.tuwien.ac.at/eeg.tuwien.ac.at_pages/publications/pdf.NAK_BOO_2006_01_summary.pdf

Dellinger, M. (2012). Ten Years of the Aarhus Convention: How Procedural Democracy is Paving the Way for Substantive Change in National and International Enviornmental Law. *Colo. J. Int'l Envtl L. & Pol'y, 23* (2), 309.

Denman, K., Brasseur, G., Chidthaisong, A., Ciais, P., Cox, P., Dickinson, R., *et al.* (2007). Couplings Between Changes in the Climate System and Biogeochemistry. In S. Solomon, D. Qin, M. Manning, Z. Chen, M. Marquis, K. B. Averyt, *et al.* (eds), *Climate Change 2007: The Physical Science Basis – Contribution of Working Group I to the Fourth Assessment Report of the IPCC*. Cambridge UK & New York USA: Cambridge University Press.

Dine, J. (2005). *Companies, International Trade and Human Rights*. Cambridge: Cambridge University Press.

Dine, J. (2012). Jurisdictional Arbitrage by Multinational Companies: A National Law Solution? *J. Hum. Rts. & Env., 3* (1), 44.

Dodds, F., Higham, A. and Sherman, R. (eds). (2009). *Climate Change and Energy Security*. London : Earthscan.

Dooley K. and Ozinga, S. (2011) Building on Forest Governance Reforms through FLEGT: The Best Way of Controlling Forests' Contribution to Climate Change? *Rev. Eur. Community & Int'l Envtl. L., 20* (2), 163.

Elkins, Z., Ginsburg, T. and Melton, J. (2009). *The Endurance of National Constitutions*. Cambridge: Cambridge University Press.

Ellerman, D. (2010). The EU Emission Trading Scheme: A prototype global system? In J. E. Aldy and R. N. Stavins (eds), *Post-Kyoto International Climate Policy – Implementing Architectures for Agreement*. Cambridge: Cambridge University Press.

Eritja, M. C. (ed.) (2004). *Sustainability Labelling and Certification*. Madrid: Marcial Pons.

Erskine, D. (2007). *The Companies Act 2006: Directors' Duties Guidance*. Retrieved 13 January 2013 from Corporate Responsibility: http://corporate–responsibility.org/wp–content/uploads/2009/09/directors_guidance_final.pdf

Esty, D. C. (1994). *Greening the GATT – Trade, Environment, and the Future*. Washington DC: Institute for International Economics.

Esty, D. C. (1994). The Case for a Global Environmental Organization. In P. Kenen (ed.), *Managing the World Economy: Fifty Years After Bretton Woods*. Washington DC: Institute for International Economics.

Esty, D. C. (2002). The World Trade Organisation's Legitimacy Crisis. *World Trade Rev., 1* (1), 7,9.

Esty, D. C. (2011). Economic Integration and Environmental Protection. In *The Global Environment – Institutions, Law and Policy*. Washington DC: CQ Press.

Fabra, A. (14–16 January 2002). *Background Paper No. 3 for the Joint UNEP–OHCHR Expert Seminar on Human Rights and the Environment, The Intersection of Human Rights and Environmental Issues: A Review of Institutional Developments at the International Level*. Retrieved 7 August 2012 from Background Paper No. 3 for the Joint UNEP–OHCHR Expert Seminar on Human Rights and the Environment, The Intersection of Humnan Rights and Environmental Issues: A Review of Institutional Developments at the International Level: www2.ohchr.org/english/issues/environment/environ/bp3.htm

Fabra, A. and Arnal, E. (14–16 January 2002). *Background Paper No. 6 for the Joint UNEP–OHCHR Expert Seminar on Human Rights and the Environment, Review of Jurisprudence on Human Rights and the Environment in Latin America*. Retrieved 7 August 2012 from Office of the United Nations High Commissioner for Human Rights: www2.ohchr.org/english/issues/environment/environ/bp6.htm

Figueres, C. (14 January2013). *GLOBE International – World Summit of Legislators*. Retrieved 2 February 2013 from GLOBE International: www.globeinternational.org/index.php/christina-figueres-unfccc

Fitzmaurice, M. (2007). Compliance with Multilateral Environmental Agreements. *Hague Yearbook of International Law, 20*, 19–51.

Fitzmaurice, M., Ong, D. M. and Merkouris, P. (eds). (2010). *Research Handbook on International Environmental Law*. Cheltenham: Edward Elgar.

Fleiner, T. and Fleiner, L. R. (2009). *Constitutional Democracy in a Multicultural and Globalised World*, 3rd edn. Berlin: Springer.

Frankel, J. (2009). *Environmental Effects of International Trade*. Expert Report No 31 to Sweden's Globalisation Council. Stockholm: Sweden's Globalisation Council.

Frankel, J. (2010). Global Environment and Trade Policy. In J. E. Aldy and R. N. Stavins (eds), *Post-Kyoto International Climate Policy – Implementing Architectures for Agreement*. Cambridge: Cambridge University Press.

French, D. (2000). Developing States and International Environmental Law: The Importance of Differentiated Responsibilities. *Int'l & Comp. L. Q., 49*, 35.

French, D., Mayson, S. and Ryan, C. (2010). *Company Law*, 27th edn. Oxford: Oxford University Press.
Garvin, S., Frisby, S. and Hudson, A. (2010). *Charlesworth's Company Law*, 18th edn. London: Sweet and Maxwell.
Glasewski, J. (2005). *Environmental Law in South Africa*. Durban: Lexis Nexis Butterworths.
Global Reporting Initiative. (2012). *Global Reporting Initiative*. Retrieved 22 October 2012 from https://www.globalreporting.org/pages/default.aspx
Globe International. (2013). Retrieved 2 February 2013 from GLOBE International: www.globeinternational.org/
Goeteyn, N. and Maes, F. (2012). The Quest for a World Environment Organization: Reflections on a failing debate as an input for future improvement. In P. Martin, L. Zhiping, Q. Tianbao, A. D. Plessis and Y. L. Bouthillier (eds). Cheltenham: IUCN Academy of Environmental Law Series, Edward Elgar.
Gomez-Echeverri, L. and Müller, B. (2009 April). *The Financial Mechanism of the UNFCCC – A Brief History*. Retrieved 3 January 2013 from European Capacity Building Initiative: www.oxfordclimatepolicy.org/publications
Gomula, J. (2010). Environmental Disputes in the WTO. In M. Fitzmaurice, D. M. Ong and P. Merkouris, *Research Handbook on International Environmental Law*. Cheltenham: Edward Elgar.
Gormley, W. P. (1976). *Human Rights and the Environment: The Need for International Cooperation*. Leiden: Sitjhoff.
Government of Bolivia (2010). *Ley de derechos de la Madre Tierra (Law 071 of the Plurinacional State 2010)*. Retrieved 9 August 2012 from www.scribd.com/Gobernabilidad/d/44900268-Ley-deDerechos-de-la-Madre-Tierra-Estado-Plurinacional-deBolivia
Government of Chile (1980 with amendments up to 2011). *Constitution of Chile*. Retrieved 20 August 2012 from Constitution of Chile: http://pdba.georgetown.edu/Constituions/Chile/vigente.html
Government of Ecuador (2008). *Title II, Chapter 7, Rights of Nature chapter of Constitution of Ecuador*. Retrieved 9 August 2012 from http://pdba.georgetown.edu/Constitutions/Ecuador/english08.html
Government of Ghana (1992). *Constitution of the Republic of Ghana*. Retrieved 21 August 2012 from Constitution of the Republic of Ghana: www.politicsresources.net/docs/ghanaconst.pdf
Government of India (1949). *Constitution of India*. Retrieved 21 August 2012 from Constitution of India: www.india.gov.in/govt/constitutions_india.php
Government of Kenya (2010). *Constitution of Kenya*. Retrieved 21 August 2012 from Constitution of Kenya: www.kenyaembassy.com/pdfs/The%20Constitution%20of%20Kenya.pdf
Government of the Kingdom of Bhutan (2008). *Constitution of the Kingdom of Bhutan*. Retrieved 21 August 2012 from Constitution of the Kingdom of Bhutan: www.constitution.bt/TsaThrim%20Eng%20(A5).pdf
Government of Madhya Pradesh (2010). *Bhopal Gas Tragedy Relief and Rehabilitation Department*. Retrieved 6 February 2013 from Government of Madhya Pradesh: www.mp.gov.in/bgtrrdmp/relief.htm
Government of Norway (1814 including amendments up to 2012). *Constitution of Norway*. Retrieved 20 August 2012 from Constitution of Norway: www.servat.unibe.ch/icl/no0000_.html
Government of the People's Republic of China (1982). *Constitution of the People's Republic of China*. Retrieved 21 August 2012 from Constitution of the People's Republic of China: http://english.people.com.cn/constitution/constitution.html
Government of Peru (1993). *Constitution of Peru*. Retrieved 21 August 2012 from Constitution of Peru: www.congreso.gob.pe/_inlges/CONSTITUTION_29_08_08.pdf
Government of the Republic of Ecuador (2008 with amendments up to 2011). *Constitution*

of the Republic of Ecuador. Retrieved 21 August 2012 from Constitution of the Republic of Ecuador: http://pdba.georgetown.edu/Consitutions/Ecuador/english08.html

Government of South Africa (1996). *Constitution of South Africa*. Retrieved 20 August 2012 from Constitution of South Africa: www.info.gov.za/documents/constitution/1996/96cons2.htm

Government of Spain (1978 modified 1992). *Constitution of Spain*. Retrieved 21 August 2012 from Constitution of Spain: www.senado.es/constitu_i/indices/consti_ing.pdf

Government of Thailand (2007). *Constitution of the Kingdom of Thailand*. Retrieved 21 August 2012 from Constitution of the Kingdom of Thailand: www.asianlii.org/th/legis/const/2007/1.html

Government of Western Australia (26 September 2011). *Western Australia Environmental Offset Policy*. Retrieved 11 November 2012 from www.epa.wa.gov.au/EPADocLib/WAEnvOffsetPolicy–270911.pdf

Gower, L. (1979). *Principles of Modern Company Law*, 4th edn. London: Stevens and Sons.

Grear, A. (2012). Human Rights, Property and the Search for 'Worlds Other'. *J. Hum. Rts. & Envt., 3* (2), 173.

Greene, J. P. (2008). Law and the Origins of the American Revolution. In M. Grossberg and C. Tomlins (eds), *The Cambridge History of Law in America – Vol I – Early America (1580–1815)*. Cambridge: Cambridge University Press.

Gutiérrez, M. (2012). Making Markets out of Thin Air. In P. Newell, M. Boykoff and E. Boyd (eds), *The New Carbon Economy – Constitution, Governance and Contestation*. Hoboken (NJ): Wiley Blackwell.

Harries, T. and Penning-Roswell, E. (2011). Victim Pressure, Institutional Inertia and Climate Change Adaptation: The case of flood risk. *Global Environmental Change, 1* (1), 188.

Harrison, J. (26 July 2012). *An Evaluation of the Institutionalisation of Corporate Human Rights Due Diligence*. Retrieved 21 Ocotober 2012 from Social Science Research Network: http://papers.ssrn.com/sol3/papers.cfm?abstract_id=2117924

Hathaway, O. A. (2006). *Strong States, Strong World: Why International Law Succeeds and Fails and what we should do about it*. Retrieved 6 October 2012 from www.law.yale.edu/documents/pdf/Faculty/BookOutline1.pdf

Hathaway, O. A. (2007). Why Do Countries Commit to Human Rights Treaties? *Journal of Conflict Resolution, 51*, 588.

Hathaway, O. and Shapiro, S. J. (2011). Outcasting: Enforcement in Domestic and International Law. *Yale L. J., 121* (2), 252–349.

Havercroft, I. and Reisberg, A. (2010). *Directors' Duties under the UK Companies Act 2006 and the impact of the Company's Operations on the Environment*. Retrieved 4 February 2013 from Social Science Research Network: http://papers.ssrn.com/sol3/paperscfm?abstract_id=1274567

Hayward, T. (2005). *Constitutional Environmental Rights*. Oxford: Oxford University Press.

Henderson, G. E. (2011). *A Fiduciary Duty to Minimize the Corporation's Environmental Impact*. Retrieved 22 October 2012 from Social Science Research Network: http://papers.ssrn.com/sol3/papers.cfm?abstract_id=1932032

Henn, H. G. and Alexander, J. R. (1983). *Laws of Corporations*, 3rd edn. West Publishing Co.

Higgins, P. (2012). *Earth is Our Business: Changing the Rules of the Game*. London: Shepherd-Walwyn.

Hiskes, R. P. (2010). Missing the Green: Golf Course Ecology, Environmental Justice, and Local 'Fulfillment' of the Human Right to Water. *Hum. Rts. Q., 32*, 326.

Hiskes, R. P. (2009). *The Human Right to a Green Future – Environmental Rights and Intergenerational Justice*. Cambridge: Cambridge University Press.

Ho, J. K. (2010). 'Director's Duty to Promote the Success of the Company': Should Hong Kong Implement a Similar Provision? *J. Corp. L. Stud., 10* (1), 17.

Hoekman, B. (2011). Proposals for WTO Reform: A Synthesis Assessment. *Minn. J. Int'l L., 20* (2), 324–64.

Holder, J. and Lee, M. (2007). *Environmental Protection Law and Policy*. Cambridge: Cambridge University Press.
Honkonen, T. (2009). *The Common but Differentiated Responsibility Principle in Multilateral Environmental Agreements*. Leiden: Wolters Kluwer.
Hoo, S. d. and Olaerts, M. (29 August 2011). *Sustainable Development and the Need for Sustainable Oriented Corporate Law and Regulation*. Retrieved 22 October 2012 from Social Science Research Network: http://papers.ssrn.com/sol3/papers.cfm?abstract_id=1926065
Hopt, K. (2006). Comparative Company Law. In M. Reimann and R. Zimmerman (eds), *The Oxford Handbook of Comparative Law*. Oxford: Oxford University Press.
Huang, L. Y. (2008). Not Just Another Drop in the Human Rights Bucket: The Legal Significance of a Codified Human Right to Water. *Fl. J. Int'l. L., 20*, 353.
Humphreys, S. (2009). Introduction – Human Rights and Climate Change. In S. Humphreys (ed.), *Human Rights and Climate Change*. Cambridge: Cambridge University Press.
Humphreys, S. (2010). Competing Claims: Human Rights and Climate Harms. In S. Humphreys (ed.), *Human Rights and Climate Change*. Cambridge: Cambridge University Press.
Humphreys, S. (ed.). (2010). *Human Rights and Climate Change*. Cambridge: Cambridge University Press.
International Business Publications. (2011). *Peru – Business Law Handbook*. Washington DC: International Business Publications.
IPCC (2007). *Climate Change 2007: Mitigation of Climate Change – Contribution of Working Group III to the Fourth Assessment Report*. (B. Metz, O. Davidson, P. Bosch, R. Dave and L. Mayer, eds) Cambridge: Cambridge University Press.
IPCC (2007). *Climate Change 2007: Synthesis Report for Policy Makers*. Retrieved 2 February 2013 from IPCC: www.ipcc.ch/pdf/assessment–report/ar4/syr/ar4_syr_spm.pdf
IPCC (2007). *Summary for Policy Makers. Climate Change 2007: The Physical Science Basis. Contribution of the Intergovernmental Panel on Climate Change*. Cambridge UK and New York US: Cambridge University Press.
IPCC (2007). *Summary for Policymakers. In: Climate Change 2007: The Physical Science Basis. Contribution of Working Group I to the Fourth Assessment Report of the Intergovernmental Panel on Climate Change*. (M. Manning, Z. Chen, M. Marquis, K. Averyt, M. Tignor and H. Miller, eds) Cambridge, UK and New York, US.: Cambridge University Press.
Irwin, D. A. (1996). *Against the Tide – An Intellectual History of Free Trade*. Princeton, NJ: Princeton University Press.
Iturregui, P. and Dutschke, M. (August 2005). *Liberalisation of Environmental Goods and Services and Climate Change*. Retrieved 2 Febraury 2013 from Hamburg Institute of International Economics: http://papers.ssrn.com/sol3/papers.cfm?abstract_id=872504
Jaffe, J. and Stavins, R. N. (2010). Linkage of Tradable Permit Systems in International Climate Policy Architecture. In J. E. Aldy and R. N. Stavins (eds), *Post–Kyoto International Climate Policy*. Cambridge: Cambridge University Press.
Jain, S. and Mishra, N., *Health Effects of the Toxic Gas Leak from the Union Carbide Methyl Isocynate Plant in Bhopal Technical Report on Population Based Long Term Epidemiological Studies (Report of Period: 1985–1994)*. Retrieved 6 February 2013 from Indian Council of Medical Research: http://icmr.nic.in/final/synopsis_tech_rep_clinical.pdf
Jefferson, T. (1999). *Jefferson: Political Writings*. (J. Appleby and T. Ball, eds) Cambridge: Cambridge University Press.
Jeßberger, C. (February 2011). *Multilateral Agreements up to 2050: Are they Sustainable Enough?* Retrieved 16 August 2012 from Institute for Economic Research at the University of Munich. Working Paper No. 98: http://papers.ssrn.com/sol3/papers.cfm?abstract_id=2004241
Kanda, H. and Milhaupt, C. J. (2003). Re-examining Legal Transplants: The Director's Fiduciary Duty in Japanese Corporate Law. *Am. J. Comp. L., 51*, 887.

Kawara, F. and Kwa, A. (2003). *Behind the Scenes at the WTO*. London: Zed Books.
Kazimova, R. (2011). Insurance as a Risk Management Tool. In S. Leader and D. Ong (eds), *Global Project Finance, Human Rights and Sustainable Development*. Cambridge: Cambridge University Press.
Kerr, M., Janda, R. and Pitts, C. (2009). *Corporate Social Responsibility*. (C. Pitts, ed.) Markham: LexisNexis.
Kinely, D. and Tadaki, J. (2004). From Walk to Talk: The Emergence of Human Rights Responsibilities for Corporations at International Law. *Va. J. Int'l L., 4*, 931.
Kingsmith, A. (26 October 2012). *Greenwashing: The Corporate Exaggeration of Environmental Consciousness*. Retrieved 13 January 2013 from The International: www.theinternational.org/articles/275-greenwashing-the-corporate-exaggeration
Kleeman, L. A. (2011). The Impact of Trade and Economic Growth on the Environment: Revisiting the Cross-Country Evidence. *J. Int'l. Dev.*, DOI: 10.1002/jid.1789.
Knox, J. (2009). Linking Human Rights to Climate Change at the United Nations. *Harv. Envtl. L. Rev. 33*, 477.
Kooper, C. (2011). New Perspectives on the 1931 Banking Crisis in Germany and Central Europe. *Business History, 53* (2), 216.
Kotzé, L. J. (2012). 'Some for all, forever' – A Southern perspective on poverty, access to water, environmental health and the North-South divide. In L. Westra, C. L. Soskolne and D. W. Spady (eds), *Human Health and Ecological Integrity*. London: Routledge.
Kotzé, L. J. (2007). The Judiciary, the Environmental Right and the Quest for Sustainability in South Africa: A Critical Reflection. *Rev. Eur. Community & Int'l Envtl. L., 16* (3), 298.
Kramer, L. (2011). *EU Environmental Law*, 7th edn. London: Sweet and Maxwell.
Kysar, D. A. (2010). *Regulating from Nowhere*. New Haven: Yale University Press.
Lancaster, K. A., Strand, C. A. and Carr, J. (2001–02). An Evaluation of the Usefulness of Web-based Financial and Environmental Performance Information Provided by Oil and gas Companies. *Oil and Gas Energy Q., 50*, 591.
Landes, D. S. (1998). *The Wealth and Poverty of Nations – Why Some are so Rich and Some are so Poor*. London: W. W. Norton and Co.
Larmuseau, I. (ed.) (2007). *Constitutional Rights to an Ecologically Balanced Environment*. Gent, Belgium: VVOR.
Larragan, J. D. (2011). *Distributional Choices in EU Climate Change Law and Policy – Towards a Principled Approach?* Leiden: Wolters Kluwer.
Lauterpacht, H. (1950). *International Law and Human Rights*. London: Stevens and Sons.
Law, D. S. and Versteeg, M. (2012). The Declining Influence of the United States Constitution. *N.Y. U. L. Rev., 87* (3), 762–858.
Law, D. S. and Versteeg, M. (2011). The Evolution and Ideology of Global Constitutionalism. *99 Cal. L. Rev., 99*, 1163.
Leary, D. and Pisupati, B. (eds). (2010). *The Future of International Environmental Law*. New York: United Nations University Press.
Lee, B., Preston, F., Kooroshy, J., Bailey, R. and Lahn, G. (December 2012). *Resources Futures*. Retrieved 2 February 2013 from Royal Institute of International Affairs – Chatham House: www.chathamhouse.org/sites/default/files/public/Research/Energy,%20Environment%20and%20Development/1212r_resourcesfutures.pdf
Leopold, A. (1949). *A Sand County Almanac – and Sketches Here and There*. New York: Oxford University Press.
Lord, R., Goldberg, S., Rajamani, L. and Brunnee, J. (eds) (2012). *Climate Change Liability – Transnatioanal Law and Practice*. Cambridge: Cambridge University Press.
Low, P., Marceau, G. and Reinaud, J. (12 January 2011). *The Interface Between the Trade and Climate Change Regimes: Scoping the Issues*. Retrieved 19 November 2012 from The World Trade Organization: www.wto/english/res_e/reser_e/ersd201101_e.pdf
Lowenfeld, A. F. (2002). *International Economic Law*, 2nd edn. Oxford: Oxford University Press.

Mackenzie, C. P. (2012). Lessons from Forestry for International Environmental Law. *Rev. Eur. Community & Int'l Env. L., 21* (2), 114.

Macmillan, F. (2001). *WTO and the Environment.* London: Sweet and Maxwell.

Macrory, R. (2008). *Regulation, Enforcement and Governance in Environmental Law.* London: Cameron May.

Maddex, R. L. (2008). *Constitutions of the World*, 3rd edn. Washington DC: CQ Press.

Mares, R. (2012). Business and Human Rights After Ruggie: Foundations, the Art of Simplification and the Imperative of Cumulative Progress. In R. Mares (ed.), *The UN Guiding Principles on Business and Human Rights – Foundations and Implementation.* Leiden: Martinus Nijhoff.

Mares, R. (2012). Preface. In R. Mares (ed.), *The UN Guiding Principles to Business and Human Rights – Foundations and Implementation.* Leiden: Martinus Nijhoff Publishers.

Marquis, C. and Toffel, M. W. (20 December 2012). *When do Firms Greenwash? Corporate Visibility, Civil Society Scrutiny, and Environmental Discolosure (Working Paper 11–115).* Retrieved 19 January 2013 from Harvard Business School: www.hbs.edu/faculty/Publication%20Files/11–115_af40ca36–f8fa–4542–b211–0ef0ebc64da3.pdf

Martin, P., Zhiping, L., Tanboa, Q., Plessis, A. D. and Bouthillier, Y. (eds) (2012). *Environmental Governance and Sustainability.* Cheltenham: IUCN Academy of Environmental Law Series – Edward Elgar.

Martin, R., Muûls, M. and Wagner, U. (2010). *Europe's Emission Trading Scheme: Taxpayers Versus the Industry Lobby.* Retrieved 7 January 2013 from Centre for Economic Performance – London School of Economics: http://cep.lse.ac.uk/pubs/download/cp311.pdf

Matsushita, M., Schoenbaum, T. J. and Marvoidis, P. C. (2006). *The World Trade Organization – Law Practice and Policy*, 2nd edn. Oxford: Oxford University Press.

Matsushita, M., Schoenbaum, T. J. and Mavroidis, P. (2006). *The World Trade Organization – Law, Practice and Policy*, 2nd edn. Oxford: Oxford University Press.

McAlinn, G. (2007). *Japanese Business Law.* Leiden: Kluwer Law International.

McCaffrey, S. C. and Neville, K. J. (2009). Small Capacity and Big Responsiibilities: Financial and Legal Implications of a Human Right to Water for Developing Countries. *Georgetown Int'l Envtl L. Rev., 21*, 679.

McDonald, S. (2013). *Behind the Scenes of British-German Climate and Energy Collaboration.* UK Government. Berlin (copy on file with the author).

McGillivray, D. (2012). Compensating Biodiversity Loss: The EU Commission's Approach to Compensation under Article 6 of the Habitats Directive. *J. Envtl. L., 24* (3), 417.

McIlwain, C. H. (1947). *Constitutionalism – Ancient and Modern.* New York: Ithaca .

McKinsey and Company. (2009). *Charting our Water Future – Economic Frameworks to Inform Decision-Making.* Retrieved 2 February 2013 from McKinsey and Company: www.mckinsey.com/App_Media/Reports/Water/Charting_Our_Water_Future_Exec%20Summary_001.pdf

McNish, T. (2012). Carbon Offsets are a Bridge too far in the Tradable Property Rights Revolution. *Harv. Env. L. Rev., 36*, 387–443.

Meltzer, J. (2012). Climate Change and Trade – The EU Aviation Directive and the WTO. *J. Int'l Econ. L., 15* (1), 111–56.

Michael Kerr, R. J. and Pitts, C. (2009). *Corporate Social Responsibility.* (C. Pitts, ed.) Markham: LexisNexis.

Moltke, K. V. (2005). Clustering International Environmental Agreements as an Alternative to a World Environment Organization. In F. Biermann and S. Bauer (eds), *A World Environment Organization: Solution or Threat to Effective International Environmental Governance.* Aldershot: Ashgate.

Morgera, E. (2009). *Corporate Accountability in International Environmental Law.* Oxford: Oxford University Press.

Morrow, K. (2012). Rio + 20, the Green Economy and Re-orienting Sustainable Development. *Envtl. L. Rev. 14* (4), 279.

Mrema, E. M. (2006). Cross Cutting Issues Related to Ensuring Compliance with MEAs. In U. Beyerlin, P-T. Stoll and R. Wolfram (eds), *Ensuring Compliance with Multilateral Environmental Agreements – A Dialogue Between Practitioners and Academics*. Leiden: Martinus Nijhoff.

Muchlinski, P. T. (1987). The Bhopal Case: Controlling Ultrahazardous Industrial Activities undertaken by Foreign Investors. *Mod. L. Rev., 50*, 545.

Muchlinski, P. T. (2007). *Multinational Enterprises and the Law*. Oxford: Oxford University Press.

Najam, A. (2005). Neither Necessary, Nor Sufficient: Why Organizational Tinkering Will Not Improve Environmental Governance. In F. Biermann and S. Bauer (eds), *A World Environment Organization: Solution or Threat to Effective International Environmental Governance*. Aldershot: Ashgate.

Narain, V. (2010). Water as a Fundamental Right: A Perspective from India. *Vt. L. Rev., 34*, 917.

Neuhoff, K. (2011). *Climate Policy after Copenhagen – The Role of Carbon Pricing*. Cambridge: Cambridge University Press.

Neumayer, E. (2001). *Greening Trade and Investment: Environmental Protection without Protectionism*. London: Earthscan.

Newell, P. (2010). Climate Change, Human Rights and Corporate Accountability. In S. Humphreys (ed.), *Climate Change and Human Rights*. Cambridge: Cambridge University Press.

Newell, P., Boykoff, M. and Newell, P. (eds). *The New Carbon Economy – Constitution, Governance and Contestation*. Hoboken (NJ): Wiley Blackwell.

Nordström, H. and Vaughan, S. (1999). *Trade and Environment*. Geneva: WTO.

OECD (2011). *OECD Guidelines for Multinational Enterprises*. Retrieved 6 February 2013 from www.oecd.org/daf/internationalinvestment/guidelinesformultinationalenterprises/48004323.pdf

Parker, C. and Howe, J. (2012). Ruggie's Diplomatic Project and Its Missing Regulatory Infrastructure. In R. Mares (ed.), *The UN Guiding Principles on Business and Human Rights – Foundations and Implementation*. Leiden: Martinus Nijhoff Publishers.

Pauwelyn, J. (2003). *Conflicts of Norms in Public International Law – How WTO Law Relates to other Rules of International Law*. Cambridge: Cambridge University Press.

Pedersen, O. W. (2008). European Environmental Human Rights and Environmental Rights: A Long Time Coming? *Geo. Int'l Envtl. L. Rev., 21*, 73.

Pedersen, O. W. (2011). A Bill of Rights, Environmental Rights and the UK Constitution. *Public Law*, July, 577.

Pedersen, O. W. (2011). The Janus-Head of Human Rights and Climate Change: Adaptation and Mitigation. *Nordic J. Int'l. L., 80* (4), 403.

Peel, J. (2011). Environmental Protection in the Twenty-first Century: The Role of International Law. In R. S. Axelrod, S. D. Vandeveer and D. L. Downie (eds), *The Global Environment – Institutions, Law and Policy*. Washington DC: CQ Press.

Penning-Roswell, T. H. (2011). *Victim Pressure, Institutional Inertia, and Climate Change Adaption: The Case of Flood Risk* (Vol. 1(1)). London: Global Environmental Change.

Petersmann, E-U. (2011). The Future of the WTO: From Authoritarian 'Mercantilism' to Multilevel Governance for the Benefit of Citizens. *Asian J. WTO & Int'l Health L. & Pol'y, 6*, 45.

Pomeranz, K. and Topik, S. (2006). *The World that Trade Created – Society, Culture, and the World Economy, 1400 – the Present*, 2nd edn. New York: M. E. Sharpe Inc.

Popovsky, M. (2011). Nanotechnology and Environmental Insurance. *Colum. J. Envtl. L., 36* (1), 125.

Porrini, D. (2008). *Law and Economics of Environmental Insurance (Editorial)*. Retrieved 12 2012 November from The International Associaton for the Study of Insurance Economics: www.genevaassociation.org/PDF/Geneva_papers_on_Risk_and_Insurance/GA2008_GP33(2)_Porrini.pdf

Porritt, J. (1973). Introduction. In E. F. Schumacher, *Small is Beautiful – A Study of Economics as if People Mattered*. Blond and Briggs Ltd (reprinted by Vintage 1993).
Posner, E. A. and Weisbach, D. (2010). *Climate Change Justice*. Princeton NJ: Princeton University Press.
Powers, A. (2010). Climate Change and Pollution: Addressing intersecting threats to oceans, coasts and small island developing states. In D. Leary and B. Pisupati (eds), *The Future of International Environmental Law*. New York: United Nations University Press.
Quirico, O. (2012). Disentangling Climate Change Governance: A Legal Perspective. *Rev. Eur. Community & Int'l Env. L., 21* (2), 92.
Rajamani, L. (2006). *Differential Treatment in International Environmental Law*. Oxford: Oxford University Press.
Rajamani, L. (2010). The Increasing Relevance and Currency of Rights–based perspectives in the International Negotiations on Climate Change. *J. Envtl. L., 22* (3), 391–423.
Rajamani, L. (2012). The Durban Platform for Enhanced Action and the Future of the Climate Regime. *Int'l & Comp. L. Q., 61* (2), 501–518.
Rayfuse, R. and Scott, S. V. (eds). (2012). *International Law in the Era of Climate Change*. Cheltenham: Edward Elgar.
Razzaque, J. (2004). *Public Interest Environmental Litigation in India, Pakistan and Bangladesh*. Leiden: Kluwer Law International.
Razzaque, J. (2010). Human Rights to a Clean Environment. In M. Fitzmaurice, D. M. Ong and P. Merkouris (eds), *Research Handbook on International Environmental Law*. Cheltenham: Edward Elgar.
Recio, E. (9 October 2012). *On the Road to Doha: Will the Bell Toll for the Kyoto Protocol*. Retrieved 28 December 2012 from International Institute of Sustainable Development: http://climate-l.iisd.org/policy-updates/on-the-road-to-doha-will-the-bell-toll-for-the-kyoto-protocol/
Redgwell, C. (2012). Climate Change and International Environmental Law. In R. Rayfuse and S. V. Scott (eds), *International Law in the Era of Climate Change*. Cheltenham: Edward Elgar.
Reid, C. T. (2011). The Privatisation of Biodiversity? Possible New Approaches to Nature Conservation Law in the UK. *J. Envt'l L., 23* (2), 203–31.
Robinson, J., Barton, J., Dodwell, C., Heydon, M. and Milton, L. (2007). *Climate Change Law – Emissions Trading in the EU and the UK*. London: Cameron May.
Rubini, L. (2012). Ain't Wastin' Time No More: Subsidies for Renewable Energy, The SCM Agreement, Policy Space and Law Reform. *J. Int'l Econ. L., 15* (2), 525.
Ruggie, J. (2004). Reconstituting the Global Public Domain – Issues, Actors, and Practices. *European Journal of International Relations, 10* (4), 518.
Sampson, G. P. (12–13 October 2011). *UNEP – First Preparatory Meeting of the World Congress on Justice, Governance and Sustainability*. Retrieved 19 November 2012 from United Nations Environment Programme: www.unep.org/delc/Portals/24151/GreenEconomyInternationalEG.pdf
Sampson, G. (2005). *The WTO and Sustainable Development*. Tokyo: The United Nations University Press.
Sands, P. (1989). The Environment, Community and International Law. *Harv. Int'l L. J., 30*, 393.
Sands, P., Peel, J., Fabra, A. and Mackenzie, R. (2012). *Principles of International Environmental Law*. Cambridge: Cambridge University Press.
Santer, A. L. (2011). A Soft Law Mechanism for Corporate Responsibility: How the Updated OECD Guidelines for Multinational Enterprises Promote Business for the Future. *Geo. Wash. Int'l L. Rev., 43*, 375.
Schipper, L. F. and Conway, D. (2011). Adaptation to Climate Change in Africa: Challenges and Opportunities Identified from Ethiopia. *Global Envtl. Change, 21* (1), pp. 227–37.
Schoenbaum, T. (1992). Free International Trade and Protection of the Environment. *Am. J. Int'l L., 86*, 700.

Scott, J. and Rajamani, L. (2012). EU Climate Change Unilateralism. *Eur. J. Int'l L., 23* (2), 469.
Shelton, D. (1991). Human Rights, Environmental Rights and the Right to Environment. *Stan J. Int'l L., 28*, 103.
Shelton, D. (1992). What Happened in Rio to Human Rights? *Y.B. Int'l Envtl L., 3* (3), 75.
Shelton, D. (1995). Environmental Protection and the Right to Food. In A. A. Trindade (ed.), *Derechos Humanos Desarollo Sustenable y Medio Ambiente*. San Jose: Instituto Interamericano de Derechos Humanos.
Shelton, D. (ed.). (2000). *Commitment and Compliance*. Oxford: Oxford University Press.
Shelton, D. (2000). Law, Non–Law and the Problem of 'Soft Law'. In D. Shelton (ed.), *Commitment and Compliance*. Oxford: Oxford University Press.
Shelton, D. (2001). Environmental Rights. In P. Alston (ed.), *Peoples' Rights*. Oxford: Oxford University Press.
Shelton, D. (14–16 January 2002). *Environmental Issues and Human Rights in Multilateral Treaties Adopted Between 1991 and 2001*. Retrieved 31 May 2012 from Joint UNEP–OHCHR Expert Seminar on Human Rights and the Environment: http://www2.ohchr.org/english/issues/environment/environ/bp2.hrm
Shelton, D. (2004). Human Rights Bodies: Decisions and Actions. *Envtl. Pol'y & L., 34* (2).
Shelton, D. (2007). Environmental Rights in the State Constitutions of the United States. In I. Larmuseau (ed.), *Constitutional Rights to an Ecologically Balanced Environment*. Gent, Belgium: V.V.O.R.
Shelton, D. (2010). Developing Substantive Environmental Rights. *J. Hum. Rts. & Envt., 1* (1), 89–120.
Shelton, D. (2010). Equitable Utilization of the Atmosphere: A rights-based approach to climate change. In S. Humphreys (ed.), *Human Rights and Climate Change*. Cambridge: Cambridge University Press.
Shelton, D. (2010). Human Rights and the Environment: Substantive Rights. In M. Fitzmaurice, D. M. Ong and P. Merkouris (eds), *Research Handbook on International Envrionmental Law*. Cheltenham: Edward Elgar.
Sindico, F. (2012). Post-2012 Compliance and Carbon Markets. In J. Brunee, M. Doelle and L. Rajamani (eds), *Promoting Compliance in an Evolving Climate Regime*. Cambridge: Cambridge University Press.
Sjåfell, B. (2012). Regulating Companies as if the World Matters – Reflections from the Ongoing Sustainable Companies Project. *Wake Forest L. Rev., 47*, 113.
Smith, A. (1776 (1993)). *An Inquiry into the Nature and Causes of the Wealth of Nations*. (K. Sutherland, ed.) Oxford: Oxford University Press.
Soltau, F. (2009). *Fairness in International Climate Change Law and Policy*. Cambridge: Cambridge University Press.
Spassov, Y., Krustev, A. and Nikolovska, V. (2011). Lowest-Cost Abatement in Light of the EU ETS and Renewable Feed in Tarrifs in the Electricity Sector in Bulgaria. *J. Energy & Nat. Resources. L., 29* (2), 281.
Speth, J. G. (2008). *The Bridge at the End of the World – Capitalism, the Environment, and Crossing from Crisis to Sustainability*. New Haven: Yale University Press.
Speth, J. G. (2012). *America the Possible – Manifesto for a New Economy*. New Haven: Yale University Press.
Srivastava, N. (2011). Changing Dynamics of Forest Regulation: Coming Full Circle? *Rev. Eur. Community & Int'l Envtl. L., 20* (2), 113.
Standing, A. (May 2011). *Corruption and REDD+: Identifying risks amid complexity*. Retrieved 3 January 2013 from U4 Anti-Corruption Resource Centre: CHR Michelsen Institute: www.u4.no/
Steinhardt, R. G. (2005). Corporate Responsibility and the International Law of Human Rights: The New Lex Mercatoria. In P. Alston (ed.), *Non–State Actors and Human Rights*. Oxford: Oxford University Press.

Stern, N. (2009). Changing Economics. In F. Dodds, A. Higham and R. Sherman (eds), *Climate Change and Energy Security*. London: Earthscan.
Stiglitz, J. E. (2001). *Globalization and its Discontents*. New York: Norton and Company.
Stone, C. D. (1972). *Should Trees Have Standing – Toward Legal Rights for Natural Objects*. California: William Kaufman Inc.
Streck, C., O'Sullivan, R., Janson-Smith, T. and Tarasofsky, R. (eds). (2008). *Climate Change and Forests – Emerging Policy and Market Opportunities*. Washington DC: Brookings Institute Press.
Sutherland, H. (1993). *Fraser & Stewart: Company Law of Canada*, 6th edn. Toronto: Carswell Legal Publications.
Taylor, C. R. (10 October2012). *United States Company Law as it Impacts Corporate Environmental Behaviour, with Emphasis on Climate Change*. Retrieved 19 January 2013 from University of Oslo Faculty of Law Research Paper No 2012–13: http://papers.ssrn.com/sol3/papers.cfm?abstract_id=2159659
Therivel, R. (2010). *Strategic Environmental Assessment in Action*. London: Earthscan.
Thornhill, C. (2011). *A Sociology of Constitutions – Constitutions and State Legitimacy in Historical-Sociological Perspective*. Cambridge: Cambridge University Press.
Tickell, O. (2008). *Kyoto 2 – How to Manage the Global Greenhouse*. London: Zed Books.
Tienhaara, K., Orsini, A. and Falkner, R. (2012). Global Corporations. In F. Biermann and P. Pattberg (eds), *Global Environmental Governance Reconsidered*. Cambridge, Massachusetts: The MIT Press.
Timmons–Roberts, J., Starr, K., Jones, T. and Abdel-Fattah, D. (November 2008). *The Reality of Official Climate Aid*. Retrieved 9 January 2013 from Oxford Institute for Energy Studies: www.oxfordenergy.org/2008/11/the-reality-of-official-climate-aid/
Transparency International (2011). *Global Corruption Report: Climate Change*. London and Wasington DC: Earthscan.
Tromans, S. (2012). *Environmental Impact Assessment*, 2nd edn. London: Bloomsbury Professional.
Tully, S. (ed.). (2012). *International Corporate Legal Responsibility*. Leiden: Wolters Kluwer.
Turner, S. J. (2009). *A Substantive Environmental Right – An examination of the legal obligations of decision-makers towards the environment*. Leiden: Wolters Kluwer.
UK Government (2012). *The Greenhouse Gas Emissions (Directors' Report) Regulations 2013*. Retrieved 22 October 2012 from DEFRA: www.defra.gov.uk/consult/files/consult–ghg–regulations–20131.pdf
UNCSD (22 June 2001). *UN Needs to Establish World Environment Organisation*. Retrieved 17 August 2012 from Rio + 20 United Nations Conference on Sustainable Development: www.uncsd2012.org/index.php?page=view&nr=138&type=230&menu=238
UNDP (2011). *Human Development Report – Sustainability and Equity. A Better Future for All*. Retrieved 26 November 2012 from United Nations Development Programme: http://hdr.undp.org/en/reports/global/hdr2011
UNEP (2005). *Register of International Treaties and Other Agreements in the Field of the Environment*. UNEP/Env.Law/2005/3, Division of Policy Development and Law. Nairobi: UNEP.
UNEP (2011). *Towards a Green Economy: Pathways to Sustainable Development and Poverty Eradication – A Synthesis for Policy Makers*. Retrieved 2 February 2013 from United Nations Environment Programme: www.unep.org/greeneconomy
UNEP (2012). *The Emissions Gap Report 2012 – A Synthesis Report*. Retrieved 24 December 2012 from www.unep.org/publications/ebooks/emissionsgap2012/
UNEP (9 December 2012). Retrieved 29 December 2012 from Doha Climate Conference Opens Gateway to Greater Ambition and Action on Climate Change: www.unep/newscentre/default.aspx?DocumentID=2700&ArticleID=9353
UNEP/Division of Technology, Industry and Economics/The International Institute of Sustainable Development (2005). *Environment and Trade – A Handbook*, 2nd edn. Winnipeg, Manitoba, Canada: International Institute for Sustainable Development.

UNEP/WCMC. (2006). *In the Front Line: Shoreline Protection and other Ecosystem Services from Mangroves and Coral Reefs*. Retrieved 2 February 2013 from United Nations Environment Programme/World Conservation Monitoring Centre: www.unep.org/publications/search/pub_details_s.asp?ID=3783

UNFCCC (1992). *United Nations Framework Convention on Climate Change*. United Nations. 9th May, in force 24 March 1994, 1771 UNTS 107.

UNFCCC (December 2009). Retrieved 29 December 2012 from Copenhagen Climate Change Conference – December 2009: http://unfccc.int/meetings/copenhagen_dec_2009/meetings/6295.php

UNFCCC (November 2010). *Cancun Climate Change Conference*. Retrieved 23 December 2012 from http://unfccc.int/meetings/cancun_nov_2010/meeting/6266.php

UNFCCC (2012). Retrieved 28 December 2012 from Status of Ratification of the Kyoto Protocol: http://unfccc.int/kyoto_protocol/status_of_ratification/items/2613.php

UNFCCC (2012). Retrieved 28 December 2012 from The Kyoto Protocol: http://unfccc.int/Kyoto_protocol/items/2830.php

UNFCCC (7 September 2012). *News Release: Kyoto Protocol's CDM passes one billionth CER milestone*. Retrieved 28 December 2012 from https://cdm.unfccc.int/CDMNews/issues/Issues/I_POQZOFWYYKFKOSAZ5GYH2250DRQK/viewnewsitem.html

UNFCCC (8 December 2012). *Report of the Ad Hoc Working Group on Further Commitments for Annex I Parties under the Kyoto Protocol*. Retrieved 28 December 2012 from Conference of the Parties serving as the Meeting of the Parties to the Kyoto Protocol Eighth SessionFCCC/KP/CMP/2012/L.9: www.unfccc.int/resources/docs/2012/cmp8/eng/109.pdf

United Nations (1972). *Declaration on the Human Environment*. United Nations Conference on the Human Environment. G.A. Res. 2997. U.N. GAOR, 27th Sess., Supp. No. 30, At 43, U.N. Doc. A/8901.

United Nations (1992). *Declaration on Environment and Development*. United Nations Conference on the Environment and Development. 31 ILM 814, UN Doc. A/Conf.151/5/Rev.1.

United Nations (2002). *Plan of Implementation*. United Nations – World Summit on Sustainable Development. Johannesburg: UN Doc. A/CONF.199/20, Res.2.

United Nations (2005). *Millennium Ecosystem Assessment – Living Beyond Our Means: Natural Assets and Human Well–Being*. Retrieved 3 February 2013 from United Nations Environment Programme: www.unep.org/maweb/documents.429.aspx.pdf

United Nations (2005). *Millennium Ecosystem Assessment, Ecosystems and Human Well–being Synthesis*. Washington, DC: Island Press.

United Nations (2010). *Millenium Development Goals*. Retrieved 26 January from 2013 United Nations' Millenium Development Goals: www.un.org/millenniumgoals/index.shtml

United Nations (2012). *Food Assistance Convention*. Retrieved 26 January 2013 from United Nations: http://treaties.un.org/Pages/ViewDetails.aspx2src=TREATY&mtdsg_no=XIX–48&chapter=19&lang=eng

United Nations (2012). *The Future We Want: Rio + 20 Outcome Document*. United Nations – Rio + 20 conference. Rio de Janeiro: UN Doc. A/Conf.216/L.1.

United Nations (2012). *Report of the United Nations Conference on Sustainable Development*. New York: United Nations A./CONF.216/XX.

United Nations Department of Economic and Social Affairs (2011). *World Economic and Social Survey – The Great Green Revolution*. United Nations, Department of Economic and Social Affairs. New York: UN Sales No. E.11.II.C.1.

United Nations FAO (2010). *Global Forest Resources Assessment 2010 – Forest Paper 163*. Retrieved 2 February 2013 from United Nations Food and Agriculture Organization: www.fao.org/forestry/fra/en/

United Nations FAO (2010). *The State of the World Fisheries and Aquaculture*. Retrieved 2 February 2013 from United Nations Food and Agriculture Organization: www.fao.org.docrep/013/i/il820e/il820e.pdf

United Nations FAO (2011). *State of the World's Forests*. Retrieved 2 February 2013 from United Nations Food and Agriculture Organization: www.fao.org/forestry/sofo/en/

United Nations GA (22 April 2009). Retrieved 9 August 2012 from U.N. G.A. Res. 63rd Sess. GA/10823 A/63/L.69: www.un.org/News/Press/docs/2009/ga10823.doc.htm

United Nations GA (24 July 2012). *Draft Resolution submitted by the President of the General Assembly, The Future we want*. Retrieved 7 August 2012 from Rio + 20 United Nations Conference on Sustainable Development: www.uncsd2012.org/thefuturewe want.html

United Nations Human Rights Council (2011). *Promotion and Protection of all Human Rights, Civil, Political, Economic, Social and Cultural Rights, including the Right to Development*. United Nations Human Rights Council, A/HRC/17/31.

Van Vuuren, D. P. and Riahi K. (2008). Do Recent Emission Trends Imply Higher Emissions Forever. *Climate Change*, 91 (3–4), pp. 237–48.

Vaughan, S. and Nordstrom, H. (1999). *Trade and Environment – Special Studies 4*. Retrieved 6 February 2013 from World Trade Organization: www.wto.org/english/res_e/booksp_e/special_study_4_e.pdf

Veel, P. E. (2009). Carbon Tarrifs and the WTO: An Evaluation of Feasible Policies. *J. Int'l Econ. L., 12* (3), 749–800.

Villiers, C. (2010). Directors' Duties and the Company's Internal Structures Under the UK Companies Act 2006: Obstacles for Sustainable Development. *Int'l Comp. Corp. L. J., 8*, 47.

Wallace, C. D. (2002). *Multinational Enterprise and Legal Control – Host State Sovereignty in an Era of Economic Globalization*. The Hague: Kluwer Law International.

Wallace, R. M. and Martin-Ortega, O. (2009). *International Law*. London: Sweet and Maxwell.

Weil, G. (2012). Subnational Climate Mitigation Policy: A Framework for Analysis. *Col. J. Envtl. L. & Pol'y, 23* (2), 285.

Weisbach, D. (2012). Carbon Taxation in the EU: Expanding the EU Carbon Price. *J. Envtl. L., 24* (2), 183.

Weston, B. H. and Bollier, D. (2013). *Green Governance: Ecological Survival, Human Rights, and the Law of the Commons*. Cambridge: Cambridge University Press.

WHO/UNICEF Joint Monitoring Programme for Water Supply and Sanitation. (2010). *Progress on Sanitation and Drinking Water: 2010*. Retrieved 2 February 2013 from WHO/UNICEF: www.wssinfo.org/

Williams, C. W. (2002). Corporate Social Responsibility in an Era of Economic Globalization. *U. C. Davis L. Rev., 35* (2), 705.

Winter, G. (2009). The Climate is No Commodity: Taking Stock of the Emissions Trading System. *J. Envtl. L., 22* (1), 1.

Wolf, S. and Stanley, N. (2011). *Wolf and Stanley on Environmental Law*. Abingdon: Routledge.

Woolley, D., Pugh-Smith, J., Langham, R. and Upton, W. (2009). *Environmental Law*, 2nd edn. Oxford: Oxford University Press.

World Commission on Environment and Development (1987). *Our Common Future*. Oxford: Oxford University Press.

World Commission on Environment and Development. (1987). *Report of the World Commission on Environment and Development*. U.N. G.A. Res. 42/187, 11 December 1987, U.N. Doc. A/Res/42/187.

Worm, B. (2009). Rebuilding Global Fisheries. *Science, 325*, 578.

Yale Center for Environmental Law and Policy, Yale University/Center for International Earth Science Information Network, Columbia University (2012). *Environmental Performance Index and Pilot Trend Environmental Performance Index*. Retrieved 2 February 2013 from Environmental Performance Index – Yale University: http://epi.yale.edu/epi2012/summary

Zeiler, T. W. (1999). *Free Trade Free World – The Advent of GATT*. North Carolina: The University of North Carolina Press.

Index